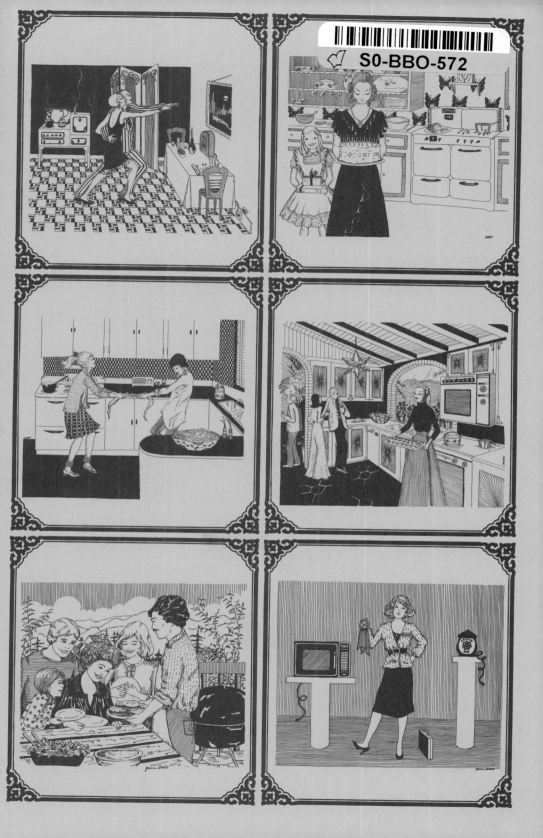

Nov 14, 1980
happy b-day Sis
all my love,

from an adobe oven to a microwave range

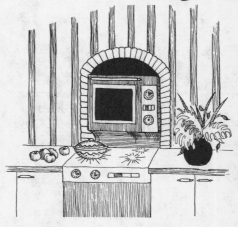

This is a cookbook born in the southwest, reflecting the fondness of a nation for good food, and illustrated with vignettes which trace the evolution of cooking from an adobe oven to a microwave range.

Published by
THE JUNIOR LEAGUE OF PUEBLO
Pueblo, Colorado

FROM AN ADOBE OVEN . . . TO A MICROWAVE RANGE

Additional copies may be obtained by sending $8.95 plus $1.50 for postage and handling to the address below. (Colorado residents add 6% or 54¢ per book sales tax.)

The Junior League of Pueblo, Inc.
P.O. Box 3326
Pueblo, Colorado   81005

First Edition	September 1972	10,000 Copies
Second Edition	July 1974	10,000 Copies
Third Edition	March 1980	10,000 Copies

Library of Congress Catalogue Card Number 79-57072

Printed in the United States
by Hart Graphics, Inc.
8000 Shoal Creek Blvd.
Austin, Texas   78758

adventure!

Everyone will not walk on the moon. There never will be another Charles Lindbergh to thrill the multitudes by being the first to fly alone across the Atlantic. Perhaps there may not be another Dwight Eisenhower to lead victorious armies and become the President of the United States.

But always with us there is some spirit of adventure. Some scale the highest peaks. Others stalk big game in distant lands. Many explore the mysteries at the bottom of the oceans. More likely we ski the steep slopes of the Rockies. Many lose their inhibitions in competitive sports while the less adept and brave cheer from the sidelines.

However, the supreme adventure in which all of us can, and do, participate is eating! Here each of us can elevate food to the highest levels of exotic adventure and palatable ecstacy. It is an experience that can be surpassed by few things in life and one which may be repeated frequently with the same sublimity.

If you think you are not an epicurist, worry not. There are those whose gourmet expeditions into the kitchen are producing delectable goodies constantly. Their willingness to share these dishes results in such delightful culinary guides as this book which has been prepared by members of the Junior League of Pueblo.

It may be true that food is the basis for survival. Since the beginning of humanity and beasts, self-preservation has been one of man's (and woman's, if Women's Liberation insists) motivations.

In Genesis we are told that God created the heavens and the earth, then put into the earth every plant and herb, brought forth the rains to make them grow, and then created Adam to till the ground, "And the Lord God planted a garden eastward in Eden; and there He put the man He had formed." And from sleeping Adam, God took a rib to create Eve. To them were born Cain and Abel, the first to bring the fruit of the ground and Abel to raise the sheep.

So God placed upon His Earth everything the people would need to sustain life, and He endowed men and women with the mentality to devise ingenious ways to crossbreed and propagate the plants to create new edibles. At the same time He encouraged all humanity, from the Stone Age to the gourmets of today to combine these elements of food and condiments to not simply satisfy hunger, but to provide supreme dining pleasure.

Great strides have been made in the past half century in the panorama of edibles, along with methods of freezing, de-hydrating and otherwise making delectable products available every day of the year. Pre-cooked and table-ready foods may entice many women out of the kitchen. The time a woman spends in the kitchen preparing meals depends upon herself—of course, providing she is willing to be 'ordinary.'

Fortunately for other members of the family, and guests, many women have tremendous pride in preparing their own special recipes. These esoteric modern queens of the range (kitchen), generously are sharing their exploits with the mundane.

Ralph C. Taylor
AUTHOR AND HISTORIAN

FORWORD

Pueblo, Colorado, is a progressive, energetic community. Pueblo Junior League is a progressive, dedicated group. This cookbook by the name "From An Adobe Oven" is a progressive gem of cookery suitable for all types of cooks and cooking, even adaptable to the microwave oven.

These recipes are the result of more than two years of work by a small devoted committee with the aid of many other members of our organization. Approximately 1400 recipes were received, each tested three times, and those best loved by the cooks and their families were chosen. Unfortunately many excellent recipes had to be omitted because of duplications, and limited space, but we hope we have achieved a well-rounded book.

The project progressed with the help of typists, proofreaders, cooks, production girls, our cross index crew, and our talented artist. A special thank you must be made to our beloved, understanding husbands who felt either overfed or neglected, depending on the time of discussion.

We are indebted to the many wonderful people in our community who have contributed to the realization, completion and success of this book, and are continuing to participate in this charitable project.

To those of you, near or far away, who may acquire "Adobe Oven," we hope you enjoy the recipes from the dear people acknowledged within, who so kindly consented to share them with us.

We also want you to know that proceeds of this book will help finance our community projects, and help us make our great city a better place in which to live.

Marjorie Birner
Suzanne Anton

cookbook committee

Editor	Marjorie Birner
Co-Editor	Suzanne Anton
Production	Jacqueline Hirsch, *Chairman* Sharon Kaufman, *Co-Chairman*
Testing	Marilyn Shomaker, *Chairman* Leah Rae Puleo, *Co-Chairman*
Typing	Barbara Vento, Marty Ardell, *Chairmen* Neta DeRose, Beverly Hurley, *Co-Chairmen*
Proofreading	Mary Jane Griffith, *Chairman* Marilyn Hunter, *Co-Chairman*
Cross-Index	Beth Thatcher, *Chairman* Judy Krause, *Co-Chairman*
Artist	Joanne McGuire Battiste
Publishing	Margaret Ann Hyde, *Chairman* Marie Vickery, *Co-Chairman*
Publicity	Nancy Bonforte, *Chairman* Colleen Hopkins, *Co-Chairman*
Promotion and Distribution	Charlotte Broome and Marjorie McGovern
Promotion Publicity	Margaret Ann Hyde, *Chairman* Susan Moore, *Co-Chairman*
Third Edition:	The Cookbook Committee wishes a sincere thank you to the many ladies who, through their dedication, have made the Third Edition a reality.

table of contents

Artwork
by
JOANNE McGUIRE BATTISTE

southwestern

It all began with the native simplicity
of the adobe oven . . . that very special
care and skill from which grew the tradition of
hearty, good-tasting food for southwesterners
of many cultural and ethnic backgrounds.

Mexican Meatloaf

2 pounds hamburger
1 can tomato paste
2 small cans of taco sauce (about 3 ounces)
1 can cream of mushroom soup
1 can chicken and rice soup
1 can diced green chilies (do to taste-maybe only ½ can)
Onion salt, garlic, salt and pepper to taste
1 package (12) corn tortillas

Brown hamburger. Mix remaining ingredients, (except tortillas) and add hamburger. Use large pan—first cover bottom with 6 tortillas; then ½ of mixture—then rest of tortillas and last half of mixture. Cover with grated Long Horn cheese.

Bake 350 degrees 45 minutes (look at it at 35 minutes). Don't overcook.

Nina Driscoll

Chili Relleno Sandwich

10 slices French bread
Sliced Monterey Jack or mild Cheddar cheese (to cover 5 slices of bread)
5 canned green chilies (4-ounce can)
2 eggs
¼ cup half and half
¼ teaspoon salt
½ cup butter or margarine
8-ounce can of tomato sauce with minced onion and lemon juice (optional)

Top each of five slices of French bread with a slice of cheese. Split canned green chilies down one side, remove seeds, rinse, and drain. Lay chilies over cheese and add top bread slice. Make a batter with eggs, half and half, and salt. Melt butter in large frying pan over medium heat. Quickly dip both sides of sandwiches in batter with tongs. Sauté on both sides in butter until golden brown and cheese is melted. Serve plain, or top with tomato sauce.

Tomato sauce:
    Heat tomato sauce just until boiling. Add instant minced onion, 1 teaspoon lemon juice and ¼ teaspoon salt. Spoon over sandwiches.

Jean Whitaker

Refritos (Mexican Beans)

1 pound pinto beans   salt
1 tablespoon lard

Wash beans thoroughly, then soak for at least one hour. Drain, cover with about 2 inches fresh water, and cook in pressure cooker for one hour. Remove cover and cook an additional half hour. (If regular pan is used, cook 3 hours, adding water as needed.) Add salt to taste. Melt lard in frying pan, drain beans, and fry to desired doneness.

Serves 10   *Gay McCabe*

Guacamole Dip

3 medium ripe avocados,   1 teaspoon onion salt
  mashed   ½ teaspoon salt
1 4-ounce can diced   ½ teaspoon pepper
  green chilies   1 teaspoon lemon juice
1 teaspoon garlic salt

Combine mashed avocados, green chilies and all seasonings. Add lemon juice, mix well. Store covered in refrigerator 2 hours before serving.

Serve with corn chips or tortilla chips (taste before serving; you may want to add more seasonings.)

Note: You may buy avocadoes 3 or 4 days in advance. Store them in a dark cool place and they will ripen just right for this dip.

Vivian Elizondo

Chili Con Queso

1 can diced green chilies   1 can crab or
1 can green chili salsa   tiny shrimp (optional)
2 pounds Old English
  processed cheese

Melt in double boiler and serve hot with taco chips.

Susie Anton

Enchilada Casserole

1½ pounds ground beef chuck
1 package (1¼ ounce)
 taco seasoning mix
10 corn tortillas
3 cups shredded Jack cheese
½ pound cooked ham, diced
1 cup sour cream

1 small onion
1 cup water
½ cup bottled taco sauce
2 packages (10 ounces each)
 frozen chopped spinach,
 thawed

Combine beef and onion in pan and brown. Stir meat until crumbled. Stir in taco seasoning and water—cover and simmer 10 minutes. Pour half the taco sauce into a 2½ - 3 quart baking dish. Turn five of the tortillas in the sauce to coat. Spread overlapping in bottom of dish.

Strain as much water from the spinach as possible and stir half into beef; spoon beef mixture over the tortillas and dish and sprinkle with half the cheese. Cover with remaining tortillas, overlapping, and spread the balance of the taco sauce over them. Distribute the ham on top and spread with sour cream. Scatter the spinach over cream; scatter cheese over top. Bake 375 degrees —50 minutes. Cover the first 25 minutes.

Serves 8-10

Jean Whitaker

Santa Fe Souffle

1¼ cups grits
1 teaspoon Tabasco
 (less if desired)
2 teaspoons salt
6 cups water

1 pound medium sharp
 cheese, grated
3 eggs, beaten
1 cube butter or margarine
2 small cans diced
 green chilies

Boil together first 4 ingredients over medium heat until water is absorbed—stirring occasionally. This will take 30 minutes or more. Stir in cheese and butter and melt. Remove from heat and add other ingredients. Pour into large (it puffs up) well-buttered baking dish. Bake at 350 degrees about 1½ hours or until puffy and brown.

Serves 8

Kay Abbot

13

Viva La Chicken

4 chicken breasts
1 can cream of mushroom soup
1 cup milk
1 can Ortega green chili salsa

1 dozen corn tortillas
1 can cream of chicken soup
1 onion, grated
1 pound Cheddar cheese, grated

Bake chicken in foil, bone and cut in large pieces. Cut tortillas into one inch strips. Mix soups, milk, onion and chili salsa. Butter baking dish. Place layer of tortillas, layer of chicken, layer of soups and repeat, ending with liquid on top. Top with cheese. Let stand in refrigerator for 24 hours.

Bake at 300 degrees for 1 — 1½ hours or until bubbly.

Yield: serves 6   *Estella McKittrick*

Chili Rice Casserole

4 cups cooked rice
  (quick brown)
2 small cans chopped
  green chilies

1 pound grated Monterey
  Jack cheese
1 pint sour cream

Pour into casserole and mix well. Heat at 350 degrees for 35 - 40 minutes or until brown and crisp on top. Mushrooms can be added.

Mary Green

Sopapillas

4 cups flour
3 teaspoons baking powder
1 teaspoon salt

3 tablespoons shortening
Water

Sift flour, baking powder and salt. Cut in shortening, adding enough water to make a stiff dough. Roll out dough until it is ¼ inch thick. Cut into 3-inch squares and deep fry until golden brown. Serve warm with honey.

Yield: 4 dozen   *Gay McCabe*

14

Chili

1 pound chili meat
2 tablespoons butter
1 large onion, chopped
2 clove garlic, crushed
1 large green pepper,
   shredded lengthwise
1 small package pre-cooked
   pinto beans

3½ tablespoons chili powder
½ cup cold water
2 cups canned tomatoes, drained
1 bay leaf, crumbled
1½ teaspoons salt
½ teaspoon cumin seed
Dash of cayenne pepper

Melt butter in large dutch oven kettle over low heat. Sauté the onion, garlic and green pepper gently for 10 minutes, stirring occasionally. Add meat and brown for 2 minutes. Put in already prepared pinto beans and lower heat.

In another pan, mix chili powder and water, then stir in tomatoes. Season this with bay leaf, salt, cumin seed and cayenne pepper. Bring this to a full boil, then pour over meat and beans. Cover and let simmer for two hours or longer.

Serves 6   *Shirley Greer*

Ensalada De Naranja
(orange salad)

1 large head Boston Lettuce
2 large oranges
1 cucumber
1 small onion
   (I prefer sweet Bermuda)

1 green pepper
3 tablespoons olive oil
1 tablespoons wine vinegar
1½ teaspoons salt

Arrange clean crisp lettuce leaves in salad bowl. Between the greens and standing on edge, set thick slices of peeled oranges with thin slices of unpeeled cucumber in between. Strew thin slices of green pepper and onion on top and season with mixture of oil, vinegar and salt.
Good complement to Mexican food.

Serves 6   *Punky Robbe*

Arroz Con Chili Jocoque
(Rice with chilies and sour cream)

1 pound Monterey Jack cheese
4 cups sour cream
4 cans peeled green
   chilies, whole
4 cups cooked rice (may be instant)
Grated Cheddar cheese
Garlic salt to taste

Cut Monterey Jack cheese in thin slices. Mix sour cream with chilies, which have been quartered lengthwise, and garlic salt. Butter 2 quart casserole (deep). Salt rice according to taste. Layer rice, sour cream mixture and cheese in three layers with additional layer of rice on top. Bake for 30 minutes at 350 degrees. During the last 5 minutes grate Cheddar cheese over rice and continue baking until cheese melts.

Serves 8

Joanne Battiste

Chili Cheese Turnovers

1 package double
   crust pie crust mix
2½ cups grated Cheddar cheese
1 egg white
1 can diced Ortega
   green chilies

Follow package directions for mixing pie crust. Add 2 cups grated cheese and blend well. Divide dough in half. Roll out 1/8 inch thick and cut into circles with *small* cookie cutter. Dab the edges of each circle with beaten egg white. Fill each with about 1/8 teaspoon grated cheese and diced chilies. Fold in half and press edges with fork dipped in flour. They can be frozen at this stage or baked and served. Arrange as many as possible on ungreased cookie sheet. Bake at 400 degrees for 8-10 minutes, or if frozen for 12-15 minutes or until golden brown.

Note: Filling may be varied with cheese and bacon, cheese and olives.

Yield: 75

Jean Whitaker

Burritos With Green Chile Sauce

SAUCE:

2 pounds boneless pork butt
2 cans mild Ortega chilies,
   diced (one can for
   milder sauce)
2 cups canned tomatoes
   (chopped)

1 teaspoon garlic powder
   or 1 large clove
   crushed garlic
1 teaspoon salt
2 tablespoons flour
1 quart water

BURRITOS:

1 number 2½ can refried beans
1 tablespoon shortening

1 cup shredded Cheddar cheese
1 dozen white tortillas

SAUCE:

Cut pork in ½ inch pieces and trim excess fat. Fry meat until well browned over medium heat and drain excess fat with exception of 3 tablespoons. After meat has been browned, add flour and brown as for gravy. Combine chili, tomatoes, garlic and salt in bowl and add to meat and flour mixture. Add water and bring to a hard boil. Reduce heat and simmer until thick (about 45 minutes).

BURRITOS:

Refry beans in hot fat. Warm tortillas on a hot griddle and spread with beans and cheese. Roll tight and place in baking pan. Before serving, heat burritos in oven for 10 minutes and serve with green chile burrito sauce.

Mrs. George Masias

Pinto Beans

1 cup beans
5 cups water
1½ teaspoons sugar

Salt pork
Clove garlic

Cook until almost done and then salt to taste. This will take at least 4 hours.

Virginia McKee

17

Kidney Beans N'Beef

1½ pounds ground chuck
2 cans kidney beans
2 tablespoons
  Worcestershire sauce
¼ cup catsup

1 small onion, chopped
1 tablespoon horseradish
1 teaspoon salt
½ teaspoon pepper

Brown ground chuck and onion in a small amount of oil. Add water to cover and put in Worcestershire sauce, catsup, horseradish and salt and pepper plus juice off of the two cans of kidney beans. Stir and allow to come to a boil - turn to simmer for about 20 minutes. Add the kidney beans, stir, and cook for 10 minutes more.

Serve in bowls with hot rolls and a salad or thicken the liquid with flour and serve wrapped in white flour tortillas with extra gravy spooned over the top.

Mrs. Shirley Cline

Burro Caldes

2 tubes pre-mixed roll
  dough (pre-cut in
  triangular shape)
6 Italian sausages

1 small can pizza sauce
3 cans green chilies
Garlic salt to taste

Cut each sausage into thirds and sauté in hot skillet until done (about 20 minutes). Drain. Cut each chili lengthwise and roll each half slice around a sausage piece. Coat each triangular shape roll mixture with pizza sauce and place sausage and chili on narrow edge and roll to large end of dough. Pinch dough together to secure sauce and sausage. Place on lightly greased baking sheet and place in 350 degree oven for 25 minutes.

Serves 6

Mrs. Aldo A. Battiste

18

Mexican Eggs

1 can Ortega chili salsa
1 corn tortilla

Monterey Jack cheese
Eggs

Pour salsa in bottom of skillet. Heat. Lay thin slices of cheese on top. Melt. Crumble tortilla (one per person) in mixture. Stir. Allow to simmer until most of the moisture is absorbed. Break eggs on top. Cover with lid. Cook until eggs are done, but not hard. Slice into pie shaped wedges.

Lillian Kellogg

Chili Squares

Whole canned green chilies
½ pound grated Cheddar
   cheese

½ pound grated mozzarella
   cheese
6 eggs

Remove seeds from chilies and lay flat in well-greased casserole. Whip eggs until foamy and combine with cheese. Pour over chilies. Bake covered for 30 minutes at 350 degrees. Lower oven to 250 degrees, uncover, and bake 30 minutes more. Cut into small squares. Wonderful with cocktails . . . cut in bite-sized pieces.

Ruth Lovelady

Vegetable Casserole Rancheros

2 cans French style
   green beans
1 can Ortega green
   chili salsa

10 strips bacon
Salt and pepper to taste

Fry bacon crisp. Break into small pieces. Drain beans thoroughly. Mix together all ingredients and heat either on top of stove in pan or in oven as casserole.

Bake at 350 degrees until warm.

Serves 8

Neta DeRose

Fiesta Burgers

½ cup finely crushed
   crackers (14 squares)
2 eggs
¼ cup chopped onions
¼ cup catsup
2 teaspoons Worcestershire
   sauce
¼ teaspoon salt

Dash pepper
1 pound ground beef
1 can condensed cream
   of mushroom soup
1 15-ounce can kidney
   beans, drained
1/3 cup green pepper or onion
½ cup shredded Cheddar cheese

Combine first 7 ingredients. Add ground beef and mix. Shape into six patties. Brown on both sides in large skillet. Pour soup over meat, top with drained kidney beans and chopped green pepper or onion as preferred. Cook, covered, over low heat for 10 minutes. Sprinkle cheese over mixture, cover and cook five minutes more.

Donna Ward

Chili Dip

1 4-ounce can chopped
   green chili
1 4-ounce can of
   mushrooms, chopped finely

¼ cup olive oil
½ teaspoon garlic salt

Mix in order given above. Set over night. Serve with crackers.

Yield: one cup

Addie Cole

Mexican Baked Beans

2 large cans chili beans
   in chili gravy
1 6-ounce package corn
   chips (not king size)

6 slices American cheese

In large casserole dish, place a layer of beans, then cheese, and then corn chips until dish is full. Bake covered at 325 degrees for 45 minutes or until heated through.

Serves 8-10

Vivian Elizondo

20

Pickled Green Chili

½ cup sugar
½ cup vinegar
1 teaspoon salt
1 teaspoon dill seed
½ teaspoon mustard seed

2½ cups fresh roasted chili
   or 5 - 4½ ounce cans
Salt to taste
Garlic buds

Make light syrup. Simmer 5 minutes. Pack chopped chilies in jars, cover with syrup, add pieces of garlic. Cover tightly and refrigerate for 3 days (may be frozen also.) Makes 2 pints. Delicious served with tostado chips, on grilled cheese, hamburgers, etc.

Yield 2 pints   *Virginia McKee*

Mexican Heartburn

1 large bag corn chips,
   crumbled
2 pounds hamburger
1 large onion, chopped
1 large can chili
   beans in chili gravy
1 green pepper, chopped

1 can or bottle taco sauce
1 can green chili salsa
1 large can tomato sauce
2 cups grated Cheddar cheese
Lettuce
Green onions
Avocado
Italian dressing

Cook hamburger, green pepper and onions together - drain well. Put in large kettle and add beans and mixed sauces - saving about 3/4 cup. Make tossed salad of lettuce, tomato, green onion and avocado using a little Italian dressing.
Layer on plate:
Crumbled corn chips
Meat mixture
Grated cheese
Salad
Top with extra sauce
Serves 4   *Kay Abbot*

21

Sangrita
(non-alcoholic cocktail mix)

46-ounce vegetable
juice cocktail (V-8)
18-ounce frozen orange
juice (undiluted)
2 ounce fresh lemon
or lime juice

2 ounce Grenadine syrup
2 tablespoons Tabasco
½-2 tablespoon salt

Mix well — strain — chill.

Mix one to one or two to one with tequila or serve plain. Makes 2 quarts.

Sangrita is Spanish for "Little Blood." Sangrita cocktail mix is used in Mexico with tequila—either mixed together or on the side. This drink is supposed to temper the effects of alcohol.

Dolph Otterstein

Wet Backs

1 pound ground round
1 chopped onion
1 clove garlic
1 tablespoon sugar
1 small can tomato sauce

1 small can tomato paste
1 small can water
1 teaspoon whole oregano,
chili powder, cumin,
Accent and salt

Combine all ingredients and simmer for 40 minutes. Serve with condiments in the following order:
Start with a handful of tortilla chips.
Cover with meat sauce in amount desired.
Top with following condiments stacked high like a tostada:

Shredded lettuce
Grated Cheddar cheese
Chopped tomato
Chopped green onion

Chopped avocado
Sour cream
Chopped black olive

Arrange condiments in bowls and let each person build his own.

Peachy Wilcoxson

Serves 4-6

22

Quiche Mexican

Prepared pastry for 9 inch pie
6 slices bacon
  fried and crumbled
4 eggs, slightly beaten
½ teaspoon ground
  coriander or cumin

2 cups Monterey Jack cheese
1½ 4 ounce cans
  chopped green chilies
1½ cups light cream
Salt and pepper

Line 9 inch pie tin with pastry . . . prick crust. Cover with foil and weight with another pie pan. Bake in 400 degree oven for 12 minutes. Remove foil. Sprinkle well with cheese, bacon and chopped chilies. Combine beaten eggs with cream and coriander. Pour into pie shell and bake at 350 degrees about 35 minutes or until set in center.

Allow to stand a few minutes before serving.

Good with cold roast beef or chicken. May be cut into small servings for cocktails.

Serves 6

Kay Abbot

Chili Rellenos Casserole

6 cans diced or whole
  Ortega brand chilies
1 pound Monterey Jack
  cheese, shredded

1 dozen eggs
1 pint sour cream
1 teaspoon salt
1 pound longhorn or
  Cheddar cheese, shredded

Layer in at least a 13 inch by 9 inch buttered baking dish. Alternate chili and one kind of cheese, then chili and second kind of cheese. Salt the mixture. Separate eggs; beat whites until just stiff. Beat egg yolks until thick. Beat in sour cream. Fold yolks and whites together. Pour over chili mixture. Bake in 350 degree oven 50-60 minutes.

Serves 8

Dottie Osburne

Tamale Pie (Mexican Casserole)

1½ pounds lean ground beef
1 medium onion
1 can stewed tomatoes
1 can pinto beans
— unseasoned
1 can chili without beans
1 can small ripe olives
(as desired)

3/4 cup grated mild cheese
(American, Monterey Jack
or longhorn)
9-12 yellow corn tortillas
or 1 package of corn
muffin mix
Salt to taste

Brown meat in salted skillet (sprinkle salt over bottom of skillet without grease). Add onions. When meat is done and onions transparent, add stewed tomatoes, drained beans, olives, chili. Mix well. Taste to assure flavor - add salt if necessary. In large baking dish, cover bottom with mixture, then layer tortillas over mixture and continue in alternate layers until mixture is used, ending with layer of mixture. Cover top with grated cheese. Bake at 350 degrees for 30 minutes or until mixture is bubbling and cheese is melted and slightly brown.

Alternate for tortillas. For corn muffin mix, mix as directed on package. Pour meat mixture into baking dish and stir muffin mix gently through - top with grated cheese. Bake at 375 degrees for 30 minutes or until corn mixture is done.

Serves 6

Mrs. George E. McKinnon

Spicy Spuds

2½ pounds potatoes
1 can cheese soup
1 soup can milk
1 4-ounce can diced
green chilies
1 4-ounce can taco sauce

1 cup grated longhorn cheese
1 small can diced
pimiento (optional)
Salt and pepper to taste
½ can French fried
onion rings

Cook potatoes until almost done. Peel and cube into casserole dish or glass loaf pan. Mix remaining ingredients (except onion rings) together. Pour over potatoes. Add onion rings the last 5 minutes of baking. Bake for 30 minutes in oven at 350 degrees.

Serves 8

Beth Thatcher

Mexican Rice

4 slices of bacon, fried crisp
1 large onion, sliced fine
1 can tomato soup
1 can red kidney beans,
    drained and rinsed

1 cup cooked rice
Salt and pepper
Cayenne

Crumble bacon. Mix all ingredients together. Add enough water, just to cover, and simmer, covered, until liquid is absorbed. May be made in your electric frying pan.

Serves 4

Kay Abbot

Spanish Omelet

2 tablespoons quick tapioca
3/4 cup milk
½ teaspoon salt

1/8 teaspoon pepper
4 eggs
1 tablespoon butter

Cook tapioca, milk, salt and pepper until slightly thick. Add butter and cool. Prepare topping while tapioca is cooling. Separate eggs. Beat yolks and add to tapioca mixture. Beat whites until stiff and fold in. Bake at 350 degrees in a preheated greased skillet about 15 minutes or until lightly browned.

TOPPING:
½ medium-sized
    green pepper, chopped
1 medium onion, cut in rings
2 tablespoons oil

1 teaspoon salt
¼ teaspoon pepper
1 No. 303 can
    sliced tomatoes

Sauté pepper and onion for 5 minutes. Add tomatoes and seasoning and cover and simmer. Serve over individual servings of omelet.

Serves 4-6

Mary Beth Jensen

Sweet Venuelos

2½ pounds enriched
   flour sifted (10 cups)
1 cup sugar

2 tablespoons lard
   or shortening.

Mix above ingredients together in a large bowl. Add enough
warm water until dough becomes manageable. Knead until soft
and pliable. Separate dough into approximately 3 inch balls. Roll
out into flat round discs the size of tortillas and set aside a few
minutes to air (about 15 minutes). Fry in deep fat until browned.
Drain. Dip immediately in a mixture of sugar and cinnamon.

Yield: 3 dozen   *Mary Ann Roldan*

Tortillas

4 cups flour
2 teaspoons baking powder
1 rounded teaspoon salt

3 tablespoons lard
1½ cups hot water (not boiling)

Mix dry ingredients. Add lard and hot water a little at a time.
Knead dough on floured board until mixed, then form dough into
balls about the size of an egg and roll out on floured board. Place
on hot griddle (not greased). Be careful not to overcook. Turn
when small areas are browned. Stack and cover with towel or
foil until ready to serve.

Yield: 18 at 8 inch diameter   *Mrs. Tony Mestas*

Green Chili Stew

1½ pounds cubed round steak
1 tablespoon garlic salt
1 cup canned tomatoes

1 cup water
4-6 cans green chili or
6 ounces of fresh chilies

Brown cubed steak, add rest of ingredients and simmer until meat
is tender. Serve with pinto beans, either mixed with stew or as
side dish.

Virginia McKee

Jerky

Cut strips from round or flank steak ¼ inch thick (6-8 inches long.) Place in casserole dish with sides touching. Sprinkle each layer with salt, pepper, two to three drops liquid smoke and chili powder. (Use seasoning you like—try garlic or onion salt or powder —possibly soy sauce or teriyaki sauce.) Put on plate with double foil over top and weight down with heavy object. Refrigerate 24 hours. Drain on paper towels. Drape strips over broiler rack with foil underneath, but not touching. (Do not overlap meat.)

Bake at 150 degrees for 8-11 hours.

(I freeze the meat and cut it partially frozen—it's easier to cut neatly.)

Bev Brill

Enchilada Casserole

1 medium onion
2 tablespoons salad oil
2 pound ground beef
1 can (12 ounces) corn with
   pimiento and green peppers
¼ teaspoon each of rosemary,
   oregano, and marjoram
2 teaspoons salt

¼ teaspoon pepper

2 cans (8 ounces) tomato sauce
1 can (10 ounce)
   enchilada sauce
12 tortillas (6 if large)
½ to 3/4 pound sharp
   Cheddar cheese, sliced

Sauté onions in oil, add beef and cook until meat is brown (drain off excess grease). Add next 6 ingredients. Combine two sauces and pour half over meat - simmer 5 minutes. In bottom of shallow 2 quart casserole arrange tortillas, pour half of meat mixture on top of tortillas, arrange half of cheese over meat. Repeat layers, pouring remaining sauce on top. Bake 350 degrees for 25 minutes.

Serves 6-8

Evelyn Streamer

Soup Mexicana

1 chicken breast
6 cups chicken broth
2 onions chopped
1 tablespoon butter
1½ teaspoon grated onion

2 cups chopped zucchini
1 cup Mexicorn
½ cup tomato puree
2 avocados sliced
Salt and pepper to taste

Cook chicken until tender in the broth with chopped onion. Remove chicken, dice, and set aside. Reserve broth.

Heat butter and onion in a large saucepan and blend in zucchini and corn. Cook about 5 minutes stirring occasionally. Mix in the broth and tomato puree. Cover and simmer about 20 minutes.

Just before serving, mix in diced chicken. Add avocado individually.

Serves 6-8

Tamzin Holman

Green Chili

1 pound pork end (remove fat)
1 tablespoon flour
½ cup fresh tomatoes

1 clove garlic (mashed)
1 dozen fresh green chilies
1½ cup water

Rinse green chilies and place on oven rack at 400 degrees. Turn when brown. Depending on your oven, this whole process should take about 15 minutes. When chilies are brown, remove from oven and place in pan, sprinkle one tablespoon water over them and cover. Wait 30 minutes and remove the stems and skin from chilies. The chilies are now ready for the sauce. (Incidentally, you may, at this point, place chilies in plastic bags and freeze for future use.)

Sauce:
Dice pork and brown in large skillet, sprinkle 1 tablespoon flour over pork and continue cooking until flour is brown. Add green chilies, tomatoes, mashed garlic and brown together. Add 1½ cups of water and simmer 45 minutes, salt to taste. This sauce has a variety of uses. You may serve with tortillas, beans, enchiladas or over a steak, Mexican style.

Jennie Espinoza

28

Gazpacho (Mexican Soup)

1 cup peeled
  tomato, chopped fine
½ cup green pepper,
  chopped fine
½ cup celery, chopped fine
½ cup cucumber, chopped fine
¼ cup onion, finely chopped
2 teaspoons parsley, snipped
1 teaspoon chives, snipped
1 garlic clove, chopped (small)

2½ teaspoons tarragon
  wine vinegar
2 teaspoons olive oil
1 teaspoon salt
¼ teaspoon black pepper,
  freshly ground
½ teaspoon Worcestershire
  sauce
4 cups tomato juice

Combine all ingredients in stainless steel or glass bowl. Cover and chill at least four hours. Serve in chilled cups with onion wafers or melba toast.

Serves 12

Mrs. James Grosso

Mexican Spoon Bread

1 can cream style corn
3/4 cup milk
1/3 cup melted shortening
2 eggs
1 cup corn meal

½ teaspoon soda
1 teaspoon salt
1 can (4 ounces) green
  chilies, chopped
1½ cups shredded
  Cheddar cheese

Mix all ingredients except chilies and cheese in order given above (wet ingredients first, then dry ones). Pour one half of the batter into greased 9 inch x 9 inch square pan and spread with peeled green chilies and one half of the cheese. Spread remaining batter on top and sprinkle with remaining cheese. Bake at 400 degrees for 45 minutes. Remove from oven and let cool just enough to set a little before cutting into serving size pieces.

Serves 8-10

Leah Rae Puleo

Sopapillas

Mix:

1½ cups warm water	1 package yeast
2 tablespoons sugar	1/3 cup oil
1 tablespoon salt	

Add:

1 cup powdered milk	3½ cups wheat flour
1½ cups flour	

Let rise in warm place until double·in bulk. Roll dough to ¼ inch thickness. Cut in squares and deep fry in a mixture of ½ oil and ½ shortening until golden brown and puffed. Serve hot with honey or jelly along with Mexican dishes.

The secret to puffing:
Air side goes down in grease. Be sure to keep submerged in hot grease when first frying. Do not use fork as it may puncture the air bubble.

Nina Palmer

Baked Chili Con Carne

1 pound ground beef (chuck or round)	1 can peeled tomatoes (number 2 can)
1 large onion, chopped	1 can kidney beans (number 2 can)
4 stalks celery, chopped	Salt and pepper to taste
½ cup cabbage, chopped	Chili powder to taste
1 green pepper, chopped	Parmesan cheese

Brown beef in large skillet. Add onion, celery, cabbage, pepper and salt and chili powder. Place in two quart casserole; add kidney beans. Sprinkle top with grated Parmesan cheese. Bake in 350 degree oven for one hour. For luncheon or Sunday supper, serve with corn muffins or corn bread and pear and grape salad.

Serves 4

Doris Flutcher

Mexican Coffee

½ teaspoon cinnamon
1½ cups strong black coffee
Sugar to taste

½ cup whipping cream
¼ teaspoon cinnamon
¼ teaspoon nutmeg

Stir cinnamon into coffee. Pour into 4 demitasse cups. Sweeten to taste, and top each cup with a generous touch of whipping cream. I use packaged whip which has been spiced with the nutmeg and cinnamon. Great with a piece of chocolate candy following a Mexican dinner.

Serves 4

Jean Whitaker

Tamale Corn

2 eggs beaten
2 No. 2½ cans
   cream style corn
3/4 cup corn meal
3/4 teaspoon garlic salt

½ teaspoon baking powder
¼ cup salad oil
2 small cans chopped
   green chilies
½ pound sharp cheese, grated

Mix all ingredients and pour into greased baking dish. Bake at 350 degrees 45 minutes or until set.

Mrs. Eldon Brown

Sopa De Aquacate Con Ajo
(Avocado soup with garlic)

4 fully ripe avocados
2 cups chicken broth
2 teaspoons lime juice
½ teaspoon salt

1/8 teaspoon garlic powder
2 cups heavy cream
Lemon slices (optional)
Whipping cream (optional)

Halve avocados lengthwise. Peel avocado halves, then puree in electric blender with broth, lime juice, salt, and garlic powder. Stir in cream. Chill throughly. Garnish with lemon slices or with heavy cream, whipped, with a dash of garlic powder.

Serves 6

Barbara Henry

Green Chili

2½ pounds lean pork
3 small cans diced chilies
   (1 hot—2 medium)

1 large can peeled tomatoes
6 to 8 cups water
1 medium egg plant

Cut off fat from meat and render in frying pan. Should have enough to brown meat and egg plant; if not add 1 to 2 tablespoons lard. Cube meat and peeled egg plant, brown meat (and remove from pan) add eggplant and lightly brown; remove from pan. Make a thin gravy by adding sufficient flour to drippings. Put all ingredients in large kettle, salt to taste, and simmer for at least 2 hours. Serve with white tortillas.

Mrs. Ed. McGuire

Green Chili

1 pound lean pork, cut in
   small pieces (cooked)
1 large can tomatoes plus
   one can water

4 cans green chili ortegas
2 teaspoons cumin, garlic
   salt and salt to taste.

Grind or chop tomatoes and green chili.
Mix all together and simmer about an hour.

Jean Ludwig

Pedro's Special

1 pound hamburger
½ chopped onion
Garlic salt to your taste
1 can (8 oz.) tomato sauce plus
   1/3 of the can of water
1 pound can of pinto beans
   with liquid

¼ teaspoon oregano
2 teaspoons chili powder
1 medium size bag of regular
   Fritos (probably won't use all)
Shredded lettuce

Brown together the meat, onion and garlic (pan off excess fat). Stir in tomato sauce, water, oregano and chili powder. Take a good size casserole, grease it, and alternate layers of this mixture with layers of beans and chips.

Bake covered at 350 degrees for 45 minutes in all (uncover the last 10 minutes). Before you serve it, strew shredded lettuce on top.

Serves a family of 4 or 5

Mr. C. N. Ogden

Ellie's Burritos

3 pounds lean cubed pork
3 cans diced green chilies
4 onions, chopped
4 peeled tomatoes, fresh
   or canned
1½ teaspoons salt
2 cloves garlic, mashed

½ teaspoon cumin
¼ teaspoon oregano
Flour tortillas
1 large can refried beans

Barely cover pork cubes with water. Add all ingredients except tortillas and beans. Simmer at least 45 minutes — be sure pork is done. Add 2 tablespoons flour mixed with cold water to make a thin paste. Cook down until thick—about 20 minutes more. Stir occasionally.

Meanwhile heat beans in a saucepan. Wrap tortillas in foil and put in 300 degree oven about 20 minutes until warm and still soft.

Place beans down the center of each tortilla, roll. Top with green chili stew.

Serves several   *Kay Abbot*

Chicken Sopa
(Mexican Casserole)

1 dozen corn tortillas
½ pound grated Cheddar cheese
1 can diced green chilies
1 or 2 cans boned chicken (left-
   over turkey can be used)

1 can cream of mushroom soup
1 can cream of chicken soup
¼ cup chopped onion

Lightly fry tortillas to soften and cut in quarters. Mix soups, chilies and onion together. Layer in casserole the tortillas, chicken, soup mix and cheese. End with tortillas and cheese.

Bake 30 minutes at 350 degrees. Ten minutes before serving spread sour cream on top.

We like this casserole hotter so I add two cans of green chilies. I never have boned chicken so I use boned, boiled fryer or leftover turkey, or canned, boned chicken.

Serves 6   *Jonnie Miller*

33

appetizers

"Home, home on the range" was often
little more than a campsite where necessity
dictated cooking over an open flame
and where using what-is-at-hand
determined the menu.

Pecan Cheese Ball

½ pound Old English cheese
½ pound sharp Cheddar, (finely
   (finely grated)
½ pound blue cheese
2 8-ounce packages cream cheese
3 teaspoons Worcestershire sauce

2 teaspoons onion, chopped
1 teaspoon salt
3 tablespoons pimiento, chopped
½ pound pecans, ground

Soften all cheeses at room temperature, and mix thoroughly with electric mixer until well blended. Add Worcestershire, onion, salt, pimiento, and half of the pecans. Mix well and chill. Shape into one large ball or four small ones. Roll in remaining pecans. This ball freezes well. Serve surrounded with crackers, and thin rye bread.

Ann Gardner

Cheese Ball

6 ounces blue cheese
1 5-ounce jar Old English
   Cheddar cheese spread
1 5-ounce jar bacon
   Cheddar cheese spread
12 ounces cream cheese
2 tablespoons finely
   chopped onion

1 teaspoon Worcestershire
   sauce
½ teaspoon Accent
1 cup ground pecans
½ cup finely chopped
   fresh parsley
½ teaspoon salt

All cheese should be at room temperature. Combine cheeses, onion, Worcestershire sauce and Accent. Mix until blended. Add ½ cup pecans and ¼ cup parsley. Mix and shape into a ball. Place in a bowl and refrigerate overnight. One hour before serving, roll in mixture of remaining pecans and parsley. Surround with crisp crackers.

Sherry Clarkin

Cheese Logs

1 cup pecans
1 clove garlic
1 6-ounce package cream cheese

1 tablespoon A-1 sauce
Chile powder

Finely grind pecans and garlic clove. Blend together with cream cheese and A-1 sauce. Shape into roll about 5 inches long and 1½ inches in diameter. Roll in chile powder to coat evenly. Wrap in foil and chill. Slice and serve with crackers.

Margie Hyde

Cheese Stuffed Rolls

1 large green pepper
1 firm ripe tomato
1 teaspoon salt
2 teaspoons grated onion

2 tablespoons butter, softened
3 packages cream cheese
4 French rolls
1 clove garlic

Peel tomato and chop fine with pepper. Drain and mix with rest of ingredients. Hollow out rolls and fill with mixture. Wrap in wax paper and chill overnight. Slice thin before serving. (Anchovy paste and pimiento may be used in place of tomato and peppers. Olives, too.

Mary Lou Hall

My Cheese Ball

1 pound Samsoe or Gruyere
   cheese, finely shredded
1 cup butter

1 tablespoon Dijon style mustard
2 tablespoons Kummel,
   Aquavit or gin

Allow ingredients to soften. Mix; form into ball and chill. Toast ¼ cup sesame seeds in oven at 325 degrees for 5 watchful minutes. Roll ball in seeds.

Mrs. Hank Williams

38

Cheese Puffs

24 to 36 stuffed olives
1 cup grated sharp
 Cheddar cheese
¼ cup butter

½ cup plus 2 teaspoons flour
½ teaspoon paprika
¼ teaspoon salt

Drain olives, dry in towel. Combine all ingredients; roll into a ball. Take one teaspoon for each olive, flatten the dough, place olive in center and roll in a ball. Bake 10 minutes in 450 degree oven.

Mrs. Herbert Shaver

Hot Snappy Wafers

1 pound sharp Cheddar,
 put through food grinder
¼ pound butter
1¼ cups flour

2 teaspoons Worcestershire
 sauce
½ teaspoon salt
Cayenne or Tabasco

Mix butter and cheese thoroughly. Add flour and other ingredients. Mix well with hands. Roll in wax paper—chill well. Slice thin and bake at 425-450 degrees for 4-5 minutes. Keep your eye on them! If you wish to make them ahead you can roll them into small balls, depress with a floured fork and freeze on a cookie sheet. Put them in a plastic bag when frozen and bake at the last minute for unexpected guests. The friend who gave me this recipe uses 8 teaspoons pepper or hot sauce. She like them to burn all the way down. If your husband or friends have an ulcer, better warn them!

Jean Looby

Teriyaki Meatballs

2 pounds ground chuck
   or lean ground beef
½ cup fine dry bread crumbs
½ cup milk

2 eggs
1½ teaspoons salt (or part
   garlic or seasoned salt)

Combine the meat, crumbs, milk, eggs and salt in a bowl. Mix lightly to blend. Shape into balls about the size of large marbles and arrange in shallow baking pans. Put into a 500 degree oven for 4-5 minutes or until lightly browned. Remove and add to the prepared sauce, including pan juices. Cool, then refrigerate until time to serve.

Teriyaki Sauce

2 tablespoons cornstarch
1/3 cup soy sauce
¼ cup sugar
1 clove garlic, minced or
   mashed (or garlic powder)

2 teaspoons minced fresh ginger
   (or ½ teaspoon ground ginger)
2¼ cups beef broth

In a pan, blend together the cornstarch, soy sauce, sugar, garlic, and fresh or ground ginger. Stir in beef broth. Cook, stirring until thickened.

Serve in chafing dish or over candle warmer. Provide toothpicks for spearing.

Yield: 100

Mary G. Shannon

Teen-Age Fondue

1 3/4 cup milk
2 8-ounce packages cream
   cheese (cubed)
2 teaspoons dry mustard

¼ cup green onions, (chopped)
1 2¼ -ounce jar sliced
   dried beef, (diced)
French bread, (cubed)

Heat milk; add cream cheese. Stir until melted. Add mustard, and onions, and beef. Cook 5 minutes. Serve in chafing dish.

Punky Robbe

Mom's Swedish Meat Balls

1½ pounds ground pork butt
   (or lean pork)
2 eggs
3/4 cup milk

3/4 cup medium onion,
   finely chopped
2 teaspoons salt
Dash pepper

Make balls the size of walnuts. Brown on at least three sides. Add additional salt while cooking if desired. After browning, add a few tablespoons water and steam for 10-15 minutes. Hints: Brown a few at a time; remove to another pan while doing others. Can be served as hors d'oeuvres or entree. Cannot be made into balls ahead—too soft. Balls are easier to form if you wet hands with cold water—shake off excess.

Yield: 80 small balls

Bev Brill

Meat Ball Appetizers

1 pound ground beef
1 teaspoon Accent
3/4 teaspoon salt
1 tablespoon minced onion
½ cup bread crumbs
¼ cup milk

1 tablespoon flour
2 tablespoons butter

3 tablespoons molasses
   (unsulphured)
3 tablespoons prepared
   mustard
¼ cup ketchup
½ teaspoon thyme

Break up meat with fork; sprinkle with Accent, salt, onion, and bread crumbs. Add milk; toss lightly. Roll into 3/4" balls, roll in flour and brown in butter. Combine remaining ingredients; blend until smooth and pour over meatballs. Simmer 8-10 minutes, stirring until sauce thickens and meatballs are glazed. Leave in refrigerator overnight if preparing in advance or serve immediately. Serve in chafing dish.

Mrs. Edward A. Pacey

Yiddish Meat Balls

1½ pounds ground beef
4 tablespoons grated onion
1 egg
2 teaspoons salt
1/8 teaspoon pepper
3 tablespoons cornstarch
2 tablespoons fat

1½ cups beefstock
2 tablespoons lemon juice
1 lemon, thinly sliced
¼ cup seedless raisins
3 tablespoons sugar
6 crushed ginger snaps

Mix meat, onion, egg, salt and pepper. Form into 1-inch balls and lightly roll in cornstarch. Melt fat in deep skillet and brown meat balls. Add remaining ingredients except snaps. Cover and cook over low heat 35 minutes. Stir in snaps and cook additional 10 minutes.

Serves 6   *Punky Robbe*

Horseradish Meat Balls

½ cup water
2 egg yolks or 1 whole egg
½ cup packaged bread crumbs
2 tablespoons horseradish

1 cup water chestnuts,
  finely chopped
1 pound ground chuck
Salt and pepper to taste

Preheat oven to 350 degrees. Beat water with egg. Stir in bread crumbs, horseradish and chestnuts. Add meat and mix gently. Shape into one-inch balls. Place in shallow pan and bake 12 minutes.

Hot marmalade soy dip:
1/3 cup orange marmalade
1 clove garlic, minced
¼ cup soy sauce

2 tablespoons lemon juice
1/3 cup water

Mix together and cook to boiling point. Serve hot over meat balls.

Yield 44 meat balls   *Rheuanna Kelly*

42

Swedish Meat Balls

2 pounds ground beef
7 Holland Rusks (rolled)
4 eggs
½ -1 cup milk
1¼ teaspoons salt
½ teaspoon pepper

2 teaspoons sugar
Dash ground allspice
    and nutmeg
2 onions, cut fine
2 tablespoons parsley, chopped

Mix well all ingredients except onions. Shape into small balls. Brown well and carefully in butter. Remove from pan. Brown onions, add small amount of flour, salt, pepper and 1 teaspoon bouillon to make gravy and simmer for 1 hour.

This makes a great hors d'oeuvre or can be served over noodles for a main dish.

Mrs. Robert McEniry

Hawaiian Ham Bits

2 pounds cooked ground ham
2 pounds cooked ground
    lean pork
1 1/3 cups fine bread crumbs

4 eggs, lightly beaten
Salt and pepper

Combine above ingredients into balls (large if for entree, small if for hors d'oeuvres). Bake at 350 degrees for 30 minutes.

Sauce: 3/4 cup brown sugar   2 tablespoons vinegar
        1 tablespoon dry mustard 1 pound crushed pineapple

Mix all ingredients, pour over cooked ham balls. Bake uncovered for 30 or 40 minutes at 350 degrees. For entree, serve with green or plain rice. For hot hors d'oeuvres, serve on warmer with toothpicks.

Nancy Tracey

Shrimp Dip

1 8-ounce package
    cream cheese
2 cans shrimp
Cocktail sauce

Tabasco
Lemon juice
Onion juice
Paprika

Place softened cream cheese in electric mixer. Add enough cocktail sauce for dip, then add shrimp; mix until spreading consistency. Add Tabasco, lemon juice, onion juice to taste. Sprinkle paprika over top.

Nancy Taylor Shivers

Shrimp Dip

1 cup mayonnaise
½ cup finely chopped celery
1 tablespoon minced onion
2 tablespoons lemon juice

Dash Tabasco
1 can broken shrimp
Seasoning salt

Mix together the day before needed. Refrigerate 24 hours, stirring occasionally. Serve with tortilla chips.

Nancy Hite

Shrimp Filling for Miniature Cream Puffs

½ pound raw shrimp, chopped
3/4 cup mayonnaise

¼ teaspoon garlic salt
½ pound American cheese,
    grated

Combine all ingredients in bowl, and beat at medium speed until smooth. Fill miniature cream puffs and bake at 375 degrees for 15 minutes.

Sandy Stein

44

"Kansas Shrimp"

¼ pound package sliced
   dried beef
1 8-ounce package
   cream cheese
1 teaspoon Worcestershire sauce

2 teaspoons prepared
   horseradish
½ teaspoon onion salt
2 tablespoons lemon juice
   or dry sherry

Combine softened cream cheese, Worcestershire sauce, horse-radish, onion salt, and lemon juice (or sherry). Mix until creamy. Spread cheese mixture on separated dried beef slices and roll each up jelly-roll fashion. Chill well in foil wrap or air tight container. Cut into bite-sized pieces. Spear each with cocktail pick.

Mrs. Carl S. Multer

Shrimp Remoulade

3 cups cooked shrimp,
   chopped fine
3 hard-cooked eggs,
   chopped fine
2 teaspoons minced capers
1 teaspoon prepared mustard
1 tablespoon tarragon vinegar
Juice of ½ lemon

1 clove minced garlic
2 tablespoons minced
   green onions
1 tablespoon minced parsley
1 teaspoon prepared
   horseradish
¼ teaspoon savory
1 cup mayonnaise

Combine all ingredients. Chill well. Serve in bowl, with spreading knives and assorted breads and crackers on the side (miniature French bread, Ritz crackers, flavored cocktail crackers, Melba toast rounds, etc.).

Rheuanna Kelly

Potted Crab

8 ounces crabmeat, cooked
   or canned, finely shredded
3 ounces butter or margarine
3 egg yolks, carefully
   separated from whites
2 tablespoons heavy cream

1 tablespoon sherry
1 tablespoon lemon juice
Salt and pepper to taste
Cayenne pepper to taste
1 tablespoon grated
   Parmesan cheese

Add the first six ingredients to a small pan and stir constantly. Cook over low heat until smooth and thick. Add salt, pepper, cayenne pepper and cheese. Stir well until smooth and well blended. Add more sherry and lemon if the taste buds say so! Pack tightly into a nonmetallic cocktail dish or other serving pot. Chill until serving time. Serve with crusty French bread broken into bite-sized pieces or with squares of crisp toast or with wheat crackers. Note: May be frozen.

Mrs. Jack Wolther

Crabmeat Puffs

6 slices bread (no crusts)
3 1-ounce slices of
   American cheese
1 cup crabmeat
2 eggs

1 cup milk
½ teaspoon salt
Dash pepper

Place three slices of bread across bottom of buttered shallow baking pan and cover each with a slice of cheese. Cover cheese with crabmeat and top with remaining slices of bread. Cut each sandwich into three strips. Beat eggs with salt, pepper and milk and pour over sandwiches. Chill 2 hours or, better yet, overnight. Bake 30 minutes at 350 degrees.

Serves 4

Ange Jagger

Hot Crab Dip

8 ounces cream cheese,
  room temperature
2 tablespoons chopped onion
1 tablespoon milk
1 teaspoon cream-style
  horseradish

1 teaspoon salt
Pepper
1/3 pound cooked crab meat
Sliced toasted almonds

Mix all ingredients and heat. Reserve a few almonds to sprinkle on top. Serve with wheat thins.

Serves 4-5

Mary Ann Sturgeon

Stuffed Mushrooms with Crab

1 cup crabmeat
1 tablespoon dry bread crumbs
1 teaspoon salt
1 tablespoon onion, parsley,
  and chives, (all chopped)

1 egg, (beaten)
1½ pound mushrooms
Parmesan cheese

Combine crab meat with bread crumbs, salt, onion, parsley, chives. Stir in egg. Wipe and remove the stems from mushrooms and fill with crab mixture. Sprinkle with buttered bread crumbs, and fresh grated Parmesan cheese. Bake at 350 degrees for 20 minutes. These can also be used as garnish around a vegetable ring or a meat platter. Allow three mushrooms per person, be sure to count.

Murial Anton

Deviled Crab Meat Pâté

½ pound fresh cooked
  crab meat
¼ cup celery
3 tablespoons butter
3 tablespoons mayonnaise
½ teaspoon lemon juice

1 teaspoon prepared mustard
½ teaspoon dry mustard
4 drops Tabasco sauce
¼ teaspoon salt
1 tablespoon scallions

Blend in mixer until smooth; chill well. Serve on crackers.

Rheuanna Kelly

Crabmeat Dip

1 cup drained crabmeat,
  chopped
½ cup sour cream
½ cup mayonnaise
1 tablespoon parsley

1 tablespoon sherry
1 teaspoon lemon juice
Salt and pepper to taste

Combine all ingredients. Mix well and allow to stand before serving. This can be made in the morning for an evening party.

Wynona Sullivan

Baked Crabmeat and Shrimp Appetizer

1 medium green pepper,
  chopped
1 medium onion, chopped
1 cup chopped celery
1 cup flaked crabmeat
1 cup cooked, cleaned shrimp

½ teaspoon salt
¼ teaspoon pepper
1 tablespoon Worcestershire
  sauce
1 cup mayonnaise or
  salad dressing
1 cup or more of bread crumbs

Combine all ingredients except bread crumbs. Place in individual sea shells. Sprinkle with buttered bread crumbs and paprika. Bake at 350 degrees for 30 minutes.

Serves 6-8

Sandy Stein

Cocktail Clam Dip

½ cube butter
1 small onion, chopped
1 pound Old English
  Cheddar cheese
½ to 1 small can Ortega
  diced peppers (chilies)

½ cup catsup
7-ounce can minced clams,
  well-drained (or shrimp,
  if desired)
½ cup sherry

In double boiler, melt butter and sauté onion. Add cheese (cut up to melt easily), peppers, catsup and clams. Add sherry last when cheese is melted. Serve hot in chafing dish with Mexican tostados or toasted rye slices.

Mrs. Owen McKinney

48

Minced Clams

1 can minced clams
3 tablespoons butter
2 tablespoons flour
2 tablespoons minced onion

Paprika
Fresh bread crumbs
from 1 slice bread

Sauté onion in butter until transparent. Add flour and cook one minute. Drain clams and heat juice. Add to butter and flour mixture. Cook until thickened. Add clams Place in shells or small cooking dishes. Top with buttered bread crumbs. Dash with paprika. Just before serving, heat in 400 degree oven for 10 minutes or until top is golden brown.

Serves 6
Mrs. T. R. Lenz

Bacon-Cheese Hors d'oeuvres

Bacon
Cream cheese

Bread slices, with
crusts cut off

Whip cream cheese and spread on bread. Roll and cut into pieces the width of a piece of bacon. Wrap ½ piece of bacon around each and broil until brown.

LaLonna Meoska

Bacon Bites

18-20 bread rounds
Melted margarine
2 stiffly beaten egg whites
1 cup grated sharp
　Cheddar cheese
1 teaspoon chopped parsley

2/3 cup finely chopped pepper
1 teaspoon chopped pimiento
½ teaspoon salt
Dash of pepper
3 bacon slices, diced

Cut bread into rounds with cookie cutter. Toast bread on one side in oven. Brush untoasted side with margarine. Fold remaining ingredients except bacon into egg whites. Spoon onto toast; sprinkle with bacon. Broil 4 to 5 inches from flame for 8-10 minutes or until bacon browns and cheese melts.

Ange Jaggar

Curry Nut Dip

2 3-ounce packages
   cream cheese
¼ cup milk
Dash Tabasco
1/3 cup chopped peanuts

¼ teaspoon curry powder
   (or more to taste)
¼ teaspoon garlic salt
   (or more to taste)

Have cream cheese at room temperature. Add milk and mix until smooth. Add remaining ingredients, blending thoroughly. Chill several hours to blend flavors. Soften to room temperature just before serving.

Marilyn Hunter

Curry Dip

½ cup sour cream
½ cup mayonnaise
1 teaspoon curry powder

1 teaspoon grated onion
2 drops Tabasco

Blend and serve with: Cauliflowerets
                      Carrot sticks
                      Celery sticks
                      Cherry tomatoes

Betty Johnson

Curry-Egg Spread for Canapes

3 minced, hard-cooked eggs
2 tablespoons mayonnaise
1 tablespoon anchovy paste
1 teaspoon lemon juice

1 tablespoon finely
   grated cheese
1 teaspoon minced onion
½ teaspoon curry powder

Combine all ingredients. Refrigerate until needed. To serve: arrange spread in bowl on tray with choice of bread rounds or crackers.

Yield: 1 cup

Rheuanna Kelly

50

Pick-Up Chicken Sticks

3 pounds chicken wings
1½ cups sifted flour
¼ cup sesame seeds

1 cup butter or margarine
1 tablespoon salt
½ teaspoon ginger

Cut off and discard wing tips. Divide each wing in half by cutting through the joint with a sharp knife. Wash and drain on paper towels. Melt butter in a large shallow baking pan. Mix flour, sesame seeds, salt and ginger in a pie plate. Roll chicken in melted butter, letting excess drip back in pan. Roll in flour mixture to coat generously and set aside on a sheet of waxed paper until all pieces are coated. Arrange coated pieces in a single layer in a shallow baking dish. Bake at 350 degrees for 1 hour or until golden brown on bottom. Place under broiler for 3 to 5 minutes until tops are golden brown.

25 servings

Ange Jagger

Indian Chicken Balls (India)

½ pound cream cheese
2 tablespoons mayonnaise
1 cup chopped, cooked chicken
1 cup chopped blanched
   almonds or pecans

1 tablespoon chopped chutney
½ teaspoon salt
1 tablespoon curry powder
½ coconut, grated

Beat together cream cheese and mayonnaise. Add chicken, almonds, chutney, salt and curry powder. Shape into walnut size balls and roll in coconut. Chill.

Makes 36 balls.

Rheuanna Kelly

French-Dressed Mushrooms

Button mushrooms

French dressing

Drain juice from mushrooms. Cover with French dressing. Chill well, drain, serve on toothpicks.

Margie Hyde

Escargot and Mushrooms

Large button mushrooms
Escargot
½ cup melted butter

1 tablespoon parsley
1 clove garlic, crushed

Remove stems from mushrooms and place escargot in buttons. Mix parsley and garlic with melted butter and pour over mushrooms. Place under broiler until brown and warm.

Leah Rae Puleo

Canapé Pasties

2 cups flour
½ pound butter

½ pound cream cheese

Work together the above ingredients, chill and roll thin. Cut into squares, sticks or fold into cones using one of the following suggested fillings:

1. Make small (marble-size) hamburgers, season to taste, cook and cool. Roll into small amount of dough.

2. Wrap around cocktail shrimp, cocktail sausages or cocktail onions.

3. Wrap around sharp cheddar cheese and crumbled bacon or cheddar cheese and onions.

4. Cut squares of dough and baked ham, roll.

5. Cut squares of dough and baked ham, sprinkle with grated cheddar cheese and roll.

6. Grated cheese mixed with green chili, rolled in dough.

Bake in moderately hot oven, 400 degrees, until light brown, 8-10 minutes. Serve with toothpicks and hot mustard sauce or cocktail sauce.

Rheuanna Kelly

Caviar Ball

1 large package
  cream cheese
1 pound braunschweiger
1 jar caviar

Sour cream
Chives
Worcestershire sauce
Tabasco

Mash cream cheese with sour cream to soften. Add chives. Form into ball. Refrigerate until firm. Mash braunschweiger. Add enough mayonnaise for spreading consistency. Add Worcestershire and Tabasco to taste. Spread over cream cheese ball; refrigerate until firm. Spread caviar over braunschweiger. Decorate with pimiento, green pepper, stuffed olives. Serve surrounded by slices of rye.

Nancy Taylor Shivers

Asparagus Rolls

1 cup pecans, finely chopped
1 pound canned ham, cut fine
1 pound butter, creamed
½ cup parsley, finely chopped
Lemon juice
3 cans asparagus, drained

8 ounces cream cheese,
  seasoned with savory salt,
  onion salt, pepper, and small
  amount of mayonnaise
2 loaves sliced sandwich bread

Mix all ingredients except asparagus and bread. Season with lemon juice to taste. Place in covered bowl in refrigerator for several hours. Prepare bread by trimming all crusts. Roll each slice on each side with rolling pin. Spread filling mixture thinly; place one spear of asparagus on one edge of bread slice and roll carefully. Place edge underneath to assure the roll will stay together. Place in container, cover and chill. Cut crosswise into small sandwiches.

Yield: 225

Rheuanna Kelly

Sombrero Dip

1 pound ground beef
¼ cup chopped onion
¼ cup hot catsup
1½ teaspoons chili powder
½ teaspoon salt
1 can refried beans
1 small can diced green chilies

Topping:
½ cup grated sharp cheese
½ cup chopped onion
¼ cup chopped green olives

Brown beef. Add remaining ingredients and heat. Pour into chafing dish and add topping.

Ruth Lovelady

Cucumber Dip

2 cucumbers, diced and drained
1 small carton firm sour cream

1 tablespoon chopped chives
Salt

Blend the above ingredients in blender.

Helen Berry

Baked Artichoke Hearts

1 can artichoke hearts
Melba toast rounds,
   rye or white
¼ pound melted butter
Salt

Freshly ground pepper
Garlic powder to taste
   (about ¼ teaspoon)
Slivered almonds or
   sesame seeds

Drain artichokes and cut in half with shears. Place each half, cut side up, on a Melba round. Arrange on oven-proof dish on which they can be served. Melt butter and add salt, pepper and garlic powder. Spoon generously over artichokes. Sprinkle with almonds or sesame seeds and bake at 350 degrees for 10 minutes.

Mrs. J. L. Sturgeon

54

Hors d'oeuvres

1 bottle chile sauce
1 jar creamy peanut butter

Partly fried bacon pieces
Bread or melba rounds

Mix chile sauce and peanut butter. Spread mixture on whole slices of bread and cut into individual shapes, or spread mixture on melba rounds. Then place a small piece of partly fried bacon on top of each serving. Heat in hot oven until they begin to bubble. May be fixed the night before and frozen.

Lolita Vidmar

Olive Tarts

2 cups grated sharp
   Cheddar cheese
½ cup soft butter
1 cup all-purpose flour

½ teaspoon salt
1 teaspoon paprika
48 stuffed olives
   or tiny anchovies

Blend cheese with butter; stir in flour, salt, paprika and mix well. Wrap teaspoon of this mixture around olive or anchovy, covering it completely. Arrange on a baking sheet or flat pan and refrigerate until firm. Place in small plastic bags, tie and freeze. To serve, bake at 400 degrees for 15 minutes (directly from freezer). Can make them without stuffing if you prefer—just make cheese balls and freeze.

Sherry Clarkin

Mrs. Phelp's Famous Bean Dip

1 #300 can refried beans
1 small can chopped
   black olives
1 small can chopped
   green chile peppers

1 small jar chopped pimiento
2 tablespoons instant
   minced onion

Mix together and heat in 350 degree oven.

Ann Phelps

55

soups

The stew pot rarely cooled in the early days of the southwest. The fireplace served as the center for cooking and heat, and the welcoming aroma of hot soup greeted a parade of peoples from Indian warrior and adventurous trapper to weary settler.

Erbsin Soupse
(German Soup)

1 pound dried split peas
2 large white onions, peeled
3 to 4 large potatoes, partially peeled

8 to 10 whole carrots, unpeeled
4 cloves garlic, chopped
2 packages Polish sausage
(or one pound sausage and one pound frankfurters)

*Whole thyme
*Whole bay leaves
*Cumin
*Cracked peppercorns (lots)
*Salt

Oregano
Celery seeds
Caraway seeds
Dry mustard
Rosemary
Mace
Red pepper

*Essential!

Marjoram
Olive oil

Soak peas in 3 quarts of water for several hours, washing three times. Use large pot. Bring peas to a rolling boil and add chopped potatoes, onions and sliced carrots. Boil for 3 to 4 hours until all of the peas and most of the potatoes are dissolved, and it begins to thicken well. Heat 1 tablespoon olive oil in double boiler and add spices and garlic cloves. Be liberal!

Cook for about 10 minutes and add to soup. Cover and cook over low heat for 45 minutes. Add sliced sausage and cook until heated through (20 to 30 minutes).

Serve with German black bread, lots of butter, assorted cheeses and dark beer. This soup gets better the longer you keep it.

Jonnie Miller

Beef Vegetable Soup

10 cups water
1 large soup bone
1 pound soup meat
1 cup mixed split peas
½ cup white beans
¼ bottle ketchup
2 tablespoons
  Worcestershire sauce

Salt and pepper to taste
6 carrots sliced
1 parsnip
6 stalks celery
Large handful of wide noodles

Put all ingredients in large soup pot and simmer for at least 8 hours.

Mrs. Phillip Hilvitz

Vegetable Soup

8 cups beef stock,
  or 5 beef bouillon cubes
  diluted in 8 cups boiling water
1 cup diced carrots
1 cup green beans
½ cup chopped onions
1½ cups peeled and
  sliced fresh tomatoes
1 cup diced celery
1 small turnip, diced

1 cup diced potatoes
1 medium sweet potato, diced
1 tablespoon salt
½ teaspoon pepper
½ teaspoon basil
¼ teaspoon marjoram
1 bay leaf
¼ cup butter
½ cup tiny macaroni (optional)

Melt butter in 6-quart pot. When hot, add onions, celery, and tomatoes. Sauté. Add all other ingredients except potatoes. Cover and simmer 45 minutes. Add potatoes and simmer ½ hour longer. One-half cup tiny macaroni may be added during last ½ hour of cooking. (My family prefers this addition.)

Sandy Stein

Ground Beef Soup

1 pound ground beef
2 cups sliced celery
2 cups sliced carrots
2 cups chopped onions

1 large can V-8 juice
1 can beef broth
Rice (if desired)
Salt and pepper to taste

Brown and drain ground beef. Add other ingredients and simmer at least one hour.

Pearl Stirling

Quick Minestrone

1 can red kidney beans
   (1 lb. 11 oz.)
1 tablespoon salt
½ teaspoon garlic salt
¼ teaspoon pepper
1 small zucchini (cut up)
2 stalks celery (chopped)
2 green onions (chopped)

1 small carrot (diced)
2 tablespoons butter
1 can tomato sauce (8 oz.)
2½ cups water
½ cup dry sherry
¼ cup cooked elbow macaroni

Place undrained beans in large saucepan, mash three quarters, and leave rest whole. Add seasoning, vegetables, butter, tomato sauce and water. Simmer 1 hour; add sherry and macaroni. Simmer 10-15 minutes longer.

Barbara Daney

Cold Soup

1 large can tomatoes
   (remove seeds)
Salt, dash
White pepper, dash
1 teaspoon sugar, heaping

Worcestershire sauce
1½ lemons, juice only
½ cup onion, chopped
½ cup green pepper, chopped

Mix and allow several hours or overnight in refrigerator to ripen.

Mrs. George Pardee

Sausage Bean Chowder

1 pound bulk pork sausage
2 16-ounce cans kidney beans
1 #303 can tomatoes, broken up
1 large onion, chopped
1 bay leaf
1½ teaspoon seasoned salt
½ teaspoon garlic salt
½ teaspoon thyme
1/8 teaspoon pepper
1 cup diced potatoes
½ green pepper, chopped
1 quart water (or less, if
 thicker soup is preferred)

Cook pork sausage until brown. Drain off fat. In large kettle combine beans, tomatoes, water, onion, and seasonings. Simmer one hour. Add potatoes and green pepper and cook 15-20 minutes longer until potatoes are tender.

Good warmed up—if there is any left.

Serves 8

Bev Brill

Mexican Rice and Bean Soup

1 pound pork sausage links
½ cup chopped onion
1/3 cup chopped green pepper
1 clove garlic (garlic powder
 may be substituted)
3 cups water
1 18-ounce can tomato juice
 (2¼ cups)
1 1-pound can kidney beans,
 drained
½ cup long-grain rice
1 teaspoon paprika
1 teaspoon chili powder
½ teaspoon salt
Dash pepper

Cut sausage links into bite-sized pieces. Brown sausage; drain off all but two tablespoons fat. Saute onion, green pepper and garlic. Add water, tomato juice, beans, rice, paprika, chili powder, salt and pepper. Simmer, covered, 25 to 30 minutes, or until rice is tender, stirring occasionally.

Serve with corn bread or hard crusty rolls.

Serves 6 to 8

Jule L. Nelson

Lentil Soup

2 - 3 small pieces of ham
   hock or 1 small ham hock
1 package dry lentils (2 cups)
5 - 6 cups water
1 bay leaf

1 stalk celery (½ cup) chopped
1 small onion (1/3 cup) chopped
1 medium carrot
   (½ cup) shredded
1 teaspoon salt
1/8 teaspoon pepper (or to taste)

Wash lentils; check for any foreign matter. Combine lentils, 5 cups water, meat, bay leaf, celery, onion, salt and pepper in large 2-3 quart pot with cover. Bring to full boil, then turn heat low enough for continuous simmering. Continue simmering for about 1 hour, stirring occasionally. Add carrot and cook until lentils soften enough to mash easily. Remove bay leaf. Cut meat into small pieces if desired; mash lentils slightly. (If liquid has decreased, add additional water to desired consistency during cooking).
Serve hot.
Freezes well.

German origin. High in protein. Can be made without meat, or with beef used instead of ham. Nice with small sausages or hot dogs added. Goes well with toasted cheese sandwiches.

Serves 6 to 8

Mrs. George E. McKinnon

Cold Avocado Soup

2 large ripe avocados
2 cans jellied consommé
2 tablespoons lemon juice
½ teaspoon salt
¼ teaspoon white pepper

1 tablespoon finely
   chopped onions
2 dashes Tabasco sauce
¼ teaspoon Worcestershire
   sauce
½ pint sour cream

Pit and peel avocados; place in blender with all ingredients except sour cream.
Blend at high speed.
Leave in blender jar; refrigerate overnight, covered.
Before serving—blend again; serve individual portions topped with sour cream.

Makes 4 servings.

Diane Larkin

Corn Chowder

1 cup salt pork, diced
2 chopped onions
1 cup celery, cut up
2 tablespoons flour
4 cups water
½ bay leaf

3 cups diced cooked potatoes
1 can creamed corn
1 can corn niblets
2 cups light cream
Parsley for garnish
Salt and pepper to taste

Cook pork until crisp; remove, leaving 3 tablespoons fat in pan. Add onion and celery. Cook 5 minutes. Add flour mixed with a little water. Add rest of water and the potatoes and bay leaf. Cover and boil 15 minutes. Add corn and cream. Season to taste. Sprinkle with parsley. Can add some of salt pork to soup—not grease.

Makes 8 one-cup servings

Priscilla S. McCabe

Tuna-Corn Bisque

1 can tuna (6½ ounce)
3 tablespoons butter
1/3 cup chopped onion
2 cups frozen or canned corn
2 tablespoons flour
1 cup water

1 #2 can tomatoes, sieved,
  or 6 tablespoons concentrated
  tomato paste with
  two cups water
2 teaspoons salt
½ teaspoon paprika
1-14½ -ounce can evaporated milk

Drain oil from tuna into large saucepan. Add butter and melt. Cook chopped onion in oil and butter until limp, but not brown. Add corn and cook for 5 minutes. Stir in flour; add water and sieved tomato or concentrated tomato paste with water. Simmer 15 minutes, stirring frequently. Flake tuna and stir into soup. Add evaporated milk and salt. Reheat but do not boil. Pour into soup bowls, sprinkle with paprika, and serve at once.

Serves 6

Betty Bullen

Borsch

2½ to 3 pounds ham
 or ham hocks
3-4 cups stringed raw potatoes
3-4 cups sliced cabbage
2 cans shoestring beets

2 cans chili beans
1 cup heavy cream
4-5 tablespoons vinegar
Salt to taste

Trim fat off ham and place in large kettle. Add ham which has been cut into small pieces and fill kettle about 3/4 full of water. Boil. Eventually, fat will rise to top and should be removed. Cook potatoes and cabbage with ham until soft. Add beets with juice and chili beans with juice and salt to taste. Simmer about one hour. Just before serving, add cream and vinegar.

Serves 10

Mrs. E. E. Kaufman

Luncheon Soup

1 can cream of asparagus soup
1 can cream of mushroom soup
1 can crab meat
1 can either shrimp cut-up
 or canned small shrimp

2½ soup cans of half and half
¼ cup sherry
Salt and pepper to taste

Beat soups together until smooth. Add 2½ cans of half and half. Add shrimp and crab. Heat slowly—do not boil. Just before serving add sherry.

Serve with toasted English muffin and dessert.

Serves 6 to 8

Ruth Gast

Cream of Potato Soup

2 medium size potatoes
1 teaspoon chopped onion
1 tablespoon flour
2 tablespoons butter

¼ teaspoon caraway seed
2 cups milk
½ cup canned milk
Salt and pepper to taste

Dice potatoes and put in sauce pan, cover with water, cook until tender. Cook onion in butter until golden, add flour and with 1 cup of milk, make a cream sauce. Add to potatoes with rest of milk, add caraway seed and seasoning. Bring just to boiling point.

Mrs. Ed McGuire

Clam Chowder

3 slices bacon
1 cup celery
1 cup onion
2 7-ounce cans clams
2 cups tomatoes

2 cups potatoes
2 cups carrots
1½ teaspoons salt
Dash of pepper

Dice bacon, celery, and onion. Partially cook bacon; pour off grease. Add celery and onions, and cook until tender. Drain liquid from clams; add enough water to make 4 cups liquid. Remove seeds from tomatoes and cut in bite-size pieces. Add tomatoes, potatoes, carrots, seasonings, and liquid. Cover and simmer for 35 minutes. To make thickening, stir 2 tablespoons water and flour into chowder and cook only until it comes to a boil. Add clams and heat through.

Mrs. George C. Pardee

Shrimp Gumbo

6 slices bacon
2 large onions
2 number 2½ cans of tomatoes
6½ cans consommé
  or chicken broth
1 carrot
4 leeks (or 8 green onions)
1½ pounds shelled shrimp

1 pound crab meat
½ teaspoon cayenne
½ teaspoon saffron (or curry)
2 pounds fresh or canned okra
2 tablespoons chopped parsley
4-6 tablespoons flour
Salt and pepper to taste

Sauté bacon, drain and crumble. Sauté onion, chopped, until golden. Transfer onion to large (4-quart) kettle, and add tomatoes and consommé. Cover and bring to a boil. Add diced, peeled carrot and sliced leeks or onions, including some of the green leaves. Simmer for ½ hour. Add shrimp and crab meat. Season with cayenne and saffron. Salt and pepper to taste. Reheat to simmering and add okra. Cook gently ½ hour more, stirring occasionally. Just before serving, add chopped parsley, and thicken with flour mixed with a little cold water to make a thin, smooth paste. Cook until slightly thickened. Add crumbled bacon.

Serve with salad and hard rolls or garlic bread.

Kay Abbot

White Fish Chowder

½ pound white fish
2 cups diced potatoes
1 small onion
1 quart milk

¼ pound butter
2 slices bacon
1 cup water
Salt and pepper to taste

Cut fish into small pieces. Fry onion and bacon. Add fish, onion, bacon and potatoes to one cup water in pressure cooker. Cook until potatoes are done. Heat milk and butter; add to other ingredients when cooked. Add salt and pepper.

Jonna Ussery

Turkey Soup

1 turkey carcass
Salt and pepper (to taste)
3 stalks of celery, diced.
1 large onion, diced
3 carrots, diced

1 cup shredded cabbage
½ cup barley
1 large can tomatoes
1 sprig chopped parsley
1 can of corn niblets

Put turkey carcass in large kettle and cover with cold water; simmer, covered, most of day. Place in cold place (garage or refrigerator) overnight. Next day, remove most of fat from top of soup, then heat to just warm. Remove from heat and remove bones and skin from broth. Leave all the meat in broth. Now, add all the remaining ingredients and simmer at least 2 hours.

This is a hearty soup, good to serve on a cold day with hot bread, as main meal of day.

Serves about 8

Mrs. Roy McKittrick

salad
dressings
and
salads

The wood stove replaced the fireplace
as focal point for household activity and the
development of irrigated southwestern land
saw bountiful harvests of crisp ingredients for
salads and fresh vegetable dishes.

Cole Slaw Soufflé Salad

1 cup hot water
1 package lemon jello
½ cup cold water
2 tablespoons vinegar
½ cup mayonnaise

¼ teaspoon
  salt-dash pepper
2 cups shredded cabbage
2 tablespoons minced
  green pepper
1 tablespoon minced onion
¼ teaspoon celery seed

Pour hot water over gelatin and stir until dissolved. Add cold water, vinegar, mayonnaise, salt and pepper; beat until well blended. Chill until firm (1 inch from edge of pan). Beat until fluffy and fold in remaining ingredients. Mold in 8x8 pan. This recipe doubled will fill a 9x12 pan and serve a large group. Especially good with ham.

Serves 8 - 10   *Mrs. R. F. Burch*

Lobster Salad

3 egg yolks, beaten
2 tablespoons sugar
2 tablespoons vinegar
1 tablespoon butter
2 tablespoons pineapple juice
Salt, dash

1 jar white cherries,
  pitted, halved, and drained
1 small can pineapple
  tidbits, drained
1 small can Mandarin
  oranges, drained
2 whole live lobsters, cooked
1¼ to 1½ cups whipped
  whipping cream, barely
  sweetened

Combine egg yolks, sugar, vinegar, butter, pineapple juice, and salt in top of double boiler. Cook and stir over hot (barely boiling) water until thick. Cool. Add fruits to cooked yolk mixture. Fold in whipped cream. Chill for several hours or overnight. Shortly before serving, add lobster meat that has been cut in bite-sized pieces. Garnish with sliced almonds if desired.

Serves 8   *Mrs. Phillip Hilvitz*

Frozen Fruit Salad

2½ cups dairy sour cream
2½ tablespoons lemon juice
1 cup sugar
1 cup drained crushed pineapple
¼ cup minced celery
¼ cup finely chopped
  maraschino cherries
1 banana diced
½ cup chopped walnuts
Dash of salt

Turn into freezing tray or loaf pan. Freeze until firm. Cut and put on lettuce leaves before serving (½ hour or longer).

12 Servings   *Mrs. Albert Ayers*

Maggie's Fruit Salad

1 can pineapple chunks
  (drained)
2 bananas, sliced
1 can Royal Anne cherries
  (drained and pitted)
½ pint whipping cream
  whipped and mixed with
  enough mayonnaise to make
  the consistency of salad
  dressing.
Miniature marshmallows
  (to taste)

Mix all together just before serving.

                                    Mrs. C. Herbert Nichols

Fruit Bowl

1 can (number 2½) peaches
1 can (number 2½) pears
1 can (number 303) Royal
  Anne cherries, pitted
1 can (number 303)
  pineapple chunks
1 1-ounce can
  Mandarin oranges
2 packages mixed
  frozen fruit
3 bananas
2 cups dry white wine

Drain all canned fruits and cut into bite-size pieces. Thaw frozen fruit and keep juice. To frozen fruit and juice, add all the rest of fruits. Do not add juice from canned fruits. Add wine and marinate 4 to 5 hours in refrigerator. About one hour before serving, add sliced bananas. Stir often.

                                    Mina Hyde

Sour Cream Dressing for Fruit Salad

1 carton sour cream
3 tablespoons honey
½ teaspoon dry mustard

Juice of small lemon
Pinch of salt

Mix gently with fork, use as desired.

Adrian Comer

Lime Cottage Cheese Salad

1 3-ounce package
   lime gelatin
1 cup fruit juice
   and water combined
   (drain juice from fruit
   used in center of mold)
1 pound carton
   cottage cheese
1 small can crushed
   pineapple
1 teaspoon lemon juice
Fresh fruit for center
   of mold (grapes,
   pineapple chunks,
   peaches, apples, etc.)

Dressing:
Whipped cream or sour
   cream sweetened with
   small marshmallows,
      or
Small carton sour cream
   flavored with 1 teaspoon
   almond extract and 3
   tablespoons honey.

Bring water and fruit juice to a boil and dissolve gelatin. Let cool and add pineapple, cottage cheese and lemon juice. Chill until firm. Unmold and fill center of ring with fruit and dressing.

Suzie Anton

73

Cranberry Salad

2 cups cranberries
1 cup sugar
2 cups cream
½ package small
  marshmallows

1 can crushed pineapple
½ cup chopped nuts

Grind cranberries; add sugar, mix and let stand 30 minutes. Whip 2 cups cream; add ½ package small marshmallows and let stand 30 minutes also. Put the mixtures together and add 1 can drained crushed pineapple and ½ cup chopped nuts. Let chill 24 hours. Serve on lettuce leaves.

Serves 12   *Wanda Glover*

Raspberry Jello Salad or Dessert

2 3-ounce packages
  raspberry gelatin
2 cups applesauce
1 10-ounce package
  frozen raspberries

2 3/4 cups boiling water
½ cup chopped pecans
  (or walnuts)

Topping:
1½ cups miniature marshmallows
1 12-ounce carton sour cream

Dissolve gelatin in boiling hot water. Add frozen raspberries, stirring to hasten thawing. Add applesauce and chopped nuts last. Cool, and allow to set in 9 x 13 inch pan. When firm, spread with a topping of miniature marshmallows mixed thoroughly with sour cream. Refrigerate overnight. May be served on lettuce leaf as a salad, or as a dessert.

Bev Hurley

Pineapple-Apricot Salad

2 packages orange gelatin
2 cups boiling water
1 cup pineapple juice
1 cup apricot juice
1 large can pineapple chunks
1 large can apricots
10 cut marshmallows

Topping:
½ cup pineapple juice
½ cup apricot juice
1 cup sugar
2 tablespoons flour (heaping)
1 beaten egg
2 tablespoons butter

1 cup whipped cream
Lettuce leaves

Drain juice from fruit and reserve this. Dissolve gelatin in water and fruit juices. Add other ingredients and let set. Use 9 x 13 pan. Combine topping and cook until thick; then cool. Fold in 1 cup whipped cream. Spread on gelatin. Chill. Cut in squares when firm; serve on lettuce leaves.

Sue Mastro

Tomato-Vegetable Mold

1 tablespoon gelatin
¼ cup cold water
1 can tomato soup
1 8-ounce carton cottage cheese
½ cup mayonnaise
½ cup sour cream

1/3 cup celery
1/3 cup green pepper
1/3 cup onion
1/3 cup cucumber

Dissolve gelatin in cold water. Heat soup and dissolve gelatin in it; add cottage cheese. Cool and add mayonnaise and sour cream. Chop celery, green pepper, onion, and cucumber and add. Pour into 2-quart mold and refrigerate.

Catherine Petersen

75

Cucumber Soufflé Salad

1 package lime gelatin
1½ - 2½ cups of
   sliced cucumbers
¼ - ½ finely chopped
   onion (or grated)

½ cup mayonnaise
3 tablespoons vinegar
½ teaspoon salt
Dash of pepper

Make gelatin, using ½ cup less water than called for. Blend all ingredients, except cucumbers. Freeze until frozen around edges. Whip until fluffy, fold in cucumbers, and pour into mold and chill.

Diane Larkin

Orange Salad

1 package orange gelatin
1 package lemon gelatin
1 pint orange sherbet
½ pint whipping cream

1 can (15¼ ounce) crushed
   pineapple (drained)
1 can Mandarin orange
   slices (well-drained)

Dissolve packages of gelatin in 2 cups boiling water. While still warm, blend in sherbet and chill until thick. Fold in fruit and whipping cream. Mold.

Marie Peake

Berry Blue Salad

1 3-ounce package
   red raspberry gelatin
1 small can crushed pineapple

1 number 303 can
   blueberries
1 envelope packaged
   whipped topping mix

Drain fruits and save juice. Mix gelatin with 1 cup boiling water. When dissolved, add 1/3 cup pineapple juice and enough blueberry juice to make one cup. Prepare packaged whip but don't whip too stiff. When gelatin begins to set, add fruit and packaged whip.

Beth Thatcher

Seven Up Salad

1 package lemon gelatin
1 cup hot water
1 cup Seven Up
½ cup crushed
   pineapple (drained)
½ cup miniature
   marshmallows
1 banana, sliced
¼ cup sugar (scant)

1 tablespoon flour
½ cup pineapple juice
1 egg (beaten)
1 tablespoon butter
1 cup whipped cream
Grated cheese
Halved cherries

Dissolve gelatin in hot water; add Seven Up. Pour into 8x8x2 dish; chill until partially thickened. Fold in pineapple, marshmallows, and banana; chill until firm. Mix sugar, flour, pineapple juice, and egg in saucepan; cook, stirring until thick. Add butter; cool. Fold in whipped cream; spread over gelatin mixture. Sprinkle with cheese; decorate with cherry halves.

Serves 6

Mrs. Doug Brown

Hawaiian Salad

1 package lemon gelatin
1 can papaya juice
   (or apricot juice)
1 cup seedless grapes
   (or small can)

½ small carton sour cream
1 tablespoon lemon juice
1 can Mandarin oranges

Heat juice and add to gelatin. When cool, add 1 can Mandarin oranges, grapes, sour cream and lemon juice. Pour into mold, greased with a little mayonnaise. If apricot juice is used instead of papaya, omit lemon juice, as the juice is already tart.

Serves 6.

Mrs. John Sturgeon

Applesauce-Cinnamon Salad

1 tablespoon gelatin
2 tablespoons cold water
2 cups applesauce
¼ cup sugar

3 tablespoons red hots
¼ teaspoon nutmeg
1 tablespoon lemon juice

Heat applesauce. Add gelatin, softened in cold water. Add sugar, red hots and nutmeg, stirring until red hots dissolve. Add lemon juice. Pour into individual molds or glass pan approximately 8 inches by 6 inches and chill in refrigerator until set. May be served on lettuce with dab of mayonnaise. Good with ham or pork. Children especially enjoy it.

Serves 6   *Marge McGovern*

Butter Mint Salad

2 tall cans crushed
  pineapple (not drained)
1 3-ounce package
  lime gelatin (dry)
1 10-ounce package
  tiny marshmallows

2 small packages dry
  whipped topping mix
1 teaspoon pineapple flavoring
¼ teaspoon mint flavoring
1 7-ounce package
  butter mints (crushed)

Mix pineapple, gelatin and marshmallows in bowl and let set overnight. Next day whip topping mix according to directions and fold in crushed butter mints. Fold this into the first mixture and pour into a 9 x 13 inch pan and freeze. This can be fixed several days ahead of time and can also be served without freezing. Cut in squares and serve on lettuce leaf.

Serves 12   *Mrs. Frank Porr*

Avocado Stuffed Tomatoes

6 medium ripe tomatoes
3 slices bacon
2 ripe avocados
2 tablespoons lemon juice
¼ cup chopped onion

3 tablespoons olive oil
¼ cup chopped green pepper
1 clove garlic
¼ teaspoon pepper

Dip tomatoes in boiling water one at a time; then peel. Scoop out seeds; refrigerate shells.

Fry bacon till crisp; crumble. Blend avocados, bacon, lemon juice, onions, olive oil, green pepper, garlic, salt and pepper. Refrigerate overnight. Fill shell. Garnish with parsley.

Serves:6   *Diane Larkin*

Avocado Salad

½ head lettuce, chopped
1 large tomato, diced
½ cup sliced black olives
¼ cup green onions, chopped
½ cup shredded Cheddar cheese
1 cup crushed corn chips

Dressing:
½ cup mashed avocado
½ cup sour cream
½ cup salad oil
1 clove garlic, crushed
½ teaspoon salt
½ teaspoon pepper
½ teaspoon sugar
½ teaspoon chili powder
Tabasco sauce to taste

Mix all ingredients, adding dressing last.

Mary Ann Broomhall

Weight Watchers's Party Salad

3 raw zucchinis,
   sliced very thin
1 can hearts of palm,
   sliced thick

Low-calorie Italian dressing

Marinate in refrigerator all day. Serve with lettuce and tomato. Crumble a little blue cheese over the top.

Fran Weaver

Caesar Salad

¼ cup salad oil
2 peeled cloves garlic,
  quartered
2 cups bread cubes,
  toasted (300 degrees)
2 quarts Romaine lettuce
  (2 heads)
6 tablespoons salad oil
1 tablespoon Worcestershire
  sauce

¼ teaspoon pepper
½ teaspoon salt
½ cup grated Parmesan cheese
¼ cup crumbled blue cheese
3½ tablespoons lemon juice
1 raw egg

Combine ¼ cup salad oil and garlic cloves; let stand at room temperature. Toss croutons with this mixture just *prior* to serving. (Discard garlic.) Mix remaining ingredients, *except* raw egg, in *morning* before serving at night so flavors will blend. Toss Romaine well with dressing; add raw egg and toss again. Add croutons (which have been tossed with oil and garlic); toss lightly. Serve and enjoy.

Bobbee Farabaugh

Sliced Cucumbers in Sour Cream

2 large cucumbers,
  pared and sliced very thin
1½ teaspoons salt
1 cup sour cream
2 tablespoons lemon juice

1 tablespoon finely
  chopped onion
¼ teaspoon sugar
Dash of pepper
1¼ teaspoons finely
  chopped parsley

Lightly toss cucumbers with 1 teaspoon salt. Combine sour cream, lemon juice, remaining salt, onions, sugar and pepper. Drain cucumbers, toss with sour cream mixture and refrigerate until well-chilled—about 2 hours. To serve, turn into shallow serving dish and sprinkle with parsley. Excellent with fish or cold cuts.

Mrs. Samuel Nelson

Liberty Cole Slaw

3/4 cup chopped
   crisp bacon
2 tablespoons lemon juice
1 scant teaspoon salt
½ cup mayonnaise
   (not salad dressing)

2 tablespoons
   chopped parsley
1 tablespoon chopped onion
4 tablespoons chopped
   green pepper (optional)
2 cups shredded cabbage

Cook bacon to golden brown and add, with other ingredients, to cabbage. Mix well and refrigerate four to six hours before serving.

Mrs. Homer Massey

Roquefort Cole Slaw

½ cup Roquefort cheese,
   crumbled
1 large head cabbage,
   shredded
¼ cup sugar

1 tablespoon salt
1/3 cup vinegar
1 cup sour cream
Dash garlic salt

Shred cabbage; combine sugar, salt, vinegar, sour cream and cheese. Pour mixture over cabbage and toss lightly. Cover and refrigerate for at least one hour before serving.

Serves: 8

Mae Vinci

Pennsylvania Cole Slaw

1 small head of cabbage
½ pint cream
1 teaspoon salt

½ cup sugar or less
½ cup vinegar

Beat cream, sugar, vinegar and salt together thoroughly until dressing is like whipped cream. Shred cabbage and combine with dressing just before serving. Shredded green and red peppers may be added for color. (Be sure to add sugar to cream *before* vinegar)

Serves: 6

Helen Snyder

Chinese Salad

1 cup cooked noodles
¼ cup chopped green onions
¼ cup chopped green pepper
¼ cup chopped celery
1 can Chinese vegetables,
    drained

½ to 1 cup mayonnaise
1 can tuna, crab or shrimp
Tabasco sauce to taste
Black olives
Hard-boiled eggs

Mix all together and chill. Serve on lettuce leaves. Garnish with black olives and hard-boiled eggs.

Serves: 4 to 6
Mrs. Dan Stevens

Gourmet Salad

½ pound fresh spinach
2/3 bunch red lettuce
½ medium-sized head lettuce
¼ pound fresh mushrooms
Lemon juice
1 can French fried onions

Italian dressing
4 tablespoons blue cheese
  (mashed with fork
  and added to dressing)
2 or 3 slices bacon,
  cooked dry and crumbled

Shred lettuce and spinach. Cut mushrooms in small pieces and sprinkle with lemon juice. Add salad dressing, then bacon and last, the French fried onions. (The onions will become soft if added too soon before serving salad.)

Serves: 12
Mrs. M. J. Clark

Greek Salad

1 medium cabbage, cut fine
1 medium green pepper,
  cut fine
3 medium carrots, cut fine
1 can ripe olives, chopped
1 jar stuffed green olives,
  cut small

¼ cup oil
¼ cup cider vinegar
Salt and pepper
Herring, marinated in sour cream

Top salad with herring in sour cream.

Lillian Meyer

82

Korean Salad

1 package fresh spinach
1 number 2 can bean
   sprouts, drained (or fresh)

8 slices bacon, fried
   crisp and crumbled
3 hard-cooked eggs, diced

Wash, clean and break up spinach. Toss all ingredients with the following dressing:

1 cup salad oil
Scant 3/4 cup sugar
1/3 cup catsup
1 tablespoon Worcestershire
   sauce

1 medium onion, grated
¼ cup vinegar
Salt to taste
3 to 4 drops soy sauce

This is also good with some lettuce added.

Mrs. J. J. Schedel

Spinach Salad

6 cloves garlic, quartered
3/4 cup French dressing
   (not creamy)
3 hard-cooked eggs, chopped

8 bacon slices,
   fried and crumbled
½ pound cleaned spinach

Marinate garlic in French dressing several hours. At serving time, sprinkle eggs and bacon over spinach which has been torn up. Remove garlic from dressing and pour over salad. Salt and pepper to taste. Toss and serve at once.

Serves:6

Peachy Wilcoxson

Swedish Sill Salad

8 cooked potatoes
8 cooked red beets
2 hard-boiled eggs
2 cups smoked herring,
   boned and skinned

1 tablespoon vinegar
1 cup thick cream
Salt, pepper and
   sugar to taste

Mix potatoes, herring, vinegar, cream and seasonings. Garnish with grated egg yolks, and beets and egg whites cut into small pieces.

Hilda Giordano

Shrimp Mousse

1 pound shrimp
1 can tomato soup
3 3-ounce packages
   cream cheese
2 tablespoons gelatin softened
   in ½ cup cold water

1 cup mayonnaise
½ cup celery, finely chopped
½ cup onion, finely chopped
½ cup green pepper,
   finely chopped

Heat the soup; add cheese and beat until creamy. Add gelatin; let cook until gelatin has dissolved. Add mayonnaise, shrimp and vegetables. Put in 2-quart mold. For dressing, use ½ cream and ½ mayonnaise.

Serve with warm rolls and relishes; delicious for a luncheon.

Serves 8 to 12
Jean Butorac

Cheese Soufflé Salad with Shrimp

1 package lemon-flavored
   gelatin (3-ounce)
1 cup hot water
½ cup cold water
½ cup mayonnaise
1 tablespoon lemon juice,
   fresh or frozen
3/4 teaspoon salt
3 or 4 drops Tabasco sauce

3/4 cup grated American cheese
3 or 4 hard-cooked eggs, sliced
½ cup diced celery
¼ cup diced green pepper
2 tablespoons diced pimiento
1 teaspoon grated onion
1 can small shrimp (optional)

Dissolve gelatin in hot water. Add cold water, mayonnaise, lemon juice, salt and Tabasco. Blend well with rotary beater. Pour into refrigerator tray. Quick chill in freezing unit 15 to 20 minutes, or until firm about 1 inch from edge but soft in center. Turn into bowl and beat until fluffy. Fold in remaining ingredients. Pour into 1-quart mold or individual molds. Chill until firm, 30 to 60 minutes. Unmold on platter. (Optional: Add one small can of small shrimp, cut in half. Place one whole shrimp on top of each serving).

Serves: 6
Mrs. Harry Amick

Hot Shrimp Salad

1 can frozen cream
of shrimp soup
1 can cream of mushroom soup
1 teaspoon Worcestershire
sauce
1 tablespoon lemon juice
2 cups diced celery
1/3 cup diced green pepper

1/3 cup diced pimiento
1/3 cup toasted
slivered almonds
3 cups diced cooked shrimp
2 large cans
chow mein noodles

Combine soups in top of double-boiler. Add Worcestershire sauce and lemon juice. Simmer till thoroughly blended. Add remaining ingredients except noodles. Season with salt and pepper. Heat and keep warm over hot water till serving time. Serve on noodles.
Serves 10 to 12

Mrs. Eugene L. Shaffer

Crab Salad

2 cups crab (2 small cans)
½ cup diced cucumber
1 cup celery, cut fine
3 hard-boiled eggs,
sliced and cut in half

¼ teaspoon salt
1/8 teaspoon pepper
Juice of one lemon
Mayonnaise to moisten

Simply toss and serve on lettuce leaf. Serve with relishes and rolls.

Mrs. Harry Amick

Shrimp-Crab Tarragon Salad

1 5-ounce can shrimp,
drained
1 5 or 7-ounce can crabmeat,
drained and flaked
½ of 5-ounce can
water chestnuts,
drained and sliced
2 ounces pimiento,
drained and chopped

¼ cup chopped
fresh green peppers
½ cup celery, finely diced
½ pound fresh frozen peas,
cooked and chilled

1. Toss with Tarragon Cream Dressing (See Tarragon Dressing)
2. Garnish with Bib lettuce
Serves: 8

Helen K. Pachak

Vegetable Salad

1 can Blue Lake green
   beans (cut, drained)
1 can tiny LeSueur
   English peas, drained
1 medium onion, chopped
1 cup finely chopped celery
1 cucumber, chopped
1 green pepper, chopped
1 small jar of
   chopped pimiento

Dressing:
1 cup sugar
1 cup vinegar
½ cup cooking oil
2 tablespoons water

Sprinkle salt over vegetables and store in refrigerator an hour or more. Mix dressing. Pour dressing over vegetables and marinate in refrigerator at least 12 hours. Drain and serve.

Doris Broughton

Thousand Island Dressing

1 cup mayonnaise
1 cup tartar sauce
1 cup tomato soup
1 pint salad dressing
2 tablespoons vinegar
2 tablespoons sweet pickle juice

2 tablespoons chili sauce
1 tablespoon sugar
1 teaspoon dry mustard
4 chopped sweet pickles
1 grated onion
1 grated garlic bud

Mix together all ingredients. Store in refrigerator.
Serve over wedge of lettuce or tossed salad.

Carol Kilstofte

Roquefort Dressing

4 ounces Roquefort cheese
2 tablespoons vinegar
6 tablespoons oil
2 tablespoons heavy
  sweet cream

Cayenne
Salt
Paprika

Mash cheese with wooden spoon until smooth; add dash of salt, paprika and cayenne. Slowly add vinegar, oil and cream, mixing well. Refrigerate to cool.

Marge Birner

Poppy Seed Dressing

1 cup salad oil
1 cup white vinegar
½ cup sugar
1 tablespoon salt
1 tablespoon coarsely
  ground pepper

1 teaspoon dry mustard
3 cloves garlic, pressed
2 tablespoons poppy seed

May be kept indefinitely. Good over lettuce wedges or any of your favorite combination salads (with a few extras like toasted almonds, etc.).

Serves 30

Jean Train

Tarragon Cream Dressing

½ tablespoon flour
1 tablespoon sugar
½ teaspoon salt
1/16 teaspoon pepper
½ teaspoon onion salt

¼ teaspoon tarragon
1 tablespoon salad oil
1 egg, beaten
2 tablespoons plus
   2 teaspoons lemon juice
2/3 cup evaporated milk

Blend flour, sugar, salt, pepper and tarragon.

Stir in salad oil, then eggs and lemon juice.

Cook and stir over low heat until thickened. Add milk and beat smooth. Chill.

Serves: 8

Helen K. Pachak

Sour Cream Salad Dressing

1 cup sour cream
1 tablespoon and
   1 teaspoon sugar
2 tablespoons vinegar
   (apple cider vinegar best)

1 tablespoon onion-grated
   (or the equivalent
   dry onion flakes)
2 teaspoons plus of horseradish
1 teaspoon salt

Combine ingredients and mix well, preferably a few hours before needed so the flavors will blend.

Use on crisp lettuce leaves or sliced cucumbers.

Yield: 1½ cups dressing

Mrs. R. E. Staats

Teton Dressing

1 cup sour cream
1 cup mayonnaise
1½ tablespoons lemon juice
1 clove garlic, minced

1½ ounces blue cheese,
   crumbled
¼ teaspoon celery salt

Blend well; refrigerate and let stand several hours before serving.

Bobbee Farabaugh

Sweet French Dressing

3/4 cup sugar
2 teaspoons salt
2 teaspoons mustard
   (dry or prepared)
2 teaspoons celery seed

2 teaspoons paprika
1 tablespoon grated onion
2 cups salad oil
½ cup vinegar
Catsup to color

Mix first six ingredients together. Add oil and vinegar slowly. Use low speed on electric mixer until thick and emulsified. Add catsup to color (about ½ cup).

Enala O. Wentworth

Sweet and Sour Dressing

1 cup salad oil
3/4 cup sugar
¼ cup vinegar
½ teaspoon salt

1/3 cup catsup
2 tablespoons
   Worcestershire sauce
1 medium onion, minced

This can be made ahead of time and stored in jar in refrigerator.

Mrs. Robert Machamer

Caesar Salad Dressing

1 egg
3/4 cup salad oil
¼ cup lemon juice
1 teaspoon salt
½ teaspoon pepper

1 teaspoon Worcestershire
 sauce
¼ cup grated
 Parmesan cheese

Submerge egg in boiling water for one minute. Break into bowl and whip until fluffy. Continue beating at high speed, slowly adding oil. Reduce speed and add remaining ingredients. Beat until mixed well.

Mary Jo Carter

Bohemian Club Dressing

Garlic clove
3/4 teaspoon salt
½ teaspoon freshly
 ground pepper
¼ teaspoon dry mustard
¼ cup finely chopped
 green onion
½ teaspoon sugar

½ teaspoon paprika
½ teaspoon Worcestershire
 sauce
1 hard-cooked egg
2½ tablespoons vinegar
¼ cup plus 2 tablespoons oil
2 tablespoons chopped parsley

Rub bowl with garlic, (or if you like garlic add some, minced or pressed, to dry ingredients). Put all dry seasonings in a bowl. Add cooked egg yolk and mash together thoroughly. Stir in vinegar, oil, parsley, ground onions, Worcestershire sauce and well-chopped egg white. Chill well. Serve on very cold wedges of head lettuce.

Serves 4

Jean Looby

wine and beverages

The preparation of ample amounts of foodstuffs and beverages mean a return to outdoor methods which accommodated large vessels. The resulting beverage provided the "soul" of the dining occasion.

Wines

For centuries, fine wines have been considered to be one of the great treasures of the world. They represent a product of nature which has been brought to its peak of perfection through generations of study, care, and battling against the elements. Men have spent their lives learning the secrets of producing great wines. It is, therefore, fitting that they should be held in esteem by people who appreciate the finer things of life.

Today, as never before, wines are being enjoyed more and more as a symbol of gracious living. Wine lends an aura of glamour and sophistication to a fine meal and enhances the flavor of good food.

When to Serve Wine

There are wines for every occasion and budget. Whether it be a formal or family dinner, a picnic or barbecue, wine will always add a little "something special" and make the occasion worth remembering.

Formal dining, of course, calls for wine. When the food is elaborately and formally served, there is a greater need for serving wine. One wine may be served at all occasions, but two or more would be more desirable.

A glass of good red wine is just the thing to complement a luscious steak or juicy hamburger at cook-outs, and a glass of white wine does wonders for fish, lobster and shrimp grilled over coals. For very little expense, such dinners can be turned into a gourmet's delight.

How to Select Wines

It always pleases the host or hostess to select a wine which will enhance the dishes to be served and which will be a "conversation piece" at the table. This is a relatively simple thing to do inasmuch as there is a tremendous variety of wines, degrees of greatness, and prices to complement each particular dish.

Drinking a fine wine is a pleasure and the worst possible mistake is to turn such an enjoyable experience into strictly regulated protocol. Generally speaking, any wine you like is a good wine for you, but you must try to insure that guests share in your pleasure of drinking a particular wine with a certain food. The "marriages" which meet with general approval are the following ones. When in doubt it is wise to abide by them.

Hors d'oeuvres: Light, dry white wine; Rosé.

Fish: Dry white wine; semi-sweet white wine.

White Meat & Poultry: Dry white wine; light red wine.

Red Meat: Full-bodied red wine.

Cheese: Red wine is best with pungent cheese, but all wines (except sweet ones) are excellent with all cheeses.

Sweet Desserts & Fruit: Sweet white wines; champagne.

Champagne and Rosé are good with all kinds of food. For true "connoisseurs" a dry white wine is always acceptable when served all during a meal, as Champagne and Rosé sometimes are.

How to Serve Wines

The proper etiquette of wine serving and drinking should be one of complete informality and ease. It does not require long planning and great care of execution, except, of course, in the case of great and old wines. These do need special handling. Some general rules to follow would be:

Serving Temperatures:

  (a) If possible, red table wines should be left standing in the dining room approximately 24 hours before the meal, allowing any sediment to settle, and the wine to reach room temperature.

  (b) White and Rosé wines are served slightly chilled (around 50 degrees F), and one hour on the shelf of a refrigerator will bring them to the right temperature.

(c) Champagnes and other sparkling wines take longer to chill and should be left in the refrigerator for a few hours.

Uncorking:

Red wine is improved if the bottle is uncorked about one hour before the meal. Wine is a living body, and as soon as the bottle is uncorked, the wine is "awakened" and starts "breathing." It absorbs oxygen from the air, and this oxidation activates the development of the "bouquet" and the aroma. One hour or so of "breathing" gives depth and smoothness to red wine.

It is the host, rather than the hostess, who serves the wine and sees to it that glasses are replenished all during the meal.

Glasses:

All experts agree that one type of wine glass is perfect for all wines, including champagne. The perfect glass is long-stemmed and tulip-shaped, with the bowl the size of an orange. It is clear, thin, without heavy ornamentation. As a matter of fact, any large glass or goblet is a good idea when no regular wine glass is available.

Serving:

Wine is poured as soon as food is brought to the table. The glasses are never filled. They are served only half-full, to allow the bouquet to fill the glass. The host should be justly proud of offering a good wine; he holds the bottle with the label up so that the guest may have a look at it.

Ted Aguilera

Beauty and The Beast

1 jigger vodka
2 dashes lemon juice

1 jigger creme de cassis
½ teaspoon grenadine

Shake all ingredients with ice and drain into a martini glass.

Barbara Henry

Bishop's Wine

1 orange
Whole cloves
1 (3-inch) stick cinnamon

1 large bottle Burgundy, zin-
   fandel, claret, or port wine
½ cup sugar

Stir whole orange with cloves and heat in wine, with cinnamon about ½ hour. DO NOT BOIL. Stir in sugar. Serve at once or keep hot in double boiler.

Peggy Capek

Chocolate Brandy Dessert

1 quart chocolate ice cream
1 cup strong black coffee

6 ounces brandy

Mix above ingredients together in blender and serve.

Fran Weaver

Green Cooler

1 6-ounce can frozen
   limeade concentrate
1 can vodka (using the frozen
   limeade can as measurer)

5 cans crushed ice

Put all ingredients in blender; cover and run on high speed for 15 seconds. Serve in highball glasses with straws.

Marty Ardell

Kahlua

4 cups sugar
4 cups water
2 ounces Spice Island
   Powdered Antiqua Coffee

1 long vanilla bean
1 fifth brandy

Combine sugar, water, and coffee, and heat until sugar dissolves. When cool, pour into a one-gallon glass jug and add vanilla bean and brandy.

Age at least one month.

Jenny Saynes

Punch

Fifth Miers Jamaican rum
Fifth Bicardi rum (green)
Fifth blended bourbon
Fifth domestic brandy
1 pint peach brandy

When ready to serve, add:
4 quarts 7-up
1 can frozen lemon juice
1 can frozen orange juice
  (large)

Be sure to purchase *quality liquor.*

Mix all alcoholic beverages at least 1 or 2 days ahead. When ready to serve, add 7-up, lemon juice and orange juice.

Center of punch bowl: Use fancy fluted mold; freeze water with maraschino cherries, fresh strawberries, and small pieces of orange sections. It is advisable to have two (2) frozen molds for this amount of punch.

In case of liquor mix left over, try:
½ large can frozen orange juice
1 can frozen lemon juice
1 can or bottle of 7-up
Add ½ of the above quantity of liquor mix. Mix all in a jar.

The liquor mix lasts indefinitely if stored in tightly sealed container.

Serves 100

Mrs. George Pardee

Champagne Punch

4 teaspoons bitters
4 tablespoons sugar
2 quarts sherry
8 ounces brandy
8 ounces maraschino cherry juice
8 ounces white Curacao
1 quart pink wine
1 quart white wine
4 quarts soda
4 bottles champagne

Garnishes:
12 orange slices
12 lemon slices
Spirals of cucumber peel
Strawberries frozen in ice cubes
Mint sprigs

Blend bitters and sugar in punch bowl; add the above ingredients, holding the soda and champagne until just before serving.

If milder potion is desired, it may be augmented with additional soda or wine.

Serves 50 adequately

Doris Flutcher

Holiday Punch

1 quart bottled
  cranberry juice
1 can (18 ounces)
  pineapple juice
1 cup orange juice

½ cup lemon juice
2 large bottles
  ginger ale, chilled
2 cups bourbon or vodka

Combine juices and bourbon or vodka. Chill. Just before serving, add ginger ale.

Serves 20-25

Betty Johnson

Milk Punch

2 raw eggs
3 ounces lemon juice
6 teaspoons powdered sugar

6 ounces gin
3 large scoops vanilla ice cream
2 handfuls shaved ice

Mix in blender and serve.

Mary Wessel

Punch Bowl

½ pineapple
1 cup sugar
1 cup lemon juice
2 cups pineapple juice

1½ bottles (fifths)
  gold Puerto Rican rum
2 quarts sparkling water
1 pint sliced strawberries

Slice pineapple; place in large pitcher with sugar, lemon juice, pineapple juice and rum. Chill at least 2 hours.

To serve, pour over a block of ice in punch bowl, add sparkling water and sliced strawberries.

Serves 20

Pete Hopkins

Paradise Punch

1 quart pineapple juice
1 quart orange juice
1 quart grapefruit juice
1 pint lemonade
1 number 2½ can
  crushed pineapple

1 10-ounce package frozen
  sliced strawberries
  (Do not thaw or drain.)
1 large bottle ginger
  ale or 7-Up

Mix all ingredients. Add ginger ale or 7-Up before serving. One gallon or 32 4-ounce servings. Vodka can be added if spiked punch is desired.

Yield: 1 gallon

Mrs. James Grosso

Christmas Punch

10 lemons
6 limes
¼ cup sugar
¼ cup grape juice

4 tablespoons grenadine
3/4 cup light rum
1 quart whiskey
2 bottles sweet soda

Put strained juice of lemons and limes into a 2-quart pitcher. Add other ingredients and pour over ice in punch bowl, adding sweet soda just before serving.

Serves 20

Hazel Wolfer

Friendly Punch

16 ounces of bottled
   lime juice
12 ounces honey

2 quarts white rum
2 quarts champagne

Pour over ice cubes.

Ruth Gast

Hot Posset

4 eggs, separated
2 cups milk
2 cups light cream
3/4 cup sugar

2 teaspoons almond extract
1 teaspoon grated lemon rind
1 cup Scotch whiskey
½ cup chopped toasted almonds

In large bowl of electric mixer beat egg yolks at high speed until thick and lemon-colored. In a large saucepan, heat milk and light cream and ½ cup sugar. Stirring to dissolve sugar, allow mixture to come to a simmer. Gradually pour mixture over egg yolks, beating constantly. Slowly beat in almond extract, grated lemon rind, and Scotch whiskey. In small bowl of electric mixer, beat egg whites (with clean beaters) until frothy. Add remaining ¼ cup sugar slowly, beating constantly, until a thick glossy meringue is formed. Quickly fold meringue into hot mixture and serve at once with a sprinkle of chopped toasted almonds on each serving.

Yield: 6 cups

Hilda Giordano

Summer Frost

1 teaspoon sugar
Juice from ½ lemon
1½ ounces bourbon whiskey
½ teaspoon green
   creme de menthe

Maraschino cherry
Lemon peel

Muddle sugar in splash of water in very tall glass. Add lemon juice. Pack glass with finely cracked ice (very important to use plenty of ice). Add bourbon whiskey and stir vigorously. Drip creme de menthe and stir. Garnish with maraschino cherry and lemon peel.

Marie Pumphrey

Mummy's Home Brew or Friendship Pot

1 cup peaches
 (drained plus 1 cup sugar)
1 cup pineapple
 (drained plus 1 cup sugar)

1 cup cherries
 with juice (plus 1 cup sugar)
1 cup apricots
 (drained plus 1 cup sugar)

Two weeks apart for addings. Never get below 3 cups. Stir in between. Keep in kitchen window or on shelf (not in refrigerator).

Serve on ice cream or custard.

Frances Ranus

Orange Julius Drink

3 cups orange juice
¼ cup sugar

¼ cup powdered milk
1 drop vanilla

Mix in blender or stir in pitcher with chopped ice cubes.

Don Pumphrey

Gluhwein

1 gallon red wine (Burgundy)
12 whole cloves
2 cinnamon sticks
1 bag or 2 cups strong tea

1½ cups sugar
1 fresh lemon
1 fresh orange

Combine all ingredients in large pan (do *not* use metal). Spiral lemon and orange and add. Simmer for at least 2 hours. Strain and serve hot.

Great for ski trips.

Mrs. Arthur Hilvitz

Hot Wine on a Cold Night

1 fifth dry red wine
1 cup apple cider
1 cup water
1 cinnamon stick
2 tablespoons sugar

1 tablespoon lemon juice
½ teaspoon nutmeg
3 cloves
1 very generous dash of bitters

Boil ingredients together 15 minutes and strain.

Serves 4

Jon Oud (Cork 'n Cleaver)

Eggnog

12 eggs
3 cups whisky
1 quart heavy cream
½ gallon vanilla ice cream

1 teaspoon vanilla
1½ cups sugar
1 quart milk

Separate eggs. Whip whites until stiff and set aside. Whip cream until stiff and set aside. Beat egg yolks with sugar until thick and lemon-colored. Add whisky slowly to yolk mixture so as not to cook eggs. To egg yolk mixture fold in egg whites, whipped cream, milk, ice cream and vanilla. Put in large eggnog bowl and sprinkle nutmeg on top.

Mina Hyde

Merry Sherry

2 cups California sherry
1 stick cinnamon

¼ cup sugar
¼ cup lemon juice

Lemon slices, extra cinnamon sticks

Heat sherry with 1 stick cinnamon and sugar, just to boiling. Add lemon juice and pour into pre-heated cups. Add thin slice of lemon to each cup with cinnamon stick for stirring.

Peggy Capek

Orange Blossom

1 scoop vanilla ice cream
½ scoop orange sherbet

1½ ounces gin (may be omitted)
½ slice orange

Put ice cream, sherbet and gin in blender container, cover and run on high speed (5) for 14 seconds. Serve in chilled champagne glasses; garnish with orange slice.

Use in place of dessert on hot summer nights.

Marty Ardell

Rum Drink

1 can frozen lemonade
1 can frozen limeade
Green food coloring

2 fruit juice cans of rum
3 fruit juice cans of water

Put in blender, then in quart jars, and put in freezer overnight. Scoop the slush into champagne glasses or wine glasses. It only takes a few seconds to melt to drinking consistency.

Nancy Bonforte

Pink Daiquiri

1 tray of ice (12 cubes)
1 small-size can of
    frozen pink lemonade

1 can rum (refill
    lemonade can)
Maraschino cherry

Blend with blender until ice is mushy.
Pour into glasses (wine or other).
Top with cherry.

Mrs. John Kilgore

meats
and
sauces

The outdoor barbeque kindles thoughts of
ranches, Indian feasts and chuckwagon suppers.
Tasty meat dishes, cooked slowly, hinting of
smoke and seasoning, rank high among the
preferences of many Americans.

Beef Stroganoff

2 pounds sirloin steak
  or beef tenderloin
4 green onions, chopped
½ cube butter
4-5 tablespoons flour
1 can beef bouillon

1 teaspoon Dijon style
  or dry mustard
1 2-ounce can mushroom
  pieces and stems
1/3 cup sour cream
1/3 cup white wine

Cut meat into bite size pieces; sauté with green onions until lightly browned. Push meat aside in pan and add flour to juice to form paste. Stir in beef broth to form gravy. Turn up heat and stir until well mixed. Add mustard. Turn down heat to low; cover and simmer 1 hour. Before serving, stir in mushrooms, sour cream and wine. Serve over buttered rice.

Kelley Kaufman

Beef Ala Mode

4-5 pound lean pot roast
1 quart water
3 carrots, chopped
3 stalks celery, chopped
1 onion, halved
½ bay leaf

2 cloves
¼ cup vinegar
½ teaspoon sugar
2 tablespoons catsup or
  3 tomatoes, seeded
1 teaspoon salt or to taste
5 whole peppercorns
2-3 tablespoons sour cream

Trim all fat from meat and set aside. Insert cloves in onion halves and add all ingredients except meat to water. Bring to boil; add meat and cook at least 2 hours or until meat is very tender. When done, remove meat and place on a platter, covered, in oven to keep warm. In a skillet, melt 2 tablespoons butter, add 3 tablespoons flour and stir until brown. Add ½ cup cold water and stir until very thick. Then start adding juice from pot, ¼ cup at a time to make gravy consistency. Add 2-3 tablespoons sour cream over low heat (it will curdle if too hot). Serve as gravy with boiled potatoes or potato dumplings.

Marge Birner

Bar-B-Q

2 pounds chuck roast
2 onions
½ can tomato sauce
¼ cup brown sugar

1 tablespoon mustard
Vinegar to taste
Salt to taste

Boil chuck roast and onions in water till very tender. Reserve about 2 cups of liquid and thicken with flour. Pick the meat into small pieces after cooled. To thickened liquid, add remaining ingredients. Ingredients need not be exact; adjust to your taste. Warm meat and sauce, serve on hamburger buns. Can be made with chicken instead of beef. Good if stands a day, also freezes well.

Nancy Tracey

Barbecued Spareribs

Meaty ribs, 1 pound per serving
Water
1 large onion, sliced

2 cloves
1 bay leaf
1 teaspoon salt

Cut ribs in serving pieces. Place in large kettle, cover with water, add remaining ingredients. Cover, bring to boil. Reduce heat, simmer until ribs are tender and almost done—1 to 1½ hours. Remove from water, brush each side with barbecue sauce, let stand 1 to 2 hours or overnight. Grill over coals, turning and basting frequently with remaining sauce. Cook until nicely browned, 15 to 20 minutes.

Barbecue sauce:
¼ cup brown sugar, firmly packed
¼ cup vinegar
1 cup catsup
¼ cup finely chopped onion

2 teaspoons prepared mixed barbecue spices
½ teaspoon salt
1 tablespoon Worcestershire sauce

Simmer slowly 15 minutes, stirring frequently.

Hazel Gist

108

"Oven Barbecued Spare-Ribs"

3 pounds spare ribs
   (country style)
2 onions, sliced
2 tablespoons Worcestershire
   sauce
1 teaspoon salt

1 teaspoon paprika
½ teaspoon chili powder
3/4 cup water
3/4 cup ketchup

Trim fat from spare ribs. Slice onions over top of meat. Mix remaining ingredients and pour over spare ribs. Cover and simmer 1½ hours on top of stove. Serve with baked potatoes.

Serves 3-4

Marilyn Hunter

Marinated Flank Steak

¼ cup soy sauce
2 tablespoons garlic salt
   (may use onion salt)

1 cup salad oil

Mix and marinate two flank steaks at least 30 minutes, piercing meat with a fork and turning them back and forth. Barbecue four to five minutes each side close to the coals.

When serving, cut very thin slices at an angle across the grain. One steak serves three people; nice to serve with fried rice.

Mrs. William Hopkins

Flank Steak

1¼ pounds steak
1/3 cup dry red wine
¼ cup soy sauce
1 tablespoon salad oil (olive oil)

¼ teaspoon monosodium
   glutamate
½ teaspoon ginger
1/8 teaspoon garlic powder
Dash cayenne

Marinate steak at least an hour (or a day), broil quickly, 3 minutes on each side. Cut diagonally and serve.

Darian Olsen

Stripped Steak

4 tablespoons butter
1 medium chopped onion
1 4-ounce can mushroom
  slices, drained
1½ pound round steak (trimmed
  of fat and cut into
  bite size strips)
2 tablespoons flour

1 can (10-ounce) beef consommé
1 cup water
1 tablespoon prepared mustard
2 tablespoons brown sugar
1-2 tablespoons Worcestershire
Salt and pepper to taste

Melt butter in large skillet. Add onion and mushrooms, sauté 5 minutes. Add strips of steak and cook until brown. Blend flour into meat mixture. Remove from heat. Add consommé, water, mustard, brown sugar, Worcestershire, salt and pepper. Return mixture to medium heat until it reaches a simmer. Cover and simmer on low heat until steak is tender, 30-60 minutes. Thicken sauce, if desired, with small amount of flour mixed to a paste with water. Serve over rice or noodles.

Serves 4   *Anita Currier*

Pepper Steak

1 pound round steak cut in
  thin slices about 2 inches long
¼ cup cooking oil
1 teaspoon salt
Dash pepper
¼ cup chopped onion
½ teaspoon garlic salt

1 large green pepper,
  cut in rings
3/4 cup sliced celery
1 cup beef bouillon
2 tablespoons cornstarch
¼ cup water
2 teaspoons soy sauce

Set fry pan on a hot burner. Add oil, salt and pepper. When oil is hot, add meat and brown, stirring frequently. Reduce heat and add onions, garlic salt, green peppers, celery and bouillon. Cover and cook until vegetables are crispy tender, about 15 minutes. Add extra hot water if necessary. Blend cornstarch, water and soy sauce. Add to meat mixture and stir until thickened. Serve with hot rice.

Serves 4   *Mrs. Harold E. Robinson*

110

Chinese Pepper Steak

1 pound round steak
¼ cup shortening
1 clove garlic, minced
½ teaspoon salt
¼ teaspoon pepper
4 tablespoons soy sauce
½ tablespoon sugar

1 cup bean sprouts
2 large tomatoes quartered
 or 1 cup cooked tomatoes
1 large green pepper
 cut in 1-inch pieces
2 tablespoons cold water
½ tablespoon cornstarch
4 green onions, sliced

Slice steak in small pieces. Heat shortening with garlic, salt and pepper. Cook steak in shortening and seasoning until brown. Add soy sauce and sugar. Cook at high heat for 5 minutes. Add bean sprouts, tomatoes and green pepper. Cover and cook for 5 minutes. Stir in cornstarch dissolved in cold water. Cook until thickened. Sprinkle with green onions and serve with rice.

Rheuanna Kelly

Round Steak—Italian Style

2 slices round steak, ½ inch
 thick, and tenderized
3 eggs, well beaten
½ cup Worcestershire sauce

2 cups Italian style
 bread crumbs
Salt and pepper to taste

Mix together eggs, Worcestershire sauce, salt and pepper. Cut meat into serving pieces, trimming fat off. Put meat into sauce mixture. Marinate 4 hours or overnight, turning meat occasionally so all pieces get soaked well. Melt shortening in fry pan (enough to cover bottom about ½ to 1 inch). I use my electric skillet about 325 degrees. Take meat and coat each piece with bread crumbs on both sides. Put pieces in skillet and fry until nice and brown. Try to turn each piece only once, and put on a paper towel to drain. These will keep well in a warm oven, covered.

Vivian Elizondo

111

Sukiyaki

2 pounds round steak
1 tablespoon meat tenderizer
1/8 cup cooking oil
1 large onion, sliced
  very thin
2 cups celery, sliced in
  3-inch pieces
12 green onions
¼ pound mushrooms, sliced

¼ pound spinach, cut
1 5-ounce can water chestnuts
1 cup bouillon
½ cup soy sauce
1 tablespoon sugar
3 cups hot cooked rice

Cut beef in thin diagonal slices, across the grain, and sprinkle lightly with tenderizer. Dip in oil and let stand ½ hour. On large serving platter, arrange sliced and slivered foods in an attractive pattern. This dish is meant to be admired before cooking as well as after.

Heat oil in large skillet or chafing dish (an electric skillet brought to table is perfect). When oil is hot, brown meat lightly, push to side of pan. Add onion, celery, green onions, mushrooms and toss minute or two. Combine soy sauce, bouillon, sugar; add to pan, mix well. Add spinach, water chestnuts; cover and steam 3 minutes. Serve over hot boiled rice.

Peg Swath

Teriyaki Steak

3/4 cup salad oil
3 tablespoons honey
2 tablespoons vinegar
1 teaspoon garlic salt

1 teaspoon ginger
¼ cup soy sauce
¼ onion, cut in small pieces
Flank steak

Marinate steak in sauce for 4 hours, then broil.

Serve with beef flavored rice and a fruit salad.

Mrs. Thomas Broome

Tenderloin of Beef

2 pounds beef tenderloin tips
1 teaspoon chopped shallots
¼ cup oil
Salt and pepper
½ cup dry white wine

8 large fresh mushrooms,
  sliced (canned will do)
¼ cup butter
1 tablespoon chopped onion
2 cups heavy cream

Cut the tenderloin into 3/4 inch cubes. Heat the oil in a saucepan and when hot, fry the beef until slightly browned. Drain off the oil, then season with salt and pepper. Heat the butter in another saucepan and add shallots, onions, and mushrooms. Simmer for 2 minutes, then add white wine and cook for 6 more minutes. Add the heavy cream and simmer *slowly* until the sauce has thickened. Pour the sauce over the beef tenderloin and serve with buttered noodles.

4 servings

Toni Feiler

Brisket of Beef, Barbecued

6 pound brisket of beef
Water (about 8 cups)
1 large onion
  (sliced ½ inch thick)
1 bay leaf
16 whole cloves
Few grains garlic salt

2 cups catsup
¼ cup Worcestershire sauce
2 tablespoons brown sugar
2 tablespoons dry mustard

Put meat into large pot or kettle. Add enough water to cover meat. Add onion, bay leaf, cloves and garlic salt. Cover, bring to boil, reduce heat and simmer about 4 hours. Cool in liquid. Drain off liquid.

Trim off excess fat. Chill in refrigerator several hours, or overnight. At this point it can be frozen for use at a later date. Cut meat into very thin slices and arrange meat slices close together (standing on end) in shallow baking pan. Pour over meat a mixture of remaining ingredients.

Heat in 350 degree oven for 40 minutes, basting occasionally with sauce in bottom of pan.

May be served as just slices of beef or put into hamburger buns.

8-10 servings

Marge McGovern

Brisket Marinade

1 can tomato paste, 6-ounce
½ cup packed brown sugar
1 tablespoon Worcestershire
  sauce
1 tablespoon cider vinegar

1 teaspoon mustard,
  hot if available
1 tablespoon margarine
1 medium onion, grated

Put paste and 1 can of water in saucepan. Add rest of ingredients and mix well. Bring to a boil, then reduce heat and simmer for 10 minutes. I use this on a brisket (rolled) which I can cook at least 9 hours at 275 degrees. Four hours before serving, I unwrap the foil from around the brisket (to which I've put salt and pepper and basil) and pour on the marinade. Wrap back up, put back into dutch oven or any roaster with a tight lid and finish baking. The meat is so tender and moist. Excellent and easy for company.

This is a good marinade for any chicken or beef.

Punky Robbe

Sweet Bread Cutlets

1 pound sweet breads
1 cup blanched almonds,
  chopped fine
1 teaspoon salt
Dash of paprika
Thick cream sauce
Cracker and bread crumbs
1 can cream of mushroom soup
1 can mushrooms

Thick cream sauce:
1 cup milk
1 tablespoon butter
2 tablespoons flour

Soak sweet breads in cold water for 1 hour before cooking. Parboil the sweet breads for 20 minutes. Clean, removing membrane. Cool, pick into small pieces, chop fine. Add one cup of almonds, chopped fine, salt and paprika. Make cream sauce and add to sweet breads. When cold, form into chop-shaped cutlet, dip in egg and bread crumbs (cracker crumbs) let set awhile. Put a piece of macaroni in the end of each cutlet and fry in deep fat. Serve with sauce made from mushroom soup and canned mushrooms.

Serves 4

Muriel Anton

114

Hungarian Goulash

2 pound ground sirloin
  or round
1 medium onion, chopped
1 medium green pepper,
  chopped
1 large can tomatoes (#2½)
4 cups cooked elbo-roni

1 large can mushroom pieces,
  drained
1 tablespoon Worcestershire
  sauce
Salt and pepper to taste
1 cup Cheddar cheese, shredded

Brown beef in butter, add onions and green pepper, sauté with mushrooms. Add tomatoes, simmer 1 hour. Season. Cook elbo-roni, add to mixture, place in casserole, cover with shredded cheese and bake at 350 degrees until cheese melts.

Patsy Kenyon

Boilermaker Corned Beef

5 pounds corned beef
2 large cans beer
2 whole cloves garlic
1 bay leaf
2 whole onions

1 teaspoon paprika
½ cup bourbon
½ cup brown sugar
1 teaspoon whole peppercorns

Place meat in large, heavy Dutch oven. Pour in beer and add enough water to just cover. Add garlic, bay leaf, peppercorns, and onions. Bring to a boil and then *immediately* turn heat way down so that liquid does not continue to boil, but only gives up an occasional bubble or two. *Anything more than a gentle simmer makes meat stringy.* Simmer beef for about 45-60 minutes per pound, but keep almost submerged by adding more beer and water if needed. When tender remove from fire and let meat stand in liquid for another hour. Remove to a roasting pan and sprinkle with paprika, bourbon and brown sugar (in that order). Bake at 350 degrees for 20 minutes, basting every five minutes with about ¼ to ½ cup of beer liquid plus roasting pan juices.

Mrs. Toni Feiler

Liberace Special Hamburgers

6 tablespoons minced onion
2 teaspoons butter
4 pounds ground sirloin
1 tablespoon Worcestershire
  sauce
½ teaspoon oregano
1 teaspoon leaf thyme
1½ teaspoons salt
½ teaspoon freshly
  ground pepper
6 round hamburger buns

Sauté the onion in butter until light brown. Mix with remaining ingredients except buns. Split the buns and put a ½ to 3/4 inch patty on the split side of the buns. Put the meat all the way to the edge. Store in refrigerator to firm the beef until ready to cook. Broil 6 inches away from the heat for 6 to 8 minutes.

Serves 12

from "Liberace Cooks"
as told to Carol Truax, Director
Broadmoor International Theatre

Hamburgers Hawaiian

2/3 cups evaporated milk
1½ pounds ground beef
½ cup chopped onion
2/3 cups cracker crumbs
1 teaspoon seasoned salt
  (garlic salt)
1 13½ -ounce can pineapple
  chunks
2 tablespoons cornstarch
¼ cup vinegar
¼ cup brown sugar
2 tablespoons soy sauce
1 cup coarsely chopped
  green pepper

Combine milk with ground beef, onions, cracker crumbs and salt. Form six 4-inch individual patties by pressing each one between pieces of waxed paper. Brown patties in skillet in a little oil. Pour off fat. Cover hamburgers with sauce (see below). Cover and simmer over low heat 15 minutes.

Sauce: Drain pineapple chunks. Combine pineapple syrup and water to make 1 cup. Mix syrup and cornstarch, vinegar, sugar and soy sauce in saucepan. Heat until thickened and clear. Add pineapple and green pepper. Easy recipe and goes over well at a Sunday evening informal patio party.

Serves 6

Mrs. Toni Feiler

Party Hamburgers

1 pound hamburger
1 cup soft bread crumbs
  (rye bread is best
  for these)
3½ tablespoons catsup
1 egg, slightly beaten
3/4 teaspoon salt

2/3 cup coarsely grated
  Cheddar cheese
2½ tablespoons chopped
  green bell pepper
1 tablespoon chopped onion
¼ cup bottled lemon juice
8 strips of bacon

Mix all ingredients together except lemon juice and bacon. Let stand 10 minutes to stiffen. Add bottled lemon juice and mix well. Divide into 8 patties and wrap a strip of bacon and secure with a toothpick. Broil either inside or on charcoal outside.

Serves 8

Punky Robbe

Cabbage Burgers
(Kraut Beorauck — German)

Sweet roll dough:
2 cups milk
1 package dry yeast
2 teaspoons salt
½ cup sugar

½ cup shortening
2 beaten eggs
6 cups flour

Scald milk. Cool. Add yeast, salt, sugar, shortening and eggs. Add flour and knead well. Set to rise in warm place.

Filling:
2 pounds hamburger
1 medium head cabbage,
  chopped fine

2 large onions, chopped
Salt and pepper to taste

Brown hamburger and drain. Add cabbage, onion and seasonings and steam until done. Cool. Roll out small pieces of dough into squares about 6 x 6 inches. Place about 2 tablespoons filling mixture on each square and seal by folding up edges. Place on baking sheet and let rise 1 hour. Bake for 30 minutes at 350 degrees.

Yield: 16 burgers

Mrs. Norman Pierce

Beef with Green Peppers

Full cup beef tenderloin
  or flank steak
  sliced bacon-thin at an angle
2 bell peppers, cut in
  1½ inch squares

1½ teaspoon ginger, sliced
Small clove garlic
2 leeks (green onions)
  cut in 1-inch lengths

Marinate: sliced beef, 15 minutes to 2 hours in 3 tablespoons water, 1/3 teaspoon soda, 2 tablespoons soy sauce, 1/3 teaspoon salt, 1 teaspoon cornstarch, 2 teaspoons oil.

Frying sauce: 2 tablespoons water, 1/3 teaspoon salt, 1 teaspoon sesame oil, ½ teaspoon cornstarch, 1 teaspoon sugar, 1 teaspoon sherry, ½ teaspoon monosodium glutamate, 2 tablespoons soy sauce.

In 1 tablespoon oil, fry-stir green peppers lightly. Set aside. In 2 tablespoons oil fry ginger, garlic and leeks. Then add beef and stir until almost done. Add green peppers and frying sauce. Add 1 tablespoon oil, stir and serve.

Mrs. Moy Annette Kennedy

Crepes with Cannelloni Filling

3/4 cup cold water
3/4 cup cold milk
3 eggs

3/4 cup flour
Dash salt
3 tablespoons butter, melted

Put water, milk, eggs and salt in mixing bowl; beat well. Blend in a little flour at a time. Add cooled melted butter. Cover mixture and cool in refrigerator at least 2 hours or overnight. Cook in 6½ inch iron skillet in oil.

Put 3 tablespoons of batter in center of pan (batter is very thin). Tilt pan so batter will cover all surface. Crepe will brown in about 70 seconds. Turn crepe over and brown other side (about 30 seconds). This should make 15 crepes. Fill crepes while warm or later, as you so desire. If later, place wax paper between each crepe.

Sauce: See page 139 for Mornay Sauce.

118

Cannelloni Filling:

10-ounce package frozen spinach
   or ½ pound fresh spinach
1 egg
1 cup grated Parmesan cheese

½ pound sausage — 1 cup
½ pound ground round steak
Salt, pepper to taste

Cook spinach in salt water, just until tender. Drain and squeeze out excess water. Chop and set aside. Brown sausage and meat in oil, remove from heat and add beaten egg, spinach, cheese, salt and pepper. Place about 2 tablespoons filling in each crepe and roll up leaving both ends open. Place in baking dish. If cooled, put in oven for 15 minutes to heat thru. Remove from oven and add about ½ of the sauce to cover crepe. Return to oven for another 15 minutes. Remove from oven and spoon the remaining sauce and sprinkle generously with Parmesan cheese and a little parsley. Brown lightly in oven or broiler.

Josephine Montera

Beef Carbonade

2½ pound rump beef sliced
   ½ inch and pounded thinner
   Swiss steak or any cut
   of beef really will do
¼ cup flour
½ cup bacon fat or butter
2 tablespoons vinegar
1 cup beer
2 cans onion soup
2 thinly sliced carrots

1 teaspoon sugar
¼ cup tomato sauce
1 teaspoon dehydrated
   celery flakes
1 teaspoon parsley flakes
½ bay leaf
¼ teaspoon dried thyme

Shake beef with about ¼ cup flour in a bag; then brown in fat. Push meat to one side in the skillet and add to the brown glaze in the pan, the vinegar, beer (the cheaper lager beer gives more flavor than the beer which is usually served for drinking), onion soup, carrots, sugar, tomato sauce and spices. Bring to a boil and simmer 2 minutes. Place meat and sauce in layers in casserole. Sauce should come to the top of the meat. If it doesn't, add consommé. Cover tightly and bake in moderate oven, 350 degrees, about 2 hours or until meat is tender. Serve with buttered carrots and boiled potatoes or rice, hominy grits or polenta.

Serves 6

Martha Whitlock

Lobster-Stuffed Tenderloin of Beef with Mushroom Sauce

3-4 pound whole beef
   tenderloin (allow ½ pound
   per person)
2 4-ounce frozen
   lobster tails

3 tablespoons melted butter
2 teaspoons lemon juice
6 slices bacon
   partially cooked

Carefully trim beef to remove silvery connective tissue and cut lengthwise to within ½ inch of the bottom. Place frozen lobster tails in boiling salted water to cover. Return to boiling, reduce heat and simmer 5-6 minutes. (It will not be fully cooked at this point). Remove lobster from shells and cut in half lengthwise. Place lobster end to end inside beef. Combine butter and lemon juice and drizzle over lobster. Close meat and tie roast securely with string at intervals of 1 inch. Place on rack in shallow pan and roast at 425 degrees for 45-50 minutes for rare beef. Lay bacon slices over top and bake 5 minutes more. (Meat thermometer should read 130 degrees.)

Mushroom sauce:
1 cube butter
1 large lemon

1 pound fresh mushrooms
1 tablespoon Worcestershire
   sauce

Wash mushrooms and place upside down on paper towel. Squeeze lemon juice into each, then cut up and place in top of double boiler. Add butter, Worcestershire sauce and remaining lemon juice. Place over hot water and cook over low heat an hour or two. Spoon over tenderloin.

Fran Weaver

Kipling Curry or Curried Beef

2 pounds lean beef cubes
   (round steak)
2 cups lukewarm water
2 large onions sliced,
   separate into rings
6 ounces butter or margarine
6 garlic cloves, chopped fine
2 large ripe tomatoes,
   chopped and skinned

1 tablespoon ground ginger
1 inch stick cinnamon
1 tablespoon ground cumin
1 teaspoon ground tumeric
¼ teaspoon ground coriander
½ teaspoon ground cardamon
1/8 teaspoon ground red pepper
   or 2-3 drops Tabasco sauce
1 teaspoon salt, or to taste

Condiments:

1 cup shredded coconut	1 cup chutney (a must)
1 cup chopped, seeded tomatoes	1 cup chopped green pepper
3 sieved hard boiled egg whites	1 cup currants or raisins
3 sieved hard boiled egg yellows	½ cup chopped ripe olives
1 cup peanuts, chopped	

These ground spices can be altered to taste. Curry powder *should not* be substituted for the spices unless you are happy with the common taste it gives. You will probably have to obtain the coriander and cardamon from a specialty shop.

Melt butter in large pan suitable for stew. Add onion rings, cardamon, and cinnamon stick. Cook until onions are golden and transparent. Add remaining spices and tomato. Stir mixture over low heat until tomatoes are done. Add beef and 2 cups of water. When mixture returns to boil, turn heat to low so that simmer is maintained. Continue cooking, stirring occasionally, until meat is tender. Serve with fluffy rice of Pilaf and 7 of the condiments listed. This will freeze well. Best made a day in advance—enhances flavor.

Serves 6-8

Mrs. George E. McKinnon

Beef Rouladen

8 slices (¼ inch thick)	1 or 2 tomatoes
lean boneless beef	1 or 2 beef bouillon cubes
½ pound sliced bacon	Margarine
1 large onion, cut in strips	2 tablespoons flour

Take a slice of beef at a time, salt and pepper it to taste. Put some strips of bacon and onions on the meat, roll and fasten with toothpick or string. Roll each meat roll in flour.

Dissolve butter or margarine in a big pot with a lid. Brown meat on each side, sprinkling 2 tablespoons flour over it. When brown and when flour is dissolved, cover rolls with water. Add bouillon cubes and tomatoes (cut up) and cook covered for 1 hour or more. If gravy is not thick enough, add cornstarch dissolved in a little water. Cook another 10 minutes. Serve with noodles.

Serves 8

Olly Birner

Sauerbraten with Gingersnap Gravy

3½ -4 pound pot roast
  (chuck or rump)
2 cups vinegar
2 bay leaves
4 whole cloves
8 peppercorns

6 medium carrots
  (cut in strips)
4 medium onions
  (sliced thin)
2 teaspoons sugar
8 gingersnaps (crumbled)

Three days before cooking, wipe meat with damp cloth and sprinkle thoroughly with salt and pepper. Place in earthenware bowl. Heat vinegar to boiling and add to meat. Add seasonings. Marinate in refrigerator for 3 days. Turn twice a day with wooden spoons. NEVER pierce with fork.

When ready to cook, drain meat and brown thoroughly on all sides in hot fat in heavy skillet. Add vegetables and marinade. Do not cover meat with marinade. Simmer slowly 3-4 hours until tender. When meat is done, add sugar and crumbled gingersnaps and cook 10 minutes longer.

Remove meat and vegetables to platter. Keep warm. Pour off marinade. Measure 2 cups and return to kettle. Shake ½ cup cold water and 2 tablespoons flour together in jar. Stir slowly into the hot marinade. Bring to boil. Season to taste.

LaLonna Meoska

Sirloin Tips Ragout Au Vin

3 pounds sirloin tip,
  1-inch cubes
3 tablespoons butter
3 ounces tomato paste
2 tablespoons wine vinegar
1 cup Burgundy
1 stick cinnamon

2 bay leaves
2 pounds tiny whole
  onions, peeled
1 teaspoon salt
¼ teaspoon pepper
1 teaspoon cornstarch
¼ cup water

Place cubes in deep saucepan with butter. Simmer over medium heat stirring constantly till meat is brown and tender. Mix tomato paste, vinegar and wine with browned meat. Add remaining ingredients except cornstarch and water. Simmer covered for 1 hour. Mix cornstarch with water and blend into flour. Serve over hot rice.

6 servings

Helen Murley

122

Sirloin Goodie

3 pounds cubed sirloin steak
½ package onion soup mix
2 cans mushroom sauce

3/4 cup sherry
1 4-ounce can mushrooms

Brown meat. Mix all of the above ingredients and place in Dutch oven. Cover and bake in a 350 degree oven for 2 hours or until tender. Serve over rice or noodles.

Serves 5-6

Jo Marikas

Grenadin of Beef

6 tenderloins, 1 inch thick
18 matchlike strips of fat pork
Dash: pepper, thyme, nutmeg
¼ cup clarified butter
¼ cup carrots
¼ cup celery stalks
¼ cup onions (green onion, white part)
1 tablespoon chives
1 bay leaf

¼ teaspoon thyme
¼ teaspoon tarragon
6 peppercorns
1½ cups dry white wine
1 cup beef bouillon
2 tablespoons sherry
Mushrooms

Add dash pepper, thyme, nutmeg to meat; lard meat with fat pork and sear meat in butter until browned. Put browned meat in casserole with carrots, celery, onion (all coarsely chopped), chives, bay leaf, thyme, tarragon and peppercorns. Add white wine and cover casserole tightly. Braise the grenadins in a 350 degree oven for 30 minutes, turn them and cook for 30 minutes longer. Arrange on a heated platter and keep hot. Strain the sauce in the casserole into a saucepan and reduce it over high heat almost completely. Add 1 cup beef bouillon and sherry. Reduce the sauce over high heat by half and season it with salt and pepper to taste. Spread the sauce over the grenadins with a pastry brush and put the platter under the broiler until the top is glazed. Garnish with mushrooms sautéed in butter.

Margie Hyde

123

Chuck Roast Spaghetti

4 pound chuck roast, boned
1 large onion, diced
1 green pepper, diced
1 clove garlic, chopped fine
2 teaspoons beef-flavored
  instant bouillon

½ package spaghetti
Salt
Pepper
1 cup boiling water

Place roast in one end of 9x13x2 inch pan. Mix together chopped onion, pepper and garlic, and cover top of roast with the mixture. Salt heavily and pepper to taste. Sprinkle with bouillon and cover tightly with aluminum foil. Place in 350 degree oven and bake for 2 hours. Remove from oven and reset temperature control to 425 degrees. Carefully lift foil from pan. Place spaghetti in juice beside roast and pour boiling water over the spaghetti, taking care to moisten every strand. Replace foil and return to oven for 30 minutes.

To serve: On a warm platter, make a nest of the spaghetti. Cut the roast into chunks and place in center of nest. Spoon juices over meat.

This simple meal can be started on timed bake and needs only a crisp salad and hard rolls to complete.

Serves 6   *Ann Leach*

Braciole
(Stuffed meat rolls cooked in spaghetti sauce)

1 slice round steak
  (tenderized twice if cut ½
  inch thick; meat should
  be tender and thin
  but not falling apart)
3-4 eggs
1½ cups bread crumbs

1 small clove garlic,
  chopped fine
1 tablespoon parsley
1 tablespoon grated
  goat cheese or Romano
Salt and pepper to taste

Mix all ingredients; mixture should be moist (all the above ingredients are approximate and may add more or less to taste). Spread mixture on rectangle of meat, approximately 2-3 x 4-5 inches, then roll up and wrap thread around the meat. Fry till brown. Cook in sauce for 2-3 hours. Before serving, cut the threads and unwind for your guests if you like.

Leah Rae Puleo

Burgoo (Civil War Stew)

2 pounds pork
2 pounds veal
2 pounds beef shank
2 pounds breast of lamb
1 fat hen
8 quarts water
1½ pound Irish potatoes
1 bunch carrots

2 green peppers
2 cups chopped cabbage
1 quart fresh or canned
　tomatoes (chopped)
2 cups fresh or canned corn
2 pods red pepper
2 cups lima beans
1 cup diced celery
Salt, cayenne pepper
　to taste

Put all meat into cold water and bring slowly to a boil. Simmer until tender enough to fall from the bones. Sift meat out of stock, cool and chop, removing bones. Return meat to stock and add all prepared vegetables. Allow to simmer until very thick. Stir frequently with long handled wooden spoon and almost constantly after the stew gets thick, to prevent burning. Just before the stew is served, add Tabasco, A-1, and Worcestershire sauces to your taste and a cup of chopped parsley.

Recipe may be cut in half for small groups.

Serves 25

Mrs. David W. Boyer

Five Hour Beef Stew

2 pound chuck or
　shoulder roast (cubed)
3 carrots, cut in large pieces
1 cup celery
1 large sliced onion

8-ounce can tomato sauce
3 tablespoons tapioca
2 tablespoons sugar
Pinch salt, pepper

Place meat in 2 quart casserole, place vegetables on top of meat, then tapioca, sugar, salt and pepper. Pour tomato sauce over all. Bake covered at 250 degrees for 5½ hours. Stir only *once*, just before serving.

Freezes well.

Serves 6

Mrs. Sue Mastro

Beef and Dumplings

2 pounds round steak
  cut in 1-inch cubes
2 medium onions, sliced
1 bay leaf
1 10½-ounce can cream
  of chicken soup
1 10½-ounce can onion soup

½ can sliced mushrooms, drained
1 tablespoon Worcestershire
  sauce
1/3 cup flour
1 10-ounce package
  frozen peas, thawed
4 green pepper rings

Place steak in 3 quart casserole, cover with onion slices, add bay leaf. Combine soups and mushrooms, Worcestershire sauce, and flour. Pour over meat. Bake at 350 degrees, covered, for 2 hours or till meat is tender. Remove bay leaf, place peas on top of casserole, place pepper rings in the center. Drop dumplings by rounded teaspoons around pepper rings, cover. Bake at 400 degrees 20-25 minutes.

Dumplings:
1 egg
1 cup flour
2 tablespoons minced parsley
¼ teaspoon sage

2 tablespoons cooking oil
1½ teaspoons baking powder
1/3 cup milk
½ teaspoon salt

Combine in small mixing bowl egg, milk, parsley, oil and sage. Add flour, baking powder and salt. Stir only until dry particles are moistened. Drop by rounded teaspoons around pepper rings.

Dagmar Borkowitz

French Pancakes Filled with Roast Beef

Crepes:
3 large eggs, beaten
½ teaspoon salt
½ teaspoon sugar

1 cup flour
1½ cup milk
Cooking oil

Combine eggs, salt, sugar. Blend in flour and 2-3 tablespoons milk, stirring with fork. Gradually add remaining milk, stirring (or beating) constantly till smooth. Brush 7-inch skillet (Teflon works beautifully) with cooking oil; heat. Add small amount (about 2-3 tablespoons) batter, tip to spread evenly over skillet. Cook over moderate heat just till pancake is firm, turn and cook 1 minute longer. Do not brown. Crepes may be stacked.

126

Filling:

2 cups (about) cooked ground roast beef
Salt and pepper to taste
¼ cup (or more) bouillon or meat stock
3 tablespoons butter
1 medium onion, chopped

Sauté onion in butter till golden; add meat, salt and pepper and enough bouillon to make meat moist. Heat through. Place a heaping tablespoon of filling near center of pancake. Fold end of pancake over filling, then fold sides toward center. Fold end over sides forming an envelope.

If you want to make these ahead, stop at this point and refrigerate if to be used same day, or freeze for future use. If frozen, thaw prior to next step.

Heat 3 tablespoons butter in skillet, add several filled pancakes, seam side down; fry until golden on both sides, turning once. Add more butter, if necessary, to fry remaining pancakes.

Serve with commercial sour cream.

(These are really worth the effort!)

Doris Neumeister

Beef with Peapods

1 package frozen peapods
2 tablespoons butter
2 pounds sirloin,
   cut in 1/8 inch strips

1 cup beef consommé
1 tablespoon cornstarch
2 tablespoons soy sauce
¼ to ½ cup sherry or white wine

Sauté peapods in butter. Remove from pan and sauté sirloin strips in butter on high heat until brown but still rare. Remove from pan. Heat consommé. Mix cornstarch in cold water until dissolved and add to consommé. Add soy sauce and sherry. Cook till thick and clear brown. Add meat and peapods. Heat and serve at once. Good with beef-flavored rice.

Joanie Hilvitz

Beef Rouladen

1 pound sirloin tip,
   sliced 3/8 inch thick
Salt and pepper
Mustard
Dill pickles

Onions
Bacon
½ cup dill pickle juice
Flour (or cornstarch)
Instant beef broth

Lay slices of meat out flat. Sprinkle with salt and pepper. Spread on each slice a small amount of mustard, diced dill pickles, diced onions and a small slice of bacon. Roll up and secure with toothpick or with thread. Brown rolls in hot fat, add pickle juice and enough water to cover. Cook over low heat about 2 hours. When tender, remove rolls, add instant beef broth and flour to make gravy.

Serves 4-6 *Ingrid Boggess*

Tourenados of Beef

4 medium size tenderloins,
   ½ inch thick
¼ cup dry white wine
1 teaspoon leaf tarragon,
   crumbled
1 teaspoon instant minced onion

1 envelope Hollandaise sauce mix
   or 1 can Hollandaise (3/4 cup)
4 toast rounds
1 can (small) artichoke hearts

Simmer wine, tarragon and onions for 5 minutes, remove from heat, strain into a 1 cup measure. Prepare Hollandaise sauce. Gradually add strained herb-flavored wine, beating constantly. Keep warm. Broil meat 4 inches from heat for 4 minutes, turn. Broil 4 minutes longer or until steaks are as done as you like them. Meanwhile, heat, drain and salt and pepper artichoke hearts. Arrange toast rounds on platter. Top each toast with meat, place one artichoke heart on each, spoon part of sauce over each one. Serve remaining artichoke hearts and sauce separately.

Margie Hyde

Chinese Casserole

2 pounds lean pork sausage
1 bunch green onions
1 large green pepper
1 small bunch celery
2 packages chicken noodle
   soup (dry)

1 cup brown rice
1 can water chestnuts
1 small can mushrooms
1 small can clams
Slivered almonds

Cook chicken noodle soup in 4½ cups water. Add one cup brown rice. Fry pork sausage until crumbly. Pour off excess grease. Remove meat and in same pan, sauté chopped green onions (include most of tops), chopped green pepper, and chopped celery (leaves and all). Mix above ingredients together and add sliced water chestnuts, mushrooms, and minced clams. Bake in covered casserole one hour at 350 degrees. Sprinkle toasted slivered almonds on top before serving.

Mary Green

Chinese Pork Dish

1 cup chopped onion
3 pounds pork tenderloin
   (cut in 1-inch cubes)
2 tablespoons shortening or oil
2 cups sliced celery
1 cup uncooked rice
1 can (7-ounce) mushrooms,
   drained
1 can cream of mushroom soup

1 can cream of chicken soup
4 cups water
½ cup soy sauce
1 teaspoon salt
½ teaspoon pepper
1 package (12-ounce) frozen peas
   thawed
1 cup blanched almonds, slivered

Sauté onions and meat in melted shortening until meat is brown. Place in a large 4-quart casserole and mix in celery, uncooked rice, mushrooms, chicken and mushroom soups, water, soy sauce, salt and pepper. Cover and bake at 350 degrees for 45 minutes. Stir in peas and cook 30 minutes longer. Remove cover, sprinkle top with almonds, and bake 15 minutes longer to brown almonds.

Serves 8-10

Rheuanna Kelly

Nona's Canederli

One half or more (I use almost a whole loaf) of crusty French bread cut into squares.

Parlsey and celery leaves, chopped
Salt to taste
Bacon, chopped into cubes —5 or 6 slices

One sausage or salami (Italian sausage—1/3 of a pound)
4 or 5 eggs, beaten
¼ - ½ cup milk

Cook bacon with sausage. Pour eggs over remaining ingredients; add cooled bacon and sausage. Eggs will be absorbed by bread. Sift about one cup flour over the mixture and blend. Shape into 3-inch balls and cook 15 - 20 minutes in hot meat or chicken broth. Test one; if it doesn't hold together, add more flour. I cook them in my beef vegetable soup.

Fran Posa

Piquant Ham Loaf

1 pound smoked ham
1½ pounds lean shoulder pork
½ teaspoon pepper

2 eggs
1 cup milk
1 cup crushed graham crackers

Grind together the ham and pork twice. Add pepper, eggs, milk and crackers. Mix well. Bake in loaf pan one hour at 325 degrees. Pour off grease.

Syrup:
½ cup brown sugar
½ teaspoon dry mustard

¼ cup vinegar
¼ cup water

Pour syrup over loaf. Bake another ½ hour, basting occasionally. Top with ½ cup crushed pineapple or pineapple chunks for the last 15 minutes.

Serves 6 or 8

Doris Flutcher

Company Ham

4 tablespoons butter
2 cups cooked ham cut in small pieces
4 tablespoons flour
1 can mushroom soup

2 cups sour cream
1 8-ounce can sliced mushrooms
Salt and pepper to taste

Melt butter in a large skillet and add ham. Stir soup until smooth and blend into ham mixture. Cook over moderate heat a few minutes. Gradually stir in sour cream. Add mushrooms. Continue to cook until mixture is just heated through. DO NOT boil or mixture will curdle. Serve over noodles.

6 servings

Ange Jagger

Ham Steak

1 slice cooked boneless ham (about 1-inch thick)
¼ cup brown sugar
1 tablespoon dry mustard
¼ teaspoon ground cloves

½ teaspoon paprika
1 clove garlic, finely chopped
1 tablespoon salad oil
1 cup dry sherry

Combine ingredients for the marinade and pour over ham. Let stand 3 or 4 hours. Remove ham and dry with paper towel. Broil 8-10 minutes on each side, basting frequently with the marinade.

Rene Holden

Baked Ham

5 or 6 pound boneless cooked ham
Whole cloves
3/4 cup brown sugar

1 tablespoon dry mustard
Vinegar
1½ cup dry sherry

Score top of ham in diamond pattern and insert a whole clove in center of each. Mix brown sugar, dry mustard and enough vinegar to make a soft paste, and spread over ham. Place in baking dish (*not* metal) and pour dry sherry into dish. Bake at 325 degrees for 1 3/4 hours, basting frequently.

Rene Holden

Gourmet Pork Chops

2 tablespoons olive oil
1 clove garlic
6 lean pork chops
Salt and pepper to taste

3 tablespoons tomato paste
½ cup dry white wine
1 green pepper, finely chopped
½ pound fresh mushrooms, sliced

Heat oil in a heavy skillet; add the garlic and cook until browned. Discard the garlic. Add pork chops and brown on both sides. Sprinkle meat with salt and pepper. Add remaining ingredients; cover and simmer until chops are tender and cooked through, about 30-35 minutes.

Serve with dry white wine.

Serves 4 to 6   *Sidney Clutter*

Shanghai Pork

2 pounds lean pork
 (cut in 2-inch strips,
 about ½ inch thick)
½ teaspoon garlic powder
½ teaspoon salt
¼ cup salad oil
2 tablespoons instant
 minced onion
2 tablespoons water
1 tablespoon salad oil

2 cups sliced carrots,
 cut in ½-inch pieces
1 6-ounce can sliced mushrooms
1 10½-ounce can cream
 of celery soup
¼ cup soy sauce
3/4 teaspoon ground ginger
¼ teaspoon pepper
3 cups shredded cabbage
¼ cup toasted slivered almonds

Rub pork with combined garlic powder and salt. Heat the ¼ cup salad oil in skillet. Add pork, a few pieces at a time, and brown on all sides. Transfer to 2½-quart casserole. Combine instant minced onion and water; let stand 10 minutes for onion to soften. Add the 1 tablespoon salad oil to skillet. Add softened onions and carrots and cook until onions are golden. Stir frequently to keep from sticking. Add mushrooms and their liquid, soup, soy sauce, ginger and ground pepper. Heat to boiling, stirring constantly. Pour mixture over pork and toss gently. Bake covered at 350 degrees for one hour or until meat is fork tender. Top with shredded cabbage. Cover and cook for another 10 minutes. Before serving garnish with slivered almonds. Serve with fluffy hot rice.

Serves 6   *Toni Feiler*

132

Szekelys Gulyas

2 tablespoons cooking oil
2 pounds lean pork, cubed
¼ cup onion — minced
2 cloves garlic — minced
1 to 2 tablespoons paprika

1½ teaspoons salt
1½ pounds sauerkraut
½ teaspoon caraway seeds
½ cup buttermilk

Heat oil in heavy pot or kettle; brown pork lightly. Add onion and paprika; cook until onion is soft. Add salt, caraway seeds and sauerkraut. Cover and simmer gently for about 3 hours. Just before serving stir in buttermilk.

Serves 8

Peg Swath

Korean Pork Platter (Curry)

1½ pounds lean boneless
    pork shoulder, cut in
    one-inch cubes
2 tablespoons flour
4 tablespoons vegetable oil
3 teaspoons curry powder
1 tablespoon sugar
1/3 cup soy sauce

3/4 cup water
2 large onions, peeled,
    sliced and separated into rings
2 cups sliced celery
1 package (9-ounce) frozen
    cut green beans
1 teaspoon celery salt

Shake pork cubes with flour to coat evenly. Brown cubes in 2 tablespoons vegetable oil in a large frying pan; remove and set aside. Stir curry powder into drippings in frying pan; cook 3 minutes. Stir in sugar, soy sauce, and ½ cup of water. Cook (until bubbly) stirring constantly and scraping cooked-on juices from bottom and sides of pan. Stir in pork and cover. Simmer one hour and 15 minutes, or until pork is tender.

While meat cooks, sauté onion rings in remaining 2 tablespoons oil for 3 minutes in a second large frying pan; put to one side. Stir in celery; cook 3 minutes. Stir in frozen green beans. Sprinkle with celery salt; toss to mix. Add remaining ¼ cup water. Cover. Steam 10 minutes or until vegetables are crispy tender; drain.

Spoon vegetables on heated large platter; spoon pork on top. Serve with steamed rice.

Serves 6

Yvonne Baitlon

133

Polynesian Pork Roast

Loin of pork, tied and boned. Sprinkle with salt, pepper and rosemary. Roast the pork in a moderate oven (350 degrees) on rack until done.

Baste with:
½ cup soy sauce
½ cup catsup

¼ cup honey
2 large cloves garlic, crushed

Use 350 degree oven or barbecue.

Serve with preserved kumquats and watercress.

Mary Ann Sturgeon

Teriyaki Smoked Pork Loin

4-5 pound boneless,
   rolled pork loin roast
2/3 cup soy sauce
¼ cup cooking oil

2 tablespoons molasses
2 teaspoons dry mustard
2 teaspoons ground ginger
2 cloves garlic, minced

Insert spit through center of roast and adjust holding forks. Insert meat thermometer. Attach spit and turn on motor. Have medium coals at rear of firebox and a drip pan under meat. Add damp hickory chips to coals and lower smoke hood. Roast three hours, adding more damp chips as needed, or until thermometer registers 170 degrees. Brush with soy mixture occasionally *after first hour.* Let stand 15 minutes before carving.

Faith Stotko

Pork Chops with Corn Dressing

6 large pork chops
1 can cream style corn
   (yellow or white)
¼ large green pepper
2 stalks celery

¼ large onion
2 to 3 sprigs parsley
1 egg
2 to 3 slices bread
Salt and pepper to taste

Chop medium-fine the pepper, celery, onion and parsley. Place in bowl with egg and corn, and blend with large spoon. Add bread, which has been crumbled into small pieces, salt and pepper and stir until the mixture is thick enough to just stand alone. Season pork chops and place in shallow baking pan. Cover each chop with equal amounts of dressing. Place in preheated 350 degree oven and bake approximately one hour.

Note: Ideal company dish. If dinner is to be delayed, the oven temperature can be reduced while the chops cook longer or may even be turned off. They do not need watching during the cooking period.

When ready to serve, the dressing should be fairly crisp on top, moist inside and the chops moist and tender.

Toni Feiler

Hawaiian Spare Ribs

4 - 4½ pounds country-style spareribs
1 can (1 pound 14 ounce) crushed pineapple
¼ cup honey
2 tablespoons soy sauce

Brown slightly in skillet and drain off grease
4 teaspoons cider vinegar
½ teaspoon ginger
1 tablespoon cornstarch
1 tablespoon cold water

Drain pineapple and place juice in a small saucepan. Add honey, soy sauce, vinegar and ginger; stir over low heat until honey becomes thin and ingredients blend. Stir cornstarch and water until smooth; add to honey mixture, and cook, stirring constantly, until thick and clear. Add pineapple. Place ribs in a large pan. Spoon mixture over ribs. Bake covered with foil at 375 degrees for 1½ hours. Baste occasionally.

Marie Pumphrey

Herbed Roast Leg of Lamb

1 teaspoon minced marjoram
1 teaspoon minced thyme
1 teaspoon minced rosemary
1 teaspoon garlic powder
1 6-pound leg of lamb

2 tablespoons olive oil
2 tablespoons flour
1 cup dry white wine
1 teaspoon salt
Freshly ground black pepper

Mix garlic powder, salt and pepper with olive oil. Spread on lamb. Sprinkle with marjoram, thyme, rosemary and flour. Pour wine and one cup of water in roasting pan with lamb. Roast in a slow oven (250 degrees) for 2½ hours or longer, basting frequently.

Serves 6
Mrs. Toni Feiler

Lamb Shoulder Roast

1 4 to 5 pound precarved
   lamb shoulder roast
1 15-ounce can tomato sauce
¼ teaspoon instant granulated
   garlic (or powdered garlic)
½ teaspoon basil

1 teaspoon salt
¼ teaspoon pepper
¼ teaspoon oregano
2 cups sliced zucchini
   (or other summer squash)

Place roast on rack in shallow pan at 325 degrees for 1 hour. Prepare sauce by combining tomato sauce, garlic, and seasoning. Lift roast to pan with tight fitting lid. Pour sauce over roast and continue to roast 1 to 1½ hours or until tender, basting occasionally with sauce. Remove roast and place on hot platter. Cook zucchini in sauce 5 minutes. Serve sauce and zucchini in gravy boat with roast.

You may use same pan for entire recipe but be *sure* to drain all grease off and wipe out the pan after the first hour or it will be very greasy.

Mrs. Gay McCabe

136

Barbecue Sauce

2 tablespoons butter
1 small onion, chopped fine
½ teaspoon pepper
½ teaspoon salt
4 tablespoons sugar
1 teaspoon prepared mustard

1 teaspoon paprika
½ cup catsup
¼ cup vinegar
3/4 cup water
4 teaspoons
    Worcestershire sauce

Sauté onion in butter until clear. Add remaining ingredients and simmer for one hour. This sauce is excellent with spareribs or chicken. If one prefers to make a larger recipe, sauce will keep indefinitely in refrigerator.

Beverly Hurley

Bordelaise Sauce

¼ cup butter
2 shallots, finely chopped
2 cloves garlic,
    finely chopped
2 slices onion
2 slices carrot
2 sprigs parsley
10 whole peppercorns
2 whole cloves
2 bay leaves

3 tablespoons flour
1 can beef bouillon
    (10½ ounce, condensed)
1 cup good burgundy wine
¼ teaspoon salt
1/8 teaspoon pepper
2 tablespoons finely chopped
    parsley

In hot butter in medium skillet, sauté shallots, garlic, onion, carrot, parsley sprigs, peppers, cloves, and bay leaves until onion is golden, or about 3 minutes. Remove from heat; stir in flour smoothly, stirring over very low heat until flour is lightly browned, about 5 minutes. Remove from heat. Stir bouillon and 3/4 cup wine into flour mixture. Cooking over medium heat, bring just to boiling, stirring constantly. Reduce heat; simmer, uncovered, 10 minutes, stirring occasionally. Strain sauce, discarding vegetables and spices. Return sauce to skillet; add salt, pepper, parsley, and remaining ¼ cup wine. Reheat gently—do not boil. Pass with filet of beef.

Yield: 2 cups

Mrs. Philip Hilvitz

137

Hollandaise

2 egg yolks
1 cube butter or margarine

½ cup lemon juice (more
    if you want it sour)
Dash of salt

Beat egg yolks until thick and light yellow. Gradually add by teaspoons melted butter, beating all the time. Keep beating and add lemon juice, drop by drop. Beat all together. Set aside until ready to use.

Does not need cooking—can be left in refrigerator 2-3 days. Delicious over green beans, asparagus, Brussel sprouts, etc. Just pour over the hot vegetables.

The secret to this sauce is to add ingredients to egg yolks so slowly that they won't separate.

Lucille Kellogg

Hollandaise Sauce (Blender)

1 stick butter
3 egg yolks
1 tablespoon lemon
    juice (or more)

Pinch cayenne
Dash salt

Heat butter till very hot—do not brown. Blend remaining ingredients on medium speed. Remove center cap of blender and pour in hot butter, blending at full speed.

This will keep in refrigerator for days. Reheat over hottest tap water, not boiling, in a double boiler.

Yield: 3/4 cup

Doris Neumeister

Shrimp Sauce

1½ cups catsup
1 teaspoon Worcestershire
    sauce
3 tablespoons lemon juice

2 tablespoons
    minced celery
1 tablespoon horseradish

Mix well. Good with fried shrimp, shrimp cocktail, etc.

Colleen Von Bermuth

138

Mornay Sauce

6 tablespoons butter
1½ cups milk
4½ tablespoons grated
   Parmesan cheese
3/4 teaspoon salt

3 tablespoons flour
1½ cups half and half
1½ tablespoons butter
Dash nutmeg, thyme

Melt butter and stir in flour. Add milk and half and half, stirring constantly until sauce is thick and smooth. Stir in cheese, nutmeg, salt and 1½ tablespoons butter. Stir until butter melts. Sauce can be made ahead, kept in double boiler and heated when ready to use.

Yield: 3 cups
Josephine Montera

Spaghetti Sauce

1 medium onion
3 cloves garlic
1 large can tomatoes
1 large can tomato sauce
1 tablespoon dried basil

2 tablespoons parsley
¼ teaspoon allspice
1 teaspoon oregano
Salt and pepper to taste

Blend onion, garlic, tomatoes in blender, and add to the rest of the ingredients in a large kettle. Simmer 3 or 4 hours. Add meat balls last hour.

Jean   Ludwig

Hot Mustard

1 cup dry mustard
1 cup white vinegar

Combine in small saucepan and let set overnight.

Next day add: 1 cup sugar mixed with 2 beaten eggs and pinch of salt. Simmer over medium heat to desired consistency. Sauce thickens some as it cools. Recipe can be cut in half.

Yield: 1 pint
Mrs. Frank Beattie

Sauce for Ham

3/4 cup butter
½ cup flour

1 cup chicken broth
1 cup sweet vermouth or sherry

Brown butter and flour; add chicken broth and heat. Add vermouth or sherry.

Yield: enough sauce for ½ ham   *Lolita Vidmar*

Mustard Sauce for Ham

2 tablespoons mustard
1 egg
¼ cup sugar

¼ teaspoon salt
¼ cup cream
¼ cup vinegar

Blend above ingredients. Cook until thickened. Add ½ tablespoon butter after sauce is taken from stove. Best cooked in double boiler. Serve with baked ham.

Carol Kilstofte

Ham Glaze

2 tablespoons butter (melted)
1 cup red wine
  (or white sherry)
1 teaspoon cloves

2 tablespoons dry mustard
2 tablespoons brown sugar
1 teaspoon paprika
2 cloves garlic—minced

Combine and heat until sugar dissolves. Baste ham occasionally, as you bake it in the oven or on outdoor grill.

Barbara McDermid

Sweet-Sour Grape Glaze (for ham)

1 tablespoon cornstarch
1 tablespoon water
½ cup grape juice
¼ cup vinegar

3/4 tablespoon grated
  orange rind
½ cup brown sugar
1 teaspoon salt
¼ teaspoon ginger

Make a paste of cornstarch and water. Add remaining ingredients and cook, stirring constantly, until it boils. Simmer 5 minutes.

Yield: 1 cup

Faith Stotko

Sour Cream Horseradish Dressing

1 cup sour cream
1 teaspoon dry mustard
2 tablespoons horseradish

¼ teaspoon salt
Dash of sugar

Combine and mix all ingredients. This sauce can be used on tongue, corned beef, and even French-fried cauliflower.

Adrian Comer

Creamy Horseradish Sauce

1 cup whipping cream
1 egg white
¼ cup mayonnaise

1/3 cup drained
  horseradish
1 teaspoon salt

Combine whipping cream and egg white and beat until stiff peaks form. Fold in mayonnaise and then horseradish and salt.

Serve with beef, corned beef or ham. Excellent accompaniment with meat fondue. Sauce should be made no more than a half hour before serving as it becomes soft on standing.

Yield: 2½ cups

Mrs. James Grosso

Marinade Sauce

2 cloves garlic
1 medium onion
½ cup parsley

2 teaspoons salt
8-ounce can tomato paste

Put above ingredients in blender and blend. Add to the above:

½ cup oil
1 cup vinegar
1 bottle Worcestershire
  sauce

3/4 cup brown sugar
4 teaspoons Tabasco
1 teaspoon rosemary
½ teaspoon thyme

Simmer for 20 minutes, cool. Sauce will keep for months in refrigerator.

Puncture roast and sprinkle with meat tenderizer. Marinate meat two days covered in refrigerator. Cover grill with aluminum foil and poke holes in it before cooking roast. This will keep sauce from burning. Cook over charcoal on grill for 40 minutes per side for a 6-pound roast, 2 and 3/4 inches thick. Chuck or blade roast is good.

Nadene Henry

Marinade for Sirloin

1 cup soy sauce
1 cup bourbon

2 tablespoons vegetable oil

Marinate sirloin (1½ to 2 inches thick) about 2 hours. Broil inside or out!

Fran Weaver

142

poultry and game birds

What fond memories are stirred by the
thoughts of fowl simmering and roasting
in the old coal stove, sending a promise to all
corners of the house that grand dining
is in store for all.

Pollo Con Jocoque
(Chicken Breasts with Sour Cream and Mushrooms)

4 extra large chicken
    breasts, halved (8 pieces)
½ cup butter
½ cup chicken bouillon
1 onion chopped fine
3/4 to 1 pound fresh
    mushrooms, sliced

1 clove garlic, minced
3 tablespoons butter
1 small container sour cream
½ cup heavy cream
Salt

Remove skin from chicken breasts and quickly brown on all sides in ½ cup butter.

Butter a large shallow casserole and arrange chicken breasts. Dot with butter, pour bouillon over chicken and bake at 350 degrees for 1 hour or until chicken is tender.

Cook the mushrooms, onions, and garlic in 3 tablespoons butter until golden. Add sour and sweet cream and salt to taste. Heat slowly. Do not boil. Pour over chicken and serve.

Joanne Battiste

French Chicken

4 large or 6
    small chicken breasts
1 can cream mushroom soup
2/3 can canned
    mushrooms and liquid

1 cup sour cream
½ cup wine

Place chicken, skin side up, in a large glass baking dish. Pour all ingredients which have been combined over the chicken. Sprinkle all generously with paprika. Bake at 350 degrees for 1¼ hours.

Garnish with parsley sprigs, serve with plain or wild rice.

Mrs. J. Roland Mathis

Freeze Ahead Chicken Kiev

4 whole chicken breasts,
   3-3½ pounds
Lemon juice
Salt and pepper to taste
¼ pound cold butter

Flour
1 egg, beaten with
   1 tablespoon milk
½ cup fine dry bread crumbs
Fat for deep frying

Have the butcher halve, and bone, and pound thin the chicken breasts. Carefully remove skin from chicken so you do not tear flesh. Place pieces between sheets of waxed paper and pound gently with flat meat mallet until each piece is very thin and doubled in size. (Butchers will not do this at times). Sprinkle with salt, pepper and lemon juice. Cut butter into 8 sticks about 2 inches long. Place a stick at small end of each piece of chicken, and roll tightly, folding in sides to enclose butter and make a compact roll. Fasten with small metal skewers or wooden picks. Coat each roll with flour, the egg mixture, the bread crumbs. Fry two at a time in deep hot fat, (350 degrees) for 5 minutes until golden brown. Drain on paper towels. When cool, remove skewers, wrap individually in foil, and freeze. To serve, unwrap rolls and let stand at room temperature for 1 hour. Bake on rack in a shallow pan at 450 degrees for 20-25 minutes until well browned.

Serves 6-8

Ann Gardner

Chicken Kiev

4 chicken breasts
8 tablespoons chopped
   green onion
8 tablespoons parsley
1 cube butter, cut in 8 pieces
Flour
2 eggs
1 cup bread crumbs
1 lemon, cut in 8 wedges

Mushroom sauce:
3 tablespoons butter
½ pound sliced mushrooms
1 tablespoon flour
1 teaspoon soy sauce
3/4 cup light cream

146

Cut away bone and remove skin from chicken breast; cut in half. Place each chicken breast between two pieces of clear plastic wrap. Pound with wooden mallet until breast is ¼ inch thick; peel off wrap and sprinkle with salt. Place one tablespoon of green onion and parsley on cutlet and one piece of butter. Roll as a jelly roll, tucking in ends. Fasten with a toothpick. Dust each roll with flour, dip into beaten eggs, and then roll in fine bread crumbs. Chill at least one hour or longer. Fry in deep hot fat or oil (340 degrees) about 5 minutes or until golden brown. Serve with mushroom sauce and lemon wedges.

Sauce: Melt butter, add mushrooms and sprinkle with flour. Cook over medium heat, stirring occasionally, 8 to 10 minutes or until tender. Add soy sauce; slowly stir in cream and cook until mixture bubbles and thickens. Season to taste.

Diane Larkin

Stuffed Chicken Breasts

6 to 8 chicken
   breasts, boned
3 ounces finely chopped
   mushrooms
2 tablespoons butter
2 tablespoons flour

½ cup half and half
   or light cream
¼ teaspoon salt
1 dash cayenne pepper
1¼ cups sharp Cheddar
   cheese, shredded

Cook mushrooms in butter for 5 minutes. Blend in flour and stir in cream. Add salt and cayenne pepper. Cook and stir until thick. Stir in cheese; cook over low heat, stirring constantly until cheese melts. Turn into a pie plate. Cover and chill for at least 1 hour.

Pound chicken breasts to ¼-inch thick and salt. Place wedge of chilled cheese mixture in each one, roll lengthwise and chill before breading. Then dust with flour, dip in egg and roll in bread crumbs. Chill an hour or overnight. One hour before serving, deep fat fry for 5 minutes at 375 degrees. Drain on paper towel. Place in shallow baking dish and bake at 325 degrees for 30 to 45 minutes.

Ange Jagger

Chicken Breasts Provencal

3 whole broiler-fryer chicken
  breasts, cut in half
Salt
Paprika
½ cup butter or margarine
½ pound mushrooms (if you
  do not use fresh, use 1 can
  of mushroom caps)
1 garlic clove, chopped
1 medium onion, chopped

1 green pepper, cut in strips
1 medium eggplant (the deep
  purple variety) cut in
  ½ -inch slices
1 cup (1 pound) tomatoes
1 can (8-ounce) tomato sauce
¼ teaspoon Tabasco sauce
¼ teaspoon dried leaf tarragon
Grated Parmesan cheese
2 tablespoons chopped parsley

Sprinkle chicken breasts with salt and paprika. Heat butter in large skillet, add chicken and brown on both sides. Remove chicken. Chop mushroom stems, reserve the caps, add to skillet with garlic, onion, green pepper strips, and eggplant. Cook 3 to 5 minutes. Add tomatoes, tomato sauce, tabasco, basil and tarragon. Return chicken to skillet; cover and simmer 15 minutes. Add mushroom caps; cook 5 minutes longer.

To serve, sprinkle with Parmesan cheese and parsley.

Note: This is a good party recipe. The chicken can be prepared early in the day and cooked after your guests arrive.

Serves 6   *Toni Feiler*

Roast Chicken Perfect

1 4-pound chicken
1 to 2 ounces brandy
1 lemon peeled
1 orange, peeled

1 medium onion, peeled
Salt
7 cloves, with heads
2 tablespoons butter

Wash and dry chicken; rinse cavity with brandy. Salt cavity and insert lemon, orange and onion. Stick with cloves. Truss with skewers. Roll outside of chicken in butter; wrap in foil. Roast chicken 1 hour 45 minutes. Unwrap foil during last few minutes to brown chicken. Temperature—450 degrees.

Garnish with parsley.

Faith Dix

Chicken Smetone

2 2½ to 3-pound
   broiler-fryer chickens
1 large clove garlic
1 to 1½ cups dairy sour cream
2 tablespoons lemon juice

1 tablespoon seasoned salt
1 teaspoon each salt and paprika
Dash pepper
1 cup fine, dry bread crumbs
½ to 3/4 cups butter, melted

Mash garlic thoroughly and combine with sour cream, lemon juice and seasoning. Coat chicken in sour cream and chill covered for several hours (or overnight) in refrigerator. Butter large shallow baking dish. Remove chicken from cream allowing as much cream as possible to adhere to pieces. Roll gently in crumbs and arrange in single layers in baking dish. Drizzle with melted butter and bake 50 to 60 minutes, or until golden brown, at 350 degrees.

Carol Zuercher

Chicken Teriyaki

Breasts, thighs and
   legs of frying chicken
2/3 cup soy sauce
½ cup dry sherry
2 tablespoons brown sugar

1 cup water
3 cloves garlic, minced,
   or garlic salt to taste
1 teaspoon ground ginger

Combine marinade ingredients and place in large bowl. Add chicken parts and marinate for 1 or 2 days in refrigerator. To prepare, place chicken in a flat baking dish and cover with the marinade sauce. Bake at 325 degrees for 1½ to 2 hours until very tender. Serve on a bed of fluffy rice to which you have added butter, parsley, and almond meats. Serve remaining marinade in a gravy boat.

When serving large crowds, this may be pressure-cooked; it doesn't detract from the flavor at all.

Mrs. Donald Abram

Chicken Cacciatore

18 - 20 pieces chicken
(thighs, legs, breasts)
Olive oil and butter
(to brown chicken)
1 large can tomatoes
(reserve ½ juice)
2 cloves garlic

1 large onion, minced
1 stalk celery
2 cans button mushrooms
3 - 4 tablespoons parsley flakes
Salt and pepper to taste
2 teaspoons sugar
½ cup white wine

Heat oil and butter in heavy dutch oven. Brown chicken. Pour off oil and arrange chicken in dutch oven. Salt and pepper. Add tomatoes with ½ of juice. Sprinkle sugar on tomatoes and chicken. Add onions, garlic on toothpicks, and parsley. Add celery, cut in half. Add mushrooms. Put on lid and simmer for 1 to 1½ hours. Last 15 minutes, add wine.

Serves 6 to 8

Petie Pryor

Chicken Creole Maybe

1 large fryer, cut in pieces
Salt and pepper
3 green onions, chopped
(tops too)
3 tablespoons olive oil
½ pound raw ham, diced
(Virginia is best)

1 pink okra, diced
1 number 2½ can Italian tomatoes
1 large can water chestnuts
(drained, sliced in ½ -inch pieces)
2 tablespoons soy sauce
½ teaspoon thyme
½ teaspoon marjoram

Flour chicken, salt and pepper. Brown in olive oil, add onions, and put in deep casserole. Brown ham in same skillet; add to casserole. Likewise okra, tomatoes, water chestnuts, soy sauce, 4 cups water and the seasonings. Cover lightly and simmer in 350 degree oven 1½ hours or until chicken is tender and liquid is reduced at least half in quantity.

Serves 4

Mrs Henry Williams

"Hahn"

1 fryer
Salt and pepper to taste
1 tablespoon olive oil
8 slices bacon
2 small onions
2 bell peppers
1 tablespoon tomato paste
1 cup strong white wine
Parsley, minced

1 bay leaf
1 teaspoon thyme
2 tablespoons black
  olives, sliced
1 can mushrooms
4 peeled and seeded tomatoes
1 stick butter

Cut the chicken in four pieces. Salt and pepper chicken, simmer in olive oil and butter until the meat is firm and white, (takes about 5-10 minutes) take the meat out of skillet. Fry bacon (diced), add the onions, (diced) until they turn yellow. Add diced bell peppers. Finally add tomato paste and pour white wine over this. Add herbs and chicken pieces into boiling gravy, cover pan and let simmer for about 3/4 or 1 hour. The chicken pieces can be put into a deep dish and kept until morning. Add to the gravy, peeled and seeded tomato slices, olives, and mushrooms. Cook gravy for a short time. If it is too thin, blend in some flour.

Serve gravy over chicken pieces with rice.

Blanka Nicoll

Easy Chicken Divan

2 10-ounce packages broccoli
2 cups sliced cooked chicken
2 cans cream of chicken soup
1 cup mayonnaise
1 teaspoon lemon juice

½ teaspoon curry powder
½ cup sharp Cheddar
  cheese, shredded
½ cup soft bread crumbs
2 tablespoons melted butter

Cook broccoli. Arrange in greased 11½ x 7½ inch dish. Place chicken on top. Combine soup, mayonnaise, lemon juice and curry powder. Pour over chicken. Sprinkle with cheese. Combine bread crumbs with butter and sprinkle over all. Bake at 350 degrees 25 or 30 minutes.

Serves 6 to 8

Doty Reyhons

Indian Curry

1 garlic bud, mashed
2 medium onions, quartered
3 tablespoons shortening or
    cooking oil—DO NOT USE
    BUTTER OR OLEO
3 rounded tablespoons
    curry powder

2 three pound chickens
    cut into small sections
2 tablespoons tomato paste or
    4 tablespoons tomato sauce
Juice of ½ lemon
1 tablespoon cardamon
    seeds, husked
2 cups of water
Salt and pepper to taste

In a 6 to 8-quart pan, put garlic, onions and shortening or oil. Over low heat stir well until the onions are transparent. Add curry powder and continue cooking over low heat, stirring well, for at least 5 minutes. Add chicken pieces and stir until well covered with paste. Add the rest of the ingredients; turn up the heat to medium and continue to cook, stirring occasionally, until meat is done. Adjust the seasoning and serve hot.

Note: The secret to good curry is the time taken to cook the powder before adding the other ingredients. This is an extremely versatile dish, since shrimp, fish, beef, lamb, hardboiled eggs, or vegetables can be substituted for the chicken. The best vegetables to use are cucumbers, cauliflower, summer squash, peas and tomatoes. This is a favorite Lenten dish for us, since I can use a combination of fish and vegetables and add ½ cup coconut to make it more tasty. When I use this recipe, I add more lemon to bring out the flavors.

Serve with boiled rice and tomato onion salad.

Serves 6 to 8   *Mrs. Jack Wolther*

Oven Barbecued Chicken

½ cup water
½ cup vinegar
½ cup brown sugar

½ cup catsup
1 stick butter

Heat above ingredients; pour over one or two cut-up chickens (or pieces desired) in a baking dish.
Bake at 350 degrees for 1½ hours.

Serves 6-8   *Ev Streamer*

152

Pheasant with Sauerkraut

1 pound sauerkraut
8 ounces dry white wine
½ teaspoon caraway seed

Pheasant
Butter
Salt and pepper

Mix sauerkraut, wine and caraway seed. Cover and simmer. Clean bird, cut into serving pieces and brown well in melted butter. Salt and pepper. Place browned bird in casserole with sauerkraut mixture. Bake at 350 degrees for 1 hour.

Mrs. D. L. Vickery

Gourmet Dressing for Poultry or Fowl

1 pound fresh mushrooms
1 cup butter
3 garlic cloves, minced

Salt to taste
4 cups fine bread crumbs
2 cups sour cream

Wash and drain mushrooms. Chop caps and stems to very fine pieces. Add to large hot skillet with ½ cup butter. Brown and add minced garlic and salt to taste. Add remaining ½ cup butter and bread crumbs. Mix well. Remove from heat and add sour cream. Season with salt and pepper to taste. Will stuff 8 to 10-pound turkey or capon or 8 cornish hens.

Joanne Battiste

Smothered Pheasant

Pheasant
Seasoned flour

½ cup butter
1 cup water, cream or milk

Clean pheasant thoroughly and cut into serving pieces. Roll in seasoned flour and brown in melted butter slowly. Place in a casserole and add water, cream or milk. Cover tightly and bake at 325 degrees for about 1 hour or until tender. Gravy may be made from drippings, if desired.

Mrs. D. L. Vickery

Roast Wild Duck and Apricot Sauce

3 wild ducks
Celery leaves
1 cup butter, melted
½ cup dry red wine
1 teaspoon salt
Freshly ground black pepper

Sauce:
2½ cups canned,
    peeled apricots, drained
1 teaspoon grated
    orange rind
2 cups dry red wine
6 tablespoons butter
Duck juice
Ground black pepper

Rub cavities of ducks with salt and pepper. Fill cavities with celery leaves; brush ducks with ½ cup butter. Roast ducks in 375 degree oven for 1½ hours, basting every 5 minutes with wine and remaining butter. Save juices to be added to apricot sauce. Keep ducks warm while making sauce.

Sauce: Press apricots through a coarse sieve. Combine apricots, orange rind, wine, butter and pepper in top of double boiler. Cook over direct heat for 5 minutes. Add duck juice; place over hot water and simmer for 5 minutes, stirring constantly until smooth and slightly thickened. Slice duck very thin and place on individual plates. Pour sauce on duck to taste.

Margie Hyde

Pheasant in Sour Cream

Pheasant
Bacon drippings
Salt and pepper

1/8 teaspoon paprika
1 pint sour cream

Clean bird and cut into serving pieces. Rub with bacon drippings. Dust with salt, pepper and paprika. Place in baking dish and brown for 20 minutes in hot oven (450 degrees). Add sour cream; reduce heat to 325 degrees and bake, covered tightly, for 30 minutes longer.

Mrs. D. L. Vickery

Roast Pheasant

1 2½ to 3-pound pheasant
¼ pound bulk sausage
½ cup chopped tart apples
1 teaspoon chopped onion
¼ teaspoon salt

1/8 teaspoon pepper
½ cup hot water
½ cup bread crumbs
½ cup cracker crumbs
Bacon slices

Clean bird, dry cavity and salt lightly. Fry sausage slightly—do not drain. Add remaining ingredients; mix well and stuff in body cavity. Place on rack in shallow pan. Lay bacon strips over bird, and bake at 325 degrees for 1½ hours.

Mrs. D. L. Vickery

fish and seafood

Frying pan sizzling atop the potbellied stove signalled the pending arrival of many a delicacy—perhaps trout, fresh from a Rocky Mountain stream.

Shrimp in Cheese Sauce

2 tablespoons butter
2 tablespoons flour
1 cup milk
¼ teaspoon salt
Dash pepper
1 teaspoon Worcestershire
 sauce

½ cup shredded
 sharp Old English cheese
1½ pounds fresh or frozen
 shrimp (cooked and cleaned)
1 10-ounce package frozen
 peas, cooked and drained
1 teaspoon lemon juice,
 fresh, frozen or canned

Melt butter; blend in flour. Add milk gradually and cook until thick, stirring constantly. Add salt, pepper and Worcestershire sauce. Add cheese; stir until melted. Add shrimp, peas and lemon juice. Heat thoroughly. Serve in bread baskets or other shells.
Serves 6   *Pat Siemsen*

Shrimp Curry

3 pounds deveined shrimp
3 tablespoons butter
¼ cup onion, chopped
½ cup carrots, thin-sliced
1 to 1 and 3/4 tablespoons curry
 (to taste)
3 tablespoons flour

2½ cups canned tomatoes,
 drained and mashed
1 cup boiling water
2 beef bouillon cubes
½ cup tart apples, chopped
1 tablespoon chutney, chopped
1 cup liquid from cooking shrimp

Melt butter; add onions and carrots and sauté until yellow. Stir in curry, flour, tomatoes, liquids and dissolved bouillon. Up to this point, recipe can be prepared early in afternoon. Shortly before serving, add chopped apple and chutney. Reheat; then add cooked shrimp and cook slowly about 5-7 minutes until heated thoroughly. Serve with rice (don't overcook), cooked in part chicken stock and part water.*

Delicious served with extra bowl of chutney, croissants or French bread, tossed salad and a good, dry sherry.

*Surround rice with canned, drained mandarin oranges and garnish with watercress.

Eleanor Evans

Halibut Shrimp Bake

2 pounds frozen,
  slightly thawed, halibut
1 can frozen cream of
  shrimp soup, thawed
¼ cup butter or
  margarine, melted

½ teaspoon grated onion
½ teaspoon Worcestershire
  sauce
¼ teaspoon garlic salt
1¼ cup crushed crackers

Place fish in greased baking dish, spoon soup over top. Bake at 375 degrees for 20 minutes. Combine remaining ingredients, sprinkle over fish. Bake 10 minutes longer.

Serves 6 to 8
Jule L. Nelson

Shrimp Creole-Caribbean

¼ cup oil
1 green pepper
2 onions
1 clove garlic
1 cup canned tomatoes
1½ teaspoons salt
¼ teaspoon black pepper

¼ teaspoon red pepper
Thyme
1 bay leaf
2 tablespoons lemon juice
1½ -pound package frozen shrimp
1 teaspoon cornstarch
½ cup dry, white wine

Mince and sauté in oil, the green pepper, onions, and garlic. Add the tomatoes, seasonings, lemon juice and shrimp, which has been cleaned and deveined. Simmer 8-10 minutes. Add cornstarch dissolved in wine. Cook 2 minutes longer. Serve with parsleyed rice.

Serves 4
Faith Stotko

Shrimp Galaxie

1 4-ounce can mushrooms,
  drained
1 tablespoon butter
1 10-ounce can frozen
  condensed shrimp soup
½ cup light cream

2/3 cup cooked seafood;
  you may use all shrimp, or
  mix shrimp, lobster and/or
  crab meat
¼ cup shredded Cheddar cheese
1/3 cup sauterne wine

Brown mushrooms in butter, add seafood and coat well. Add remaining ingredients, except wine. Add wine just before serving and mix well.

Serves 6
Rheuanna Kelly

160

Cheese Shrimp Casserole

8 slices of white bread
  (cut off crusts)
Butter
3 eggs
2 cups half and half
2 cups nippy Old English
  Cheddar cheese

Shrimp (use canned, large-size,
  but cooked fresh may
  be used.)
½ teaspoon salt
¼ teaspoon dry mustard
Worcestershire sauce, cayenne
  pepper, etc. as desired

Butter slices of bread generously and cube. Put in bottom of glass baking dish (12 x 8 x 2). Add layer of the cubed Cheddar cheese, layer of shrimp, placed close together (the more the better). Beat eggs thoroughly; add the half and half and seasonings. Pour liquid over all and set in refrigerator overnight and until time to bake. Set in pan of water and bake at 325 degrees over an hour. Be sure to allow plenty of time. When it is done, it will be bubbly, brown and crusty.

Helen S. Ackerly

Rolled Fish Fillets with Shrimp

4 tablespoons butter
1 clove garlic
1 onion, minced
10 cooked shrimp or ½ pound
  fresh salmon (8 diced
  fine, 2 cut in half)
½ green pepper, diced

¼ cup bread crumbs
1 tablespoon parsley and chives
  (or ½ to 1 tablespoon dried)
¼ teaspoon salt
1/8 teaspoon pepper
4 fillets (flounder or sole)

Melt 2 tablespoons butter and sauté garlic and onion. Add green pepper, 8 diced shrimp, crumbs, herbs and seasonings. Remove from flame. Place 2 tablespoons of mixture on boned side of fillet. Roll up fillet and enclose stuffing. Heat an oven dish with 2 tablespoons butter in 350 degree oven. When butter is melted, roll fillets in butter and place flap side down. Fasten with toothpicks. If there is additional filling, poke it into sides of rolls. Bake at 350 degrees for 25 minutes. Before serving, top with Hollandaise sauce. Garnish with ½ shrimp on each fillet.

Serves 4

Rose Pluss

161

Sole 'N Shrimp

¼ to ½ cup half and half
1 package frozen sole
1 can frozen shrimp soup
½ cup good white wine

1 can or ¼ pound very
  small shrimp (optional)
Salt and pepper to taste
Butter
Chopped parsley

Poach sole in small amount of half and half, about 10 minutes in slow oven. Pour off excess cream. Dot with butter and sprinkle with salt and pepper and chopped parsley.

Heat wine with soup and pour over fish (with shrimp if desired). Cook about 10 to 15 minutes in 325 degree oven.

Serve with potatoes covered with butter and chopped parsley.

Mrs. J. L. Sturgeon

Swedish Pickled Shrimp

2 to 2½ pounds fresh or
  frozen shrimp in shells
½ cup celery tops
¼ cup mixed pickling spices

1 tablespoon salt
2 cups sliced onions
7 or 8 bay leaves
1 recipe pickling marinade

Cover shrimp with boiling water; add celery tops, spices and salt. Cover and simmer for 5 minutes. Drain. Peel and devein under cold water. Alternate the cleaned shrimp, onion and bay leaves in shallow baking dish (9x9). Cover with marinade.

Pickling marinade:
1½ cups salad oil
3/4 cup white vinegar
3 tablespoons capers
  and juice (optional)

2½ teaspoons celery seed
1½ teaspoons salt
Several drops Tabasco

Mix well. Pour over shrimp; cover. Chill at least 24 hours. Spoon over shrimp occasionally.

Six appetizer-size servings

Gay McCabe

Scalloped Crab

1 pound crab meat or
   2 cans crab
½ cup dry sherry
¼ cup butter
2 tablespoons finely
   chopped onions
¼ cup flour
½ cup milk

1 cup light cream
1 tablespoon Worcestershire
   sauce
1 teaspoon salt—dash pepper
2 egg yolks, lightly beaten
1 can button mushrooms
Buttered bread crumbs

Preheat oven to 350 degrees. Lightly grease 6 or 8 scallop shells or a one-quart casserole. Drain crab meat; remove cartilage. Sprinkle crab with ¼ cup sherry. Toss to mix. In ¼ cup butter, sauté onion. Remove from heat. Stir in flour. Gradually stir in milk and cream. Bring to boil, stirring; reduce heat and simmer until quite thick, 8 to 10 minutes. Remove from heat, add Worcestershire, salt, pepper and rest of sherry. Stir a little sauce into egg yolks; return to rest of sauce, mix well. Stir in crabmeat mixture. Add drained mushrooms. Put in shells or casserole. Sprinkle with buttered crumbs. Bake about 20 to 25 minutes until brown, at 350 degrees. (A dry white wine may be used instead of sherry.)

Kay Abbot

Crab Stuffed Trout

12 medium trout — washed
   (preferably boned)
6 slices of bacon,
   diced and fried
1 small onion, chopped
1 can crab meat

1 cup bread crumbs
Parsley
Avocado wedges
Lemon wedges
Salt and pepper to taste

Pick over crab meat and toss with bread crumbs and onions. Put in trout. Put bacon on trout and wrap in foil.

Cook over slow heat on grill or in 350 degree oven for 25 to 30 minutes. Garnish with parsley, avocado and lemon wedges.

Serves 6 to 10

Muriel Anton

Quick and Easy Crabmeat

8 ounces whipped
 cream cheese
8 ounces crab meat,
 canned or frozen
½ teaspoon Worcestershire
 sauce

½ lemon, squeezed
Tabasco dash
Salt and pepper to taste
Paprika

Clean and crumble crab meat. Mix with remaining ingredients. You may want to add more lemon. Put in greased crab shells or greased casserole. Sprinkle paprika on top. Bake at 350 degrees for ½ hour. Casserole will take longer.

Serves 4   *Kay Abbot*

Crab Tuna Fondue Casserole

1 7-ounce can crab meat
1 4-ounce can tuna
5 cups cubed French bread
1 8-ounce package
 Muenster cheese, cubed
2 tablespoons chopped parsley
1 teaspoon grated onion

4 eggs
3 cups milk
3 tablespoons butter, melted
2 teaspoons dry or
 prepared mustard

Drain crab and tuna. Combine in a small bowl. Layer 1/3 each of bread, seafood, cheese and parsley into a buttered 1½ -quart casserole. Repeat to make two more layers. Beat eggs with milk, butter, mustard and onion. Pour over seafood mixture, cover; chill at least three hours or overnight. Bake, uncovered, at 350 degrees, 1 hour 15 minutes, until puffed and golden.

Delightful and so easy for ladies luncheon as it may be made the day before.

Serves 6   *Ruby Robbe*

164

Luncheon Dish

Slices of bread
Hard boiled eggs
Sliced peeled tomatoes
Old English cheese

Crab meat
Mayonnaise
Lemon juice
Salt and pepper to taste

Butter slices of bread. On this, put a hard boiled egg, sliced lengthwise. Salt and pepper. Next, put slices of peeled tomatoes. Salt and pepper. On this, put a thick slice of Old English cheese. Salt and pepper. Top with crab meat which has been mixed with mayonnaise and lemon juice. Be generous with the crab meat. Salt and pepper. Bake in medium oven (375 degrees) for 35 to 40 minutes or until cheese has melted and the whole thing is brown.

For "the ladies" for lunch. Can be done ahead and covered with wax paper until ready to serve.

Ruth Gast

Sour Cream Halibut

1 cup white wine
1 teaspoon salt
1 pound fish fillet (halibut)
1 cup mayonnaise

½ cup sour cream
¼ cup chopped onions
Bread crumbs
Paprika

Mix wine and salt, add fish and marinate 2 hours minimum (I prefer all day).

Drain fish on paper towel. Dip both sides in bread crumbs and place in greased baking dish.

Mix mayonnaise, sour cream and onions and spread over fish. Sprinkle bread crumbs thickly on top and sprinkle with paprika.

Bake at 500 degrees for 10 minutes or until fish flakes with a fork.

Sandy Stein

Fillet of Sole Casserole

2-3 pounds fillet of sole,
  fresh or frozen (thawed)
½ medium onion, chopped
2 tablespoons flour
½ stick butter or
  margarine (or less)
1½ cups milk
½ package Old English cheese,
  grated (about ¼ cup)

Salt and pepper
Worcestershire sauce
½ cup sauterne
1 can green grapes
Cheese and garlic croutons
Parsley and dill

Brown sole in butter and place in greased casserole. Brown onion in 2 tablespoons of the butter. Add flour and milk to make a cream sauce. Add cheese and stir until melted. Add a dash of Worcestershire, salt and pepper to taste, Sauterne, chopped parsley and ½ teaspoon dill weed and drained grapes. Pour over sole. Roll cheese and garlic, croutons in plastic bag. Sprinkle crumbs over casserole. Bake 40 minutes at 350 degrees.

Serves 4   *Kay Abbot*

Herbed Fish Bake

1 pound frozen fish fillets (or
  1 piece fish, fairly thick)
1/3 cup of onion flakes
1 small clove garlic, minced
  (or ½ teaspoon garlic powder)

¼ cup water
1 bouillon cube
½ teaspoon tarragon
¼ teaspoon thyme
¼ teaspoon salt
Dash of pepper

Thaw fish; place in baking dish. Cook onion flakes and garlic in bouillon and water until tender. Stir in other seasonings and cook 1 minute. Spread over fish. Bake at 470-475 degrees for 12 minutes or until fish flakes.

Good diet dish.

                                            Toni Feiler

Fabulous Flounder
(Snapper sole)

2 pounds flounder
2 cups frozen shrimp soup
Salt
Pepper
1½ tablespoons Worcestershire
   sauce

Tabasco sauce
1½ tablespoons cooking
   sherry or red wine
1 small onion, chopped

Thaw fish and place in shallow baking dish. Pour remaining mixed ingredients over fish. Bake at 350 degrees for 30 minutes. Serve hot over rice.

Serves 8

Mrs. Dirk McGuire

Steamed Curried Trout

3 large 2-pound trout (clean,
   keep whole and do not
   remove heads
2 fresh lemons

Curry powder (about
   3 to 5 tablespoons)
½ stick butter or margarine
Salt to taste

Coat each whole trout copiously with soft butter, inside and out. Sprinkle each trout *generously* with curry powder. Line inside cavity of each trout with whole thin slices of lemon. Wrap each trout securely with aluminum foil (heavy weight). Be sure to seam edges so steam and sauce will not escape. Place on center rack in oven preheated to 350 degrees for 40 minutes. Allow more time for exceptionally large trout. When done, remove fish from foil reserving sauce in separate bowl. Carefully bone trout. Place ½ trout (skin side down) on individual serving plate; arrange lemon slices attractively over fish. Distribute extra sauce evenly over trout; salt to individual taste.

Serves 6

Mrs. Aldo A. Battiste

Sautéed Trout with Mushrooms

4 cleaned trout
4 tablespoons butter
2 tablespoons vegetable oil
8 slices bacon, cut
   into ½ -inch pieces
1 small chopped onion

1 can mushrooms
1 tablespoon lemon juice
½ teaspoon salt
Pepper to taste
Flour (small amount)

Sprinkle trout inside and out with salt and pepper, roll in flour to coat lightly.

Heat 2 tablespoons butter and oil until hot. Add trout and cook 6 to 7 minutes on medium heat, then turn and cook other side.

Cook bacon in separate skillet until almost crisp. Drain off fat and add 2 tablespoons butter and onions and cook several minutes. Add mushrooms, lemon juice, salt and pepper. Cook long enough to heat mushrooms, stirring occasionally.

Place trout on platter and cover with sauce.

Serves 4
Laura Mattoon

Lobster and Wild Rice

1 and 3/4 cups wild rice
4 packages of small lobster
   tails (2 in a package)
2 cans cream of
   mushroom soup
2 4-ounce cans
   button mushrooms

1 pound grated sharp cheese
3 tablespoons
   Worcestershire sauce
3 teaspoons dry mustard
Salt and pepper to taste

Wash and cook wild rice according to directions on package and drain. Cut up lobster; set aside. In large saucepan put rest of ingredients. Add drained rice and lobster meat. Place in a large buttered casserole. Cook at 325 degrees for 1 hour, after sprinkling bread crumbs in a thin layer on top and dotting with butter.

Serves 12
Alysmai Ward

Lobster Tails Bar-B-Q (On outdoor grill)

6 to 8 lobster tails
¼ cup lemon juice
1 can frozen orange
   juice concentrate
½ teaspoon dry mustard
¼ teaspoon rosemary

½ teaspoon celery salt
½ teaspoon onion powder
½ teaspoon salt
¼ teaspoon bitters
½ cup butter

Heat all ingredients. Baste lobster tails with sauce and turn several times. Will take only 20 minutes or less (leave tails in shells). Use remaining sauce for dipping of lobster meat.

Jo Ann Bertholf

Lutfish
(Traditional Christmas Eve Fare in Sweden)

4 pounds lutfish (Start at Thanksgiving if you want it by Christmas)
Soak dry fish in water for 7-10 days.
Saw dry fish in pieces to fit container you are using to soak fish in.
Make lime solution:
   1 gallon slacked lime (from lumber yard)
   1 package sal soda
This is enough solution to soak 5 pounds dry fish which will yield four times this much prepared fish . . . 15 to 20 pounds.

Put lime in water and add soda. Pour solution over dry fish; add water to completely cover fish. Leave in solution until fish gets thick, 1½ to 3 inches. This will take approximately two weeks or longer. When it is ready, pour solution off. Wash fish to remove all lime solution. Put in clear fresh water, leaving until ready for use. Change fresh water every 24 hours.

Rinse fish 3 or 4 times in cold water. Remove fins and cut crosswise into 3 or 4-inch pieces. Tie in a white cloth to keep fish firm and place in a pan of boiling water for 20 minutes. The fish should be soft and flaky when done. If overcooked, it becomes gelatinous. Serve hot with creamed white potatoes.

Hilda Giordano

Restaurants

The ostentatious creations produced
during the Victorian heyday in the legendary
kitchens of famed restaurants and resorts were
at least partially possible because of the
equally legendary institutional ranges
from which they originated.

Cape Cod Clam Chowder

1 large onion (grated)
½ cup butter
½ cup chopped parsley

6 large potatoes
(diced—add water to cover)

Saute' onion in butter, add 1 small can cream of celery soup, cook until potatoes are done. Add 1 small can minced clams, let boil for about 30 minutes; add 1 cup of milk mixed with ½ cream. Heat until ready to serve.

Minnequa University Club

Cheese Soufflé

5 eggs (separated)
5 tablespoons flour
1½ cups boiling milk
2½ tablespoons butter

6 ounces shredded Cheddar
or American cheese
Salt

Melt butter in small pot, add flour, stir for a few minutes. Take off flame. Under steady stirring, add boiling milk. Let boil for 3-4 minutes; add cheese. Let boil for 4-5 minutes until cheese is completely melted. Slowly add 5 egg yolks. Take completely off flame; let cool off. Beat 5 egg whites stiff; gently mix under cheese mixture. Put in buttered dish (glass bowl, casserole etc.). Bake at 275 degrees for 50-60 minutes.

Pueblo Country Club

Roquefort Dressing

3/4 quart mayonnaise
1 cup roquefort cheese
(shredded)
1 teaspoon dry parsley
½ teaspoon mustard
(prepared)

1 teaspoon garlic salt
½ cup buttermilk
½ cup onions (shredded)
1 cup sour cream

Mix together. Can be thinned to the desired consistency with additional buttermilk or sour cream.

Minnequa University Club

Gonzales Tacos with Chicken

Cooking oil
Canned, frozen, or
 fresh tortillas
Shredded chicken (see below)
Shredded lettuce
Little chopped Bermuda onion
Shredded mild Cheddar cheese

2 large whole chicken breasts
1 cup chicken broth
1 teaspoon salt

Pour ½-inch oil into skillet. When oil is hot, add tortilla. It will go limp almost immediately. Fold it in half (using tongs) keeping the edges of the tortilla apart, until it becomes crisp. Turn and lightly cook the other side. Paper towels are good drainers. Repeat until you have all the taco shells you'll need. Figure 2-3 per person.

Place chicken in large skillet with broth and salt. Cover and simmer about 30 minutes. Let it get tender. Let cool to finger temperature, remove skin and bones, and shred the meat. Refrigerate until ready to use. Fill each taco shell with shredded chicken, lettuce, onion and Cheddar.

Serves 4

Bob Gonzales
Cork 'N Cleaver, Boulder

Ramirez Special Tacos

2 pounds beef
1 package corn tortillas
1 large can green
 chili salsa

2 cans tomato sauce
½ teaspoon onion powder
½ teaspoon oregano
½ teaspoon garlic powder

Boil beef until tender. Shred it and brown in small amount of shortening. Add tomato sauce and seasonings. Simmer about one hour. Fry tortillas in hot oil, then fold. Fill with meat. Individuals may add: shredded Cheddar cheese, diced tomatoes, chopped onion, and green chili salsa to taste.

Serves 4

Ramirez Restaurant
Patsy A. Ramirez

Filet of Beef en Croute Penrose

4 pounds prime
  filet of beef
2 pounds fresh Pennsylvania
  mushrooms, sliced
6 heads of shallots,
  chopped fine
½ pint Glacé de Viande
  (veal stock well reduced)

6 ounces Foie Gras
  de Strasbourg
¼ pint old sherry wine
¼ pound butter
2 cups white bread crumbs
Pastry dough
  (puff dough preferred)
Egg yolk

Sauté butter until it turns golden and add mushrooms, cooking for 5 minutes; add shallots and sauté for 2 minutes; add Glacé de Viande and reduce to half. Remove from stove, add sherry and bread crumbs; mix well and set aside to cool. Over a hot flame, melt a small amount of butter in a roasting pan and sear filet on all sides. Then place pan in oven for 8 minutes at 400 degrees; remove pan. Beginning and ending 2 inches from each end of filet, slit meat to form a pocket. Fill with cooled filling and Foie Gras. Wrap filet in puff pastry dough; decorate top with fancy cut pieces of leftover dough and make 2 small holes for steam. Brush with egg yolk and bake in 385 degree oven for 25 minutes. Serve with truffle sauce flavored with sherry.

Serves 6

Edmond C. Johnsen
Chef de Cuisine
The Penrose Room
The Broadmoor

Steak "17"

3 large Bermuda onions
¼ pound butter
¼ pound fresh mushrooms,
  thickly sliced
3-4 tablespoons cream sherry

Dash salt
2 pounds top sirloin steak
Splash cognac
  (about 3 ounces)

Peel and slice onions. Sauté them, covered, over low heat in ¼ pound butter. Add mushrooms. Just before you serve, add cognac, pour over charbroiled steak, sliced diagonally, and light for a few seconds (a minute at the most).

Serves 2

Cork & Cleaver

Special Pepper Steak

8-10 ounce filet steak
Crushed whole black pepper
Salt, pepper to taste

Mango chutney
Brandy

Melt a little butter in skillet, salt and pepper filet steak, put in skillet, basting steak with drippings and butter until done to desired way, turning only once. Put 1 tablespoon crushed whole black pepper on top, basting for a few minutes more. Add 2-3 tablespoons mango chutney, add a good shot of brandy. Take out steak, simmer down chutney and brandy to heavy syrup; pour over steak.

Pueblo Country Club

Lamb Shisk-Ka-Bob

1 7-pound double rack of lamb
Marinade
4 cloves garlic, crushed
1 tablespoon mint leaves
1 tablespoon parsley
2 tablespoons curry powder
1 teaspoon marjoram

1 tablespoon crushed pepper
2 bay leaves
1 pint lemon juice
1 quart olive oil

Remove the eye (center meat) from the double rack of lamb and trim off excess fat from the two pieces. (The remainder of the meat on the rack can be cut off and used another time.) Slice meat into 32 slices, 1 piece each. Cut the lean fat covering of the rack into 1-inch squares, the thickness of a bacon slice. Peel one medium eggplant, cut in ¼-inch slices, then in triangles. Quarter 4-5 medium onions and tomatoes. On a skewer, starting with ¼ tomato, alternate (using 6 pieces of meat per skewer) the lean fat, eggplant and onion, finishing with tomato. Put skewers in stainless steel pan (not aluminum), pour marinade over, and marinate in refrigerator for 48 hours. (Meat will keep in marinade for over 4 weeks as long as submerged.) Broil over charcoal, serve with rice Pilaff, buckwheat groats or Pilaff made of peeled wheat grains.

Makes 5

Edmond C. Johnsen
Chef de Cuisine
The Penrose Room
The Broadmoor

176

Cole Slaw

3/4 quart cabbage (white)
1/4 quart red cabbage
1/3 cup vinegar
1/3 cup oil

½ teaspoon salt
½ teaspoon sugar
Small amount shredded
carrots for color.

Mix vinegar, oil, salt, and sugar. Add to cabbage. Pepper as desired. Note: Slice cabbage very thin.

Minnequa University Club

Rata Fia of Colorado Raspberries

1 pound fresh raspberries
1 quart brandy

3/4 pound sugar
½ cup water

Place brandy and raspberries in glass jar, cover tightly, and set container in place exposed to sun for 40 days. Strain through paper filter and mix with simple syrup made of sugar and water. The remaining fruit pulp may be mixed with sugar and served as a topping for desserts.

Yield: 32 ounces of after-dinner cordial.

Edmond C. Johnsen
Chef de Cuisine
The Penrose Room
The Broadmoor

Beef Stroganoff

1 6-ounce filet
(cut in small strips)
1 tablespoon finely
chopped onion
1 tablespoon sliced
mushrooms

½ tablespoon finely
chopped dill pickle
4-5 tablespoons sour cream
Salt and pepper to taste

Heat skillet very hot with few drops of oil, put meat in stirring with a fork quite frequently. When brown on all sides, add onion, mushrooms, pickles, and salt and pepper. Cook and stir for a few minutes, then add sour cream, again cook and stir for 4-5 minutes, serve with buttered noodles or rice.

Pueblo Country Club

Vermont Christmas Goose
Colonel Schiffeler

1 oven-ready goose, 8-12 pound
1 pound chopped onion
2 pounds dry rolls, crumbled
   or 1 loaf dry white bread
6 eggs
1 quart sauterne wine

6 apples, peeled and sliced
1 tablespoon salt
1/8 teaspoon pepper
1/8 teaspoon thyme
1 cup goose fat

Soak the goose overnight in water with a little salt, drain. To prepare stuffing, sauté onions in goose fat; add apples. Remove from fire when apples are tender-crisp. Beat eggs into sauterne, add seasoning and pour over crumbled rolls. Let rolls absorb wine mixture, add cooked onions and apples. Stuff goose and sew up cavity. Roast at 375 degrees for 4½-5 hours, basting occasionally.

Delicious served with red cabbage.

Edmond C. Johnsen
Chef de Cuisine
The Penrose Room
The Broadmoor

Red Cabbage

5 pounds sliced red cabbage
3 apples, peeled and sliced
½ pound sliced onions
½ cup goose fat

1 pint red wine
1½ teaspoons salt
¼ teaspoon pepper
½ teaspoon caraway seeds

Place sliced cabbage in boiling water for 2 minutes; drain. Smother sliced apples and onions in goose fat, add drained cabbage, red wine and seasoning. Let this cook slowly for 2 hours, adding more liquid if necessary. Cook until cabbage is well done. (Reheated red cabbage has a better flavor, so may be prepared two or three days in advance and refrigerated until served).

Edmond C. Johnsen
Chef de Cuisine
The Penrose Room
The Broadmoor

178

vegetables

The ongoing responsibility for carefully planning and preserving the foods for the annual needs of the home was an important and serious task, given numerous benefits in efficiency and ease with the advancements made in the development of the stove.

Patio Potatoes

2½ pounds potatoes
3 cups medium cream sauce
2 cups shredded mild
  cheddar cheese

1 4-ounce can peeled green
  chilies, rinsed and diced
2 teaspoons salt
2 cloves garlic, pureed
Buttered crumbs

Cook potatoes, peel, slice (or cube) and put into a 1½ quart baking dish. Combine cream sauce, cheese, chilies, salt and garlic. Cook, stirring until cheese is melted; pour over potatoes. Sprinkle top with buttered crumbs and bake at 350 degrees until hot and brown.

This savory casserole is an especially satisfying accompaniment to charcoal-grilled meats.

Serves 6 to 8

Mary Wessel

Delmonico Potatoes

4 tablespoons butter
1½ tablespoons flour
1 cup milk
½ teaspoon salt
¼ teaspoon pepper

1 quart boiled potatoes
  peeled and sliced
3 hard boiled eggs,
  coarsely chopped
3/4 cup grated
  American cheese
Chopped pimiento (optional)

Melt 2 tablespoons of the butter and stir in flour. Gradually add milk, stirring over medium heat until thickened. Add salt and pepper. Pour half of the white sauce into greased 2 quart casserole. Add half of the potatoes, eggs and cheese. Sprinkle with pimiento, salt and pepper, and dot with one tablespoon butter. Repeat layers. Bake at 350 degrees for about 20 minutes.

Serves 6

Jule L. Nelson

Sweet Potato Pone

4 cups grated, raw
  sweet potatoes
2 tablespoons corn meal
1 teaspoon salt
1 teaspoon cinnamon
1 teaspoon ginger

1 teaspoon nutmeg
3 eggs
1 cup evaporated milk
1½ cups sugar
½ stick butter or margarine

Combine salt, spices and corn meal with eggs. Add milk, grated sweet potatoes and butter. Pour into buttered 10 inch square baking pan. Bake at 350 degrees for 45 minutes. Serve warm, not hot, with pork or other meat.

This is my mother's own recipe, which won a prize in a contest sponsored by a newspaper.

Serves 6   *Vera McDermid*

Polynesian Sweet Potatoes

½ lemon, sliced
½ orange, sliced
6 cups sliced sweet
    potatoes (cooked or canned)
1 cup crushed pineapple

½ cup brown sugar
½ cup melted butter
    or bacon drippings
½ teaspoon salt
½ cup shredded coconut

Arrange sliced lemon, orange and sweet potatoes alternately in shallow baking dish. Combine pineapple, sugar, butter and salt and pour over dish. Sprinkle coconut over top. Bake at 350 degrees for 30 minutes.

Rheuanna Kelly

Filled Potato Dumplings
(Kroppkakor)

1 egg and 2 yolks
3 cups mashed potatoes
1 1/8 cups flour
1 teaspoon sugar
1½ teaspoons salt

¼ teaspoon pepper
3 tablespoons minced
cooked ham
4 tablespoons minced
salt pork
1/8 teaspoon ground cloves
2-3 slices onion, minced

Beat egg and yolks and combine with potatoes. Add a little flour and beat until mixture holds its shape. Add remaining flour, sugar, salt and pepper. Turn onto lightly floured board and knead for a minute or two. Roll out to 3/8 inch thickness and cut with a round cookie cutter. Dice or mince the ham and salt pork, fry until tender and season with cloves. Remove from pan and sauté the onion; combine meat and onion. On half of the cut-out dough, place a teaspoon of the meat mixture, cover with remaining dough pieces and press edges together. Shape into round balls. Make a hole in each with a teaspoon, add a little meat mixture and close the openings. Drop the dumplings, one at a time, into rapidly boiling water. Cook 10 to 12 minutes, turning as they rise to the top. Serve with browned butter or butter mixed with parsley. (These may be fried in hot fat instead of water, or placed in a shallow buttered pan, basted with butter and baked).

Mrs. N. J. Brothers

Dill Potatoes

Potatoes
Butter
Dill weed

Salt and pepper
1 pint half and half
1½ pints whipping cream

Boil potatoes with their skins on. When cool, peel and slice. Place a layer of potatoes in baking dish, dot with butter and sprinkle with dill weed, salt and pepper. Repeat layers several times, then cover with half and half and whipping cream. Let stand in cream and refrigerate several hours before baking. Bake at 350 degrees until bubbly.

Ruth Gast

Sour Cream Scalloped Potatoes

3 or 4 slices
  bacon, chopped
½ cup chopped green
  onions, including tops
½ cup chopped green pepper
1 can cream of chicken soup

1 package frozen
  hash brown potatoes
1 cup sour cream
1 cup grated Cheddar cheese
Crushed corn flakes
Salt and pepper to taste

Fry bacon until crisp. Add potatoes and cook until tender but do not brown. (You may have to add butter depending on amount of fat from bacon). Add soup, onions, pepper, cheese and sour cream. Pour into greased casserole and sprinkle with crushed corn flakes. Bake at 350 degrees for 30 to 40 minutes.

Mrs. Eldon Brown

Potato Niochi

4 boiled, peeled potatoes
1 egg, if desired

Flour
Salt to taste

Add flour to mashed potatoes to make thick dough. Add egg if desired (this makes niochi stiffer) Salt to taste. Place ball of dough on floured board, cut off piece about size of egg and roll into long strips, the size of a thick rope. Cut into pieces ½ inch long. When all dough is prepared, pull each piece across rough grater with index finger. (If done properly this resembles a small shell). Drop into boiling, salted water and cook until they all rise to top. Drain and serve with tomato sauce or butter and cheese.

Mrs. Charles Battiste

Potatoes Italian Style

6 medium potatoes
2 bell peppers
2 large white onions
1/3 cup vegetable oil

½ cup vinegar
1 clove garlic
Salt and pepper to taste

Peel potatoes and slice as thin as possible. Core and seed peppers and slice in narrow rings. Slice onions and break into rings. Arrange potatoes, peppers and onions in a 9 by 11 inch baking pan. Add the oil, vinegar, garlic, salt and pepper. Toss as you would a salad and bake in 400 degree oven for one hour. Turn occasionally with a spatula.

Serves 6

Mrs. Aldo A. Battiste

Baked Asparagus

1 package frozen asparagus
Grated cheese to taste

Butter to taste
Salt and pepper to taste

Cook asparagus according to directions until tender. Drain and place in a baking dish, laying spears side by side so they touch. Salt and pepper to taste, sprinkle generously with grated cheese and dot with butter. Place under broiler until cheese is lightly browned.

Helen Berry

Oriental Asparagus

2 pounds fresh asparagus
3/4 cup chicken broth

1 tablespoon cornstarch
1 tablespoon soy sauce

Cut asparagus into ¼ to ½ inch thick pieces diagonally. Cook 2 to 3 minutes in small amount of water. Make a sauce by combining broth, cornstarch and soy sauce. Bring to a boil and add to asparagus; cover and cook 1 minute more. (Sauce may be prepared ahead of time). Asparagus should be crunchy.

Mrs. John Sturgeon

Baked Beans

2 cans baked beans
1 onion, chopped
Green pepper, chopped
½ cup catsup
Dash of Worcestershire sauce

1 cup brown sugar
2 tablespoons dry mustard
Salt and pepper to taste
Bacon

Place strips of bacon in bottom of loaf pan or casserole. Combine all other ingredients and pour over bacon. Top with additional bacon strips. Bake uncovered in a slow oven for 2 hours; do not stir. Let stand awhile before serving.

Serves 6 to 10   *Judy Krause*

Sweet-Sour Baked Beans

8 slices bacon,
  fried and crumbled
2 to 4 large onions,
  peeled and cut in rings
½ to 1 cup brown sugar
1 teaspoon dry mustard
½ teaspoon garlic powder
  (optional)
1 teaspoon salt

½ cup cider vinegar
2 15-ounce cans dried
  lima beans
1 1-pound can green
  lima beans
1 1-pound can red
  kidney beans
1 1-pound, 11-ounce
  can baked beans

Drain all beans except baked beans. Place onions in skillet; add sugar, mustard, garlic, salt and vinegar. Cover and cook for 20 minutes. In a 3-quart casserole, combine beans, onion mixture and crumbled bacon. Bake at 350 degrees for 1 hour.

Serves 12   *Carol Kilstofte*

186

Green Bean Pizza

1 can French green
  beans, drained
1 medium can mushrooms
  and stems, drained
1 can tomato paste
1 can water
½ green pepper, chopped

½ medium onion, chopped
4 strips bacon, diced
Pinch of oregano and
  sweet basil
Salt and pepper to taste
Parmesan cheese
Velveeta cheese

Brown onion, bacon and green pepper until soft. Add remaining ingredients except cheese and mix well. Place in greased casserole and sprinkle generously with Parmesan cheese; top with layer of Velveeta cheese. Bake at 350 degrees for 30 minutes.

Mrs. Thomas Broome

Green Bean Casserole

2 packages frozen
  French cut green beans
1 can soy beans,
  well drained*
1 cup grated Cheddar cheese

1 can water chestnuts, chopped
1 can cream of mushroom soup
1 package frozen French
  fried onion rings
Season to taste

Partly cook beans and drain well; mix with all other ingredients except onion rings. (Mixture will be dry). Arrange onion rings over top and bake at 350 degrees for about 45 minutes. May be prepared for baking a day ahead if desired.

*If soy beans are not available, omit them and water chestnuts and substitute 3/4 to 1 cup toasted, slivered almonds.

Rheuanna Kelly

Beans and Sour Cream

1½ pounds fresh green beans
¼ pound butter
2 tablespoons bread crumbs
Parsley

1 clove garlic, crushed
Black pepper
1 cup sour cream

Cook green beans and drain. Melt butter. When golden, add bread crumbs and brown. Mix parsley with garlic, season with pepper and mix with bread crumbs. Remove pan from heat. Combine parsley mixture with green beans and pour into casserole. Pour sour cream over top and bake for 15 minutes at 350 degrees, stirring once or twice.

Mrs. Arthur Hilvitz

Cavatelli Macaroni

5 cups flour,
    or more if needed
2 potatoes, peeled and
    boiled 5 to 7 minutes

4 eggs
Salt
1 tablespoon oil (optional)

Place eggs, potatoes, salt and oil in blender; blend for 3 to 5 minutes. Pour into well of flour in large mixing bowl. Mix and knead until dough is stiff. If too hard to knead, place in tightly covered bowl to rest, then knead more. Roll dough in rope-like strands. Macaroni may then be put through a Cavatelli machine or made this way: Cut rope macaroni into 1-inch pieces, place on fine part of grater one at a time and press through, pulling down with thumb. These are best if cooked soon after making.

Leah Rae Puleo

188

Pea Casserole

3 packages frozen peas
2 cans water chestnuts,
  drained and sliced
2 small cans bamboo
  shoots, drained

1 pound mushrooms or
  1 large can, sliced
Butter
2 cans cream of mushroom soup
2 cans French fried onion rings

Sauté mushrooms in butter Pre-cook peas briefly. Mix all ingredients except onion rings in a casserole and bake for 30 minutes at 350 degrees. Crumble onion rings over top and bake 5 to 10 minutes longer.

Note: Bean sprouts may replace bamboo shoots. May be prepared early in day and kept in refrigerator until 30 minutes before serving.

Serves 12   *Pat Siemsen*

Squash Casserole

2 pounds fresh or
3 packages frozen squash
1 green pepper, chopped
1 small can green chilies
1 chopped onion

2 beaten eggs
½ cup mayonnaise
½ cup grated cheddar cheese
Salt and pepper to taste
Parmesan cheese

Place squash, green pepper, chilies and onion in a saucepan with small amount of water. Cover and steam until tender. Drain well. Put into mixing bowl; add eggs, mayonnaise, grated cheese, salt and pepper. Mix well. Pour into buttered casserole and sprinkle top with Parmesan cheese. Bake at 325 degrees for 45 to 60 minutes.

Serves 6 to 10   *Ruth Lovelady*

Stuffed Artichokes

3 artichokes
2 cups bread crumbs
¼ cup grated Romano cheese
1 egg

1 clove garlic, mashed
Salt and pepper to taste
Olive oil

Wash artichokes; cut off stems and tips of leaves. Mix stuffing ingredients with enough olive oil to make a paste. Separate leaves and place a teaspoon of the stuffing between each, pushing down to tender part of leaf. Steam in a large kettle for 1 hour.

Mrs. Charles Battiste

Artichoke and Spinach Casserole

1 can artichoke bottoms
3 packages frozen,
  chopped spinach
1 cup sour cream
1 package dehydrated
  onion soup

1 "squirt" lemon juice
Parmesan cheese
Hard boiled egg, grated
Pimiento

Line bottom of 6 by 11 inch casserole with artichokes. Cook spinach, then press *all* water out. Combine sour cream, onion soup and lemon juice with spinach and spread over artichokes. Sprinkle with Parmesan cheese and bake at 350 degrees for 30 minutes. Garnish with grated hard boiled egg and pimiento, if desired.

Serves 6

Tory Thatcher

Spinach Casserole

2 cartons small curd
  cottage cheese
6 eggs
6 tablespoons flour
½ pound Velveeta cheese

1 package frozen,
  chopped spinach, thawed
¼ pound butter
Salt and pepper to taste

Cut the cheese and butter into chunks. Combine all ingredients in greased casserole and bake at 350 degrees for 1 hour or less.

Serves 8

Pat Siemsen

190

Cheese-Baked Spinach and Tomatoes

4 slices bacon
1 pound fresh spinach
3 medium tomatoes,
   peeled and sliced

¼ pound sliced Swiss cheese
Salt and pepper

Cut bacon into two inch pieces, cook until crisp, drain. Wash spinach, shake off moisture and remove stems. Arrange spinach in bottom of greased, shallow casserole, about 1½ quart size. Salt and pepper. Place tomato slices in a single layer over spinach and cover with cheese slices. Top with bacon. Bake uncovered for 20 minutes at 350 degrees, or until cheese is melted and spinach is tender.

4 small servings

Mrs. John Love

Swiss Spinach

3/4 cup sliced mushrooms
1 tablespoon plus
   1 teaspoon margarine
7/8 cup cream of celery soup
2 tablespoons plus
   2 teaspoons grated
Swiss cheese

2 tablespoons plus
   2 teaspoons light cream
4 1/3 cups drained spinach
Paprika

Sauté mushrooms in margarine until tender. Stir in soup, cheese and cream. Heat, stirring until cheese melts. Place spinach in baking dish, pour sauce over and sprinkle with paprika. Bake at 375 degrees for 30 minutes, or until hot.

Helen Pachak

Crumby Spinach

2 packages frozen
   chopped spinach
2 tins cream cheese, whipped
Garlic powder to taste
Salt and pepper to taste

½ package prepared dry
   dressing (poultry)
·3 tablespoons
   butter or margarine

Cook spinach according to package directions and drain well. Mix with cream cheese, add garlic powder, and salt and pepper to taste. Put in a flat buttered casserole. Spread dry dressing over top. Pour melted butter over dressing and put under the broiler until brown and bubbly. Watch carefully. If you wish to make this ahead, heat spinach and cheese in oven about 10 minutes, then add dressing and broil.

Serve immediately as it cools quickly.

Serves 4 *Kay Abbot*

Sweet-Sour Zucchini Squash and Tomatoes

2 tablespoons oil
4 tablespoons cornstarch
1 tablespoon sugar
1 tablespoon onion flakes
2 tablespoons dry mustard
3/4 teaspoon salt
½ teaspoon garlic salt

½ cup water
¼ cup vinegar
4 cups zucchini, cut
   in ½ inch diagonal strips
1 cup celery, cut
   in diagonal strips
2 tomatoes, quartered

Make a paste of oil and cornstarch; add seasonings, sugar, water and vinegar. Cook until slightly thick; add more water if necessary. Add squash, celery and tomatoes and simmer until tender. May be made ahead of time and placed in casserole for reheating in low oven.

Serves 6 *Jean Train*

Italian Zucchini

Zucchini, washed and diced
3-4 cloves garlic, minced
2 large onions,
    chopped fine
6 stalks celery, diced
1 green pepper, diced

1 #2 can tomatoes or
    4 fresh tomatoes
1 can tomato sauce
    with cheese
½ cup catsup
6 tablespoons butter
Salt and pepper to taste

Sauté garlic, onions and celery in 2 tablespoons butter. Add remaining ingredients, and simmer for 30 to 60 minutes, adding remaining 4 tablespoons butter just before serving.

8 generous servings

Bev Hurley

Spaghetti Sauce with Egg Plant

2 12-ounce cans tomato paste
5 cans water (12 ounce)
2 tablespoons oregano
1 tablespoon sweet basil

½ cup sugar
1 teaspoon salt
1 large clove garlic
1 quart tomato puree
    (use 2 #2 cans tomatoes,
    put through ricer)

Combine first seven ingredients and cook slowly for 3 to 4 hours. Add tomato puree and cook 1 to 2 hours longer. If meat is desired, add it when sauce has reached desired consistency.

2 egg plants
Garlic
¼ pound goat cheese or Romano cheese

Peel egg plants, leaving peeling strips on until finished. Cut four slits in eggplants, placing small piece of garlic in one, and small piece of cheese in the other. Salt heavily and place in collander to drain for 4-6 hours. Add cheese and garlic and fry until brown. Add to sauce ½ hour before serving.

Leah Rae Puleo

Baked Celery

2 bunches celery, sliced
½ cup sliced almonds
½ cup grated, sharp
   Cheddar cheese

½ to 1 teaspoon salt
1/8 teaspoon pepper
½ teaspoon paprika
1 can cream of celery soup

Place celery in casserole (1-3/4 quart baking dish). Sprinkle almonds over top, then cheese. Combine seasonings with soup and mix until smooth. Spoon mixture over celery and bake at 375 degrees for 45 minutes.

Mary Beth Jensen

Sweet Beets

1 tablespoon cornstarch
½ teaspoon salt
1 tablespoon beet juice
2 tablespoons vinegar

¼ cup honey
2 tablespoons butter
2 cups diced beets,
   cooked or canned

Mix the cornstarch and salt; blend in beet juice. Add vinegar, honey and butter. Cook slowly over medium heat, stirring constantly until thick. Pour over drained beets and allow to stand at least 10 minutes to absorb flavor. Reheat and serve.

Serves 4   *Beth Thatcher*

Broccoli Casserole

¼ cup chopped onion
6 tablespoons butter
   or margarine
2 teaspoons flour
½ cup water

1 8-ounce jar Cheese Whiz
2 packages chopped broccoli,
   thawed and drained well
3 eggs, well beaten
Cracker crumbs

Sauté onion in 4 tablespoons butter. Add flour and water; when thick add cheese. Combine sauce with broccoli and add well beaten eggs. Pour into greased casserole and top with buttered crumbs, using the remaining 2 tablespoons butter. Bake at 350 degrees for 45 to 50 minutes.

Serves 8   *Jean Adams*

Broccoli with Rice

2 tablespoons salad oil
½ cup chopped onions
½ cup chopped celery
1 package frozen, chopped
  broccoli
1 can cream of chicken soup

3/4 cup milk
1 cup water
1 8-ounce jar Cheese Whiz
1 cup Instant rice

Sauté onions and celery lightly in salad oil at low heat. Add frozen broccoli, cover and steam for 10 minutes. Add remaining ingredients, cover and bring to a boil. Pour into well-buttered baking dish and bake, uncovered, for 40 minutes at 350 degrees.

Mary Beth Jensen

Broccoli with Shrimp Sauce

1 package frozen
  broccoli spears
1 can frozen shrimp soup
1 small package
  cream cheese

2 tablespoons milk
1 tablespoon chives (or
  tops of green onions, diced)
2 tablespoons slivered almonds

Cook broccoli in salted water until just tender. Blend cream cheese and milk in heavy saucepan; add the soup. Cook until thoroughly blended. Drain broccoli and place in shallow serving bowl. Pour sauce over and sprinkle chives and almonds over top.

To make a luncheon dish, add shrimp to sauce and serve on buttered toast.

Serves 4

Betty Bullen

California Corn Casserole

2 cans cream style corn
1 large onion, sliced
1 clove garlic, crushed
2 tablespoons salad oil
½ green pepper, sliced thin
1 pound mushrooms, sliced
½ pound grated sharp cheese

1 teaspoon salt
1 cup minced parsley
½ cup dry bread crumbs
1 teaspoon grated cumin
½ teaspoon oregano
Pinch coarse pepper

Sauté onion, green pepper and mushrooms in oil; cook slowly for 5 minutes. Grease 1½ quart casserole, layer corn, then onion mixture. Cover with one-half of the cheese, and remaining ingredients mixed together (half). Repeat layers. Bake covered at 300 degrees for 45 minutes. Uncover and bake 25 minutes more. May be browned under broiler before serving.

Serves 4 to 6   *Catherine Petersen*

Scalloped Corn with Oysters

1 #2 can whole kernel
  or cream style corn
1/2 to 3/4 cup milk
1 cup cracker crumbs
½ small onion, chopped

Salt and pepper to taste
2 tablespoons butter
1 small can oysters or fresh
  oysters if available

Combine whole kernel corn and 3/4 cup milk or cream style corn and ½ cup milk. Add all other ingredients except butter; chop oysters into small pieces and add small amount of liquid. Place in casserole and dot top with butter. Bake at 350 degrees for 30 minutes.

Jule Nelson

196

Stuffed White Turnips

12 medium-sized turnips
1 tablespoon salt
1½ tablespoons butter
1 tablespoon bread crumbs

Stuffing:
1 tablespoon butter
¼ cup bread crumbs
¼ cup chopped almonds

Wash and scrape or pare turnips; cook in boiling water until soft. Let cool. Remove a small portion from center and fill the cavity with the stuffing. Place in a casserole. Brown 1½ tablespoons butter in frying pan and pour over turnips. Sprinkle crumbs over top. Bake at 350 degrees for 20 minutes or until golden brown, basting occasionally with butter.

Mrs. N. J. Brothers

Polish Cabbage

1 pound ground beef
1 pound pork sausage
1 large onion, chopped
1 medium head cabbage,
  chopped coarsely
1 teaspoon salt

½ teaspoon pepper
1 6-ounce package
  egg noodles, cooked
1 pint sour cream
½ teaspoon garlic salt

Steam chopped cabbage about 3 minutes in boiling, salted water; drain. Brown meats and onion and place in 9 by 13 inch cake pan. Add cabbage and seasonings. Combine cooked noodles, sour cream and garlic salt; pour over top of meat and cabbage. Bake for 45 minutes at 350 degrees.

Serves 8 to 10

Dagmar Borkowitz

Barley Bake

½ cup butter
1 medium onion, chopped
3/4 cup barley

1 quart chicken broth
  (4-5 bouillon cubes
  per quart water)
2 cups fresh or
  1 cup canned mushrooms

Melt butter; add chopped onion and barley. Cook, stirring until barley is golden and onion translucent. Stir in broth. Bake at 375 degrees to 400 degrees, stirring occasionally until barley is tender and moisture is absorbed. Add mushrooms in the last half hour of baking.

Serves 6 *Mary Lou Hall*

Baked Mushrooms

2 pounds fresh mushrooms
3 sticks butter (1½ cups)
2 teaspoons finely
  chopped onion
1 clove garlic, minced
3/4 teaspoon Worcestershire
  sauce

½ teaspoon each of salt
  and pepper
½ teaspoon dried rosemary
  (or ¼ teaspoon fresh)

Stem mushrooms and place caps in baking dish. Melt butter in a small saucepan. Stir in onion, garlic and all seasonings. Pour over mushrooms and bake, uncovered, at 325 degrees for 40 minutes or until butter is absorbed. Serve with fondue forks as an appetizer or to accompany meat.

Serves 8 *Annette Knudsen*

Carrot Mold

2 cups grated carrots
2 tablespoons water
2 eggs, separated
1 cup brown sugar
1 cup flour

1 teaspoon lemon juice
Pinch of salt
½ teaspoon baking powder
¼ teaspoon baking soda
3/4 cup melted butter

Separate eggs and set whites aside. Combine egg yolks and all other ingredients as you would a cake. (The carrots may be grated in a blender if desired). Fold in stiffly beaten egg whites last. Grease the bottom only of an angel food pan or any fairly deep, round pan. Pour in batter and bake at 350 degrees for 1 hour.

This resembles a cake but is served as a vegetable.

Mrs. Arthur Hilvitz

Oven Medley

2 cups tiny cooked
  carrots, drained
1 package frozen peas,
  thawed
1 pound can green
  beans, drained
1 8-ounce can water chestnuts, drained and sliced
1 green pepper, diced

1 can cream of mushroom
  soup
1 teaspoon Worcestershire
  sauce
Dash of Tabasco sauce
2 cups grated cheddar cheese
1 heaping tablespoon
  brown sugar

Combine in a 2-quart, greased casserole the carrots, peas, beans, water chestnuts and green pepper. Combine mushroom soup, Worcestershire sauce, Tabasco sauce and grated cheese. Pour over vegetables and sprinkle top with brown sugar. Bake uncovered at 350 degrees for 30 minutes. This recipe keeps well if dinner is late.

Nancy Bonforte

Egg Plant Creole

1 medium size egg plant,
   cut into small pieces
3 tablespoons butter
3 tablespoons flour
1 can tomatoes
1 green pepper, chopped fine

1 onion, chopped
1 teaspoon salt
1 tablespoon brown sugar
½ bay leaf
2 cloves
Buttered bread crumbs

Place egg plant into boiling, salted water; resume boil, cook 10 minutes and drain. Place in buttered baking dish. Melt butter in a saucepan; add flour, tomatoes, green pepper, onions, salt, brown sugar, bay leaf and cloves. Cook until tender. Pour over egg plant and top with buttered bread crumbs. Bake at 350 degrees for 30 to 40 minutes until tender.

Rheuanna Kelly

Italian Style Eggplant Casserole

1 medium eggplant
4 tablespoons flour
Salt and pepper to taste
2 cups canned tomatoes
   (stewed may be used)

1½ cup grated scamorze
   or mozzarella cheese
½ teaspoon garlic salt

Slice eggplant ¼ inch thick, then pare. Dip into mixture of flour, salt and pepper. Fry slices in hot salad oil or olive oil until crisp and brown. Place several layers of eggplant in lightly greased casserole. Top with 1 cup tomato sauce and ½ cup cheese. Place remaining eggplant, then remaining tomato and cheese. Sprinkle lightly with garlic salt. Cover and bake at 350 degrees for 40 minutes.

Mrs. Don Vickery

Braised Vegetables

1 large firm head cabbage
1 medium onion
1 tablespoon margarine
1 tablespoon oil
Pepper to taste

½ stalk celery
2 green peppers
4 medium carrots
3/4 teaspoon salt

Shred all vegetables very fine. Heat margarine and oil in heavy skillet with a tight lid. Add vegetables and cook about 5 minutes over hot fire, tossing occasionally. Add salt and pepper and serve at once.

Helen K. Pachak

Vegkebabs

1 cup oil
½ cup lemon juice
1 teaspoon Worcestershire
   sauce
½ teaspoon salt
¼ teaspoon pepper

¼ teaspoon dried basil
2 6-inch zucchinis, cubed
3 tomatoes, quartered
2 green peppers,
   cut into eighths
12 mushrooms, halved

Combine oil, lemon juice, Worcestershire sauce, pepper, salt and basil. Allow marinade to stand at room temperature for 1 hour. Marinate vegetables in mixture for several hours in refrigerator. Thread marinated vegetables alternately on skewers. Broil over hot coals for about 10 minutes, brushing occasionally with marinade to prevent drying. Turn to cook on all sides.

Great for outdoor cookouts served with steak!

Serves 12

Bettie Jean Cozzi

Vegetables Oriental

2 tablespoons oil
2 carrots, sliced diagonally
2 stalks celery,
  sliced diagonally
½ green pepper, cut
  into 1-inch pieces

1 medium onion, sliced
2 tablespoons soy sauce
2 tablespoons catsup
2 tablespoons water

Heat oil. Add carrots, celery, green pepper, and onion slices separated into rings. Cook over medium heat only until onion is half-cooked (about 3 minutes). Add soy sauce, catsup and water. Cover and cook over low heat about 10 minutes. Vegetables should remain slightly crisp.

Serves 4   *Bettie Jean Cozzi*

Ratatouille

2 cloves garlic
1 sliced onion
½ cup olive oil
1 large diced eggplant,
  unpeeled
3 sliced zucchini squash

1 sliced green pepper
1 28-ounce can Italian tomatoes
1 teaspoon fresh basil
  or dried oregano
Salt and pepper

Sauté garlic and onion in olive oil; add diced eggplant and mix. Add zucchini and green pepper and cook for 10 minutes. Add remaining ingredients and cook, covered, for 30 minutes. Uncover and simmer 30 minutes longer.

Mrs. Henry Williams

Rice and pasta

Large and cumbersome
by the standards of the eighties, perhaps,
but the large, improved cooking stove
was a blessing to families of all sizes and
cultures, making the enjoyment of traditional
feasts the greater for the cook and partaker.

Lasagne

1 pound ground chuck
1 pound Italian sausage
1 tablespoon oil
1 tablespoon parsley flakes
1 tablespoon oregano
1 teaspoon salt
1 number 2 can tomatoes
1 6-ounce can tomato paste
1 clove garlic, minced

1 10-ounce package
  lasagne noodles
2 12-ounce cartons
  large curd cream
  style cottage cheese
2 beaten eggs
1 teaspoon salt
½ teaspoon pepper
2 tablespoons parsley flakes
½ cup grated Parmesan cheese
1 pound mozzarella cheese,
  sliced thin

Brown meat in hot oil. Add 1 tablespoon parsley, salt, tomatoes and paste and garlic. Simmer uncovered until thick, about 1 hour, stirring occasionally. Cook noodles in boiling salted water until tender. Drain, rinse in cold water. Meanwhile, combine cottage cheese with eggs, 1 teaspoon salt, pepper, remaining parsley and Parmesan cheese. Place half the noodles in 13 x 9 x 2 inch dish or baking pan; spread half the cottage cheese mixture over. Add half the mozzarella cheese and half the meat mixture. Repeat layers. Bake at 375 degrees for 30 minutes. Let cool for 10 minutes for easier serving.

Makes 12 conservative servings   *Mrs. Allen Griffith*

Noodle Kugel

12-ounce package noodles
3 eggs
Small carton sour cream
1½ pints milk
½ teaspoon cinnamon

½ cup sugar
1 teaspoon salt
Handful seedless raisins
Crushed corn flakes
Butter

Mix eggs, sour cream, milk and spices and set aside. Boil noodles until tender in salted water. Add raisins and let stand for 5 minutes to soften. Drain in collander, blanching lightly, and add to first mixture. Pour into buttered baking dish 13 x 9 x 2 inches. Sprinkle top with crushed corn flakes and dot with lots of butter. Bake at 350 degrees for 1½ hours.

Mrs. Arthur Hilvitz

Noodle Casserole

1 package thin noodles (large)
1 can mushroom soup
1 can celery soup
1 4-ounce can mushrooms,
  stems and pieces
2 2-ounce packs of
  grated American cheese

1 cup milk
6 stalks celery, cut up
1 teaspoon minced onion
Onion salt
1 tablespoon Worcestershire
  sauce
Bread crumbs

Cook noodles in salted water, according to directions on package. Drain thoroughly in collander. Place noodles in buttered baking dish; add other ingredients and mix thoroughly. Top with bread crumbs. Bake 1 hour at 300 degrees.

May be prepared the day before and baked one hour before serving.

Serves 20   *Alysmai P. Ward*

Wild Rice Casserole

1 cup wild rice
1 cup brown rice
1 pound mild bulk sausage
1 8-ounce can mushrooms
2 onions, chopped
¼ cup flour
½ cup cream
2½ cups chicken broth (may
  use chicken bouillon cubes)

1 teaspoon monosodium
  glutamate
Pinch oregano
Pinch thyme
Pinch marjoram
1½ teaspoons salt
1/8 teaspoon pepper
½ cup toasted
  slivered almonds

Sauté the sausage; drain and break the meat into small pieces. Sauté the onions in the sausage drippings until soft. Add the mushrooms and the cooked sausage. Wash the rice and cook in boiling water (salted) until done. Drain. Mix the flour with cream until smooth. Add the chicken broth and cook until thickened. Season with MSG, oregano, thyme, marjoram, salt and pepper. Combine with rice, sausage, onions and mushrooms. Toss together lightly. Pour into casserole and bake for 30 minutes at 350 degrees.

Sprinkle with almonds just before serving.

Serves 10 to 12   *Mrs. Joseph A. Bullen, Jr.*

Wild Rice with Mushrooms and Almonds Casserole

¼ pound butter
1 cup wild rice
½ cup slivered almonds
2 tablespoons chives,
   onions or green pepper

½ pound sliced mushrooms
3 cups chicken broth (canned)

Melt butter in skillet. Add all ingredients except broth, stirring constantly until yellow. Add broth. Pour into casserole and cover tightly. Bake at 325 degrees for about one hour.

Serves 6   *Mrs. Don Vickery*

Rice Casserole

1 stick butter
1 large onion
1 3/4 cups raw rice
1 can mushrooms

2 cans consommé
½ pound grated cheese
1 cup roasted slivered almonds

Sauté chopped onion in butter and add to other ingredients in large casserole. Cover tightly.

Bake at 325 degrees about 1½ hours. Stir frequently.

This is good served with ham.

Serves 8   *Jonnie Miller*

Sour Cream Pilaf

3 cups chicken stock
1 tablespoon lemon juice
1½ teaspoons salt
¼ teaspoon pepper
½ bay leaf

½ cup butter
1½ cups uncooked rice
½ cup mushroom slices (canned)
½ pint sour cream
2 tablespoons chopped parsley

Put chicken stock, lemon juice, salt, pepper, bay leaf and ¼ cup butter in pan. Heat until stock starts to simmer. Add rice; cover and cook slowly for 35 minutes, or until rice is tender and liquid is absorbed. Remove bay leaf and stir in remaining butter, drained mushrooms and sour cream. Heat through. Sprinkle with parsley before serving.

Diane Larkin

Gnocchi
(Grit Casserole)

1 quart milk
½ cup margarine or butter
1 cup hominy grits
1 cup grated Swiss cheese

1 teaspoon salt
Additional 1/3 cup melted butter
Grated Parmesan cheese

Melt butter or margarine in milk. Add grits and cook until thick like cream of wheat. Remove from heat and add salt. Beat for 5 minutes, adding Swiss cheese near end of beating. Pour into greased 2-quart casserole. Pour melted butter over top. Sprinkle with Parmesan cheese.

Bake at 350 degrees for 45 minutes or an hour, depending on type of casserole, or until nicely browned.

Serves 6 to 8 *Gretchen Backlund*

Italian Spaghetti and Meat Balls

Sauce:
2 large cans tomatoes
1 can tomato paste
1 link pepperoni or
  Italian sausage
4 chicken wings
1 onion, chopped fine
1 green mango, chopped fine
  (remove seeds)
6 cloves (remove before serving)
1 sprig oregano
  or 1 teaspoon oregano
2 cloves garlic, minced
2 bay leaves
  (remove before serving)
1 tablespoon sugar
½ teaspoon sweet basil
¼ teaspoon pepper
Salt to taste

Meat balls:
1 pound ground beef
½ pound ground veal
½ pound ground pork
1 cup finely rolled cracker
  or bread crumbs
2 eggs well beaten
½ cup tomato juice
¼ teaspoon allspice
¼ teaspoon sweet basil
½ teaspoon salt or to taste
½ teaspoon black pepper
½ onion, chopped fine
2 cloves garlic, minced

208

Sauce: Boil very slowly for 3 hours with meat balls. Remove chicken wings before serving; they are used only for flavoring. Cut sausage in small slices.

Meat balls: Mix ingredients together and brown in skillet, using olive oil. Put into sauce and cook slowly for 3 hours.

Cook 2 pounds of spaghetti as directed on package. Place on plate; top with sauce, meat balls and grated Parmesan cheese.

Mrs. Harold Townsend Low

Meat Balls and Spaghetti Sauce

Meat balls:
1½ pounds ground round steak
1 pound ground lean pork
4 slices dry bread,
  crumbled fine
2 good-sized garlic
  cloves, minced
2½ teaspoons salt
¼ teaspoon pepper
1/3 cup grated cheese,
  (Parmesan, Romano)
Few leaves parsley
  (minced finely)
4 eggs

Spaghetti Sauce:
2 large cans (12-ounce)
  tomato paste
2 15-ounce cans tomato sauce
2 cans water
1 large onion, minced
1 bunch parsley (tied together)
2 bay leaves
2 pinches basil
1 teaspoon Worcestershire
  sauce
1 teaspoon sugar
Salt and pepper to taste
Olive oil to cover
  bottom of pan

Meat balls: Mix together with hands; add eggs and mix well. Shape into small balls and brown slowly in olive oil.

Sauce: Slowly cook onion in olive oil; add tomato paste, sauce and water. Add parsley, bay leaves, basil, Worcestershire, sugar, salt and pepper. Mix well and simmer 2 hours. If sauce is too thick, add water. Add meat balls and cook 20 minutes. Serve over cooked spaghetti.

Makes 24 meat balls

Mrs. W. T. Dardis, Sr.

Homemade Manicotti

Marcaroni:

1 and 3/4 cups flour	5 eggs
1 cup water	½ teaspoon salt

Put the eggs in blender and mix for 1 minute; add flour and water alternately until all is mixed, then add salt. Batter resembles thin pancake batter. Place lightly greased small skillet on stove at medium temperature. Put 2 tablespoons of batter in skillet at a time; spread thin in a round circle. Cook about 10 to 15 seconds, and then turn over and cook 2 to 5 seconds. These are not to be browned. Place them on a platter until all are made. Grease skillet after cooking each two or three noodles.

Meat filling:

1½ pounds hamburger	2 tablespoons parsley
1 small clove garlic	Salt
2 eggs	1 tablespoon of grated
½ cup bread crumbs	Romano or goat cheese

Steam and brown hamburger for 20 minutes. Cool; add the rest of the ingredients and mix thoroughly. Spread about 1 heaping tablespoon on each of the fried macaroni. Roll up and place them in a 9 x 13 inch pan that has a small amount of tomato sauce in the bottom of it. When dish is full, pour about 1 cup of the tomato sauce on macaroni. Bake covered for 30 minutes at 350 degrees. This dish may be frozen before cooking; if so, thaw and bake 30 to 45 minutes at 350 degrees uncovered.

Cheese filling:

1 pound ricotta	1 tablespoon grated
2 eggs	goat cheese or Romano
1 tablespoon parsley	1 clove garlic, chopped fine

Mix all ingredients together and spread about 1 heaping tablespoon on macaroni. Roll up. Place in dish with sauce on the bottom; then put 1 cup of the sauce on the macaroni. Bake as you do for the meat-filled macaroni. May be treated just as the meat-filled macaroni.

Barbara Comianni

breads

Assembly line manufacturing made it possible for more modern ranges to appear in even the humblest of kitchens so that the daily task of baking "the staff of life" could be considered less of a chore than a pleasurable interlude.

Refrigerator Raisin Bran Muffins

3 cups sugar
1 cup shortening
4 cups buttermilk
4 eggs
5 cups sifted flour
5 teaspoons soda

1 teaspoon salt
2 cups Nabisco 100% Bran
2 cups boiling water
4 cups Kelloggs All-Bran
2 cups raisins

Cream and mix first four ingredients. Sift together and add dry ingredients; then add next three ingredients which have been soaked, then raisins.

Mix and store in refrigerator at least overnight. Will keep 3-4 weeks if covered tightly. Bake in well-greased muffin pans at 400 degrees for 15 minutes.

Yield 6 dozen   *Mrs. Harry Amick*

English Muffins

1 package dry yeast
¼ cup warm water
2 tablespoons sugar
1½ teaspoons salt

3 tablespoons cooking oil
1¼ cups scalded buttermilk
3-3 3/4 cups sifted flour
¼ cups cornmeal

Soften yeast in water. Put sugar, salt and oil in large mixing bowl. Stir in milk until sugar dissolves and cook to lukewarm. Blend in two cups of the flour and beat with electric mixer until smooth. Add yeast and beat at medium speed for 5 minutes. Stir in enough more flour to make moderately stiff dough. (It will take nearly all of the flour called for.) Roll dough out into 12-inch square on lightly floured surface. Fold square in half, then in half again. Roll folded dough into 12-inch square again and repeat process 5 times. Cover and let rest 10 minutes. Carefully lift the dough and sprinkle cornmeal over rolling surface. Place dough on cornmeal and roll to about 3/8-inch thickness. Cut circles with three inch cutter. Cover and let rise in warm place until double, about 1¼ hours. Heat buttered griddle or skillet and brown muffins slowly on both sides, watching carefully to prevent burning.

Yield: 12-16   *Susan S. K. Daniels*
Publicity and Advertising
The Broadmoor

213

Basic Bread Dough

2 packages dry yeast
1 3/4 cups warm water
½ cup sugar
2 teaspoons salt

1 egg
¼ cup shortening
   or salad oil
5-5½ cups Flour

Dissolve yeast in warm water and put in large bowl. With fork, stir in sugar, salt, egg and shortening. Add flour and knead until dough is no longer sticky. (Dough will be lumpy if shortening is used, but will become smooth while rising.) Put dough in greased bowl and cover with cloth. Let rise 45 minutes; punch down and let rise again. Roll out and let rise in pans. Bake at 400 degrees for 10 minutes (for rolls).

This makes hot rolls, bread, sweet rolls or pizza dough. For pizza dough, however, use only ¼ cup sugar.

Crescent rolls may be filled with Cheddar cheese.

Mae Vinci

Swedish Refrigerator Rolls

1 cup hot milk
2/3 cup sugar
2 packages yeast
1 cup lukewarm water

3 well-beaten eggs
3/4 cup soft margarine
2 teaspoons salt
7½ cups flour

Pour milk over margarine, sugar and salt in large mixing bowl and cool until lukewarm. Dissolve yeast in lukewarm water, add to mixture in bowl. Add eggs and 4 cups flour. Beat mixture with large spoon or electric mixer. Stir in remaining 3½ cups flour. Dough will seem soft, but it will stiffen in refrigerator where it may be kept 4 or 5 days. Roll out on floured board and form desired shapes. Place in greased baking pan. Allow at least 2 hours for rising after rolls are in pans. Bake at 350 degrees for 15-20 minutes.

For variety, add raisins, nuts and cinnamon. Frost with plain sugar icing.

Eula Hurtig

Dilly Casserole Bread

1 package yeast
¼ cup warm water
1 cup creamed cottage cheese
  (heated to lukewarm)
2 tablespoons sugar
1 teaspoon instant onion

1 tablespoon butter
2 tablespoons dill seed
1 tablespoon salt
¼ teaspoon soda
1 unbeaten egg
2¼ - 2½ cups flour

Soften yeast in water. Combine all ingredients except flour. Add to softened yeast. Add flour to form stiff dough, beating well after each addition. Cover. Let rise for one hour or until double in bulk. Stir down. Turn into 8-inch round casserole well buttered.

Bake at 350 degrees for 40-50 minutes until golden brown. Brush with butter. Sprinkle with salt.

Agnes Enright

Rich White Butter Bread

1 package yeast
½ cup warm water
1/8 teaspoon ginger
3 tablespoons sugar

1 can evaporated milk
1 teaspoon salt
2 tablespoons salad oil
4 to 4½ cups flour

Dissolve yeast in warm water containing the ginger and 1 tablespoon sugar. After 15 minutes add the remaining ingredients. Put in 2 one pound coffee cans, well greased or one 2 pound coffee can. Bake at 350 degrees—2 cans—45 minutes; 1 can-60 minutes.

Ruth Lovelady

Spoon Bread

1 cup corn meal
½ teaspoon salt
1 pint scalded milk

6 tablespoons butter
4 beaten eggs
2 cups milk (cold)

Stir corn meal and salt gradually into milk. Cook one minute. Remove from stove. Add remaining ingredients. Bake in buttered casserole 25-30 minutes at 400 degrees. Serve with butter.

Wonderful substitute for potatoes.

Mrs. George Pardee

Onion Bread

1 loaf French bread, unsliced
Butter or margarine, softened
Chopped green onions,
   including the greens
Mustard
Sesame seeds

Cut bread lengthwise. Mix soft butter with chopped green onions. (Use own judgement on amount of onion and butter to use.) Spread onion mixture generously over bread halves. Then spread mustard sparingly over this. Top with sesame seeds and broil to desired doneness. Slice at an angle almost all the way through loaf half.

Nan Stevens

Brown Bread

1½ cups white flour
2 cups graham flour
1 teaspoon soda
1 teaspoon salt
1 cup molasses (dark)
1 egg
1½ cups buttermilk
   (or sour milk)

Mix thoroughly—put in 2 or 3 well-greased "no. 2" cans. Steam 1½ hours.

Rachel K. Curless

Whole Wheat Bread

1 package yeast
2 cups warm water
2 tablespoons sugar
2 teaspoons salt
4 cups flour
½ cup brown sugar
½ cup hot water
6 tablespoons shortening
   (use butter)
4 cups whole wheat flour

Stir first 5 ingredients together until smooth. Keep in warm place (82 degrees) until light and bubbly, approximately one hour. Heat brown sugar, water and butter until the butter is melted. Cool to lukewarm, add to yeast mixture. Add flour—knead until smooth. Last of flour will have to be kneaded into the dough. Place in greased bowl and set aside to double in bulk—about one hour. Form into two loaves; put into greased loaf pans. Let double in bulk about one hour. Bake at 375 degrees for 50 minutes.

Yield: 2 loaves

Mrs. George Pardee

Swedish Limpa

2 tablespoons fennel seed
1 12-ounce can beer
¼ cup dark molasses
¼ cup maple syrup
1 tablespoon white vinegar
½ teaspoon dry orange peel

2 packages dry yeast
1 cup white flour
2 teaspoons salt
2 tablespoons melted butter
4 cups rye flour

Mix fennel seed and beer; heat to lukewarm. Pour into large mixing bowl, and combine with molasses, syrup, vinegar and orange rind. Sprinkle yeast onto warm liquid, and add white flour, beating well. Let dough stand until bubbly; add salt, melted butter and enough rye flour to make a smooth, soft dough. (Sometimes it doesn't take quite the 4 cups called for.) Knead until smooth and elastic. Let rise 1½ to 2 hours or until double. Punch down and let rise again. Divide into halves, knead 5 minutes, and shape into round loaves. Let rise about 50 minutes or until double. Bake at 350 degrees for 35-40 minutes.

Yield: 2 loaves
Ruth Stenmark

Kanettles
(German Dumplings)

3 to 4 slices finely
chopped bacon
1 cup ham, chopped finely
½ cup hard salami,
chopped finely
½ loaf white bread
½ medium onion, chopped
very finely
2 tablespoons dehydrated
parsley

4 beaten eggs
Accent, salt and
pepper to taste
Flour
Broth (boil 4 nice short
ribs in enough water
to make 2-3 quarts broth)

Sauté in skillet, the bacon, ham and salami. Cool. Add rest of ingredients and mix lightly by hand. Add enough flour to hold together (not too much). Roll into balls about the size of golf balls. Drop into hot broth, cover and boil gently 15 to 20 minutes, covered.

Yield: 16
Grandmother Covey

217

Herb Bread Deluxe

1 loaf frozen sandwich
   bread, unsliced
½ pound soft butter
2 tablespoons grated onion
1 teaspoon prepared mustard

2 tablespoons lemon juice
1 tablespoon poppy seed
½ teaspoon beau monde
   (Spice Island)
8-ounce package Swiss cheese

Remove all crusts from the frozen bread. Cut large X's through the top of the bread—almost to the bottom—thus forming serving size pieces. Make a sauce of the remaining ingredients except the cheese. Spread this over the bread. Take the Swiss cheese, cut into strips to stuff down all the "X's." Tie with string if necessary to hold together. This is hard to do the first time.

Bake at 350 degrees for 30 minutes.

Mrs. Frank Beattie

Baking Powder Biscuits

2 cups flour
4 teaspoons baking powder
2 teaspoons sugar
½ teaspoon salt

½ teaspoon cream of tartar
½ cup butter (1 stick)
   at room temperature
2/3 cup milk

Sift flour and measure; then sift all dry ingredients together. Cut in butter until like coarse crumbling meal. Then add milk all at once and stir with fork only until dough follows fork. Knead ½ minute on lightly floured board. Bake 450 degrees 12-15 minutes. If possible, refrigerate an hour or longer before baking.

Mrs. George Pardee

Pizza Dough

1 package yeast
¼ cup warm water
6 tablespoons boiling water
1 tablespoon lard

1 teaspoon sugar
¼ teaspoon salt
Pepper to taste
2 cups flour

Add yeast to warm water to dissolve. Mix remaining ingredients, except flour, together. Cool. Add dissolved yeast and flour. Place in greased bowl and let rise ½ hour or until doubled. Press on pizza pan or cookie sheet. Add favorite pizza topping.

Leah Rae Puleo

Cranberry Bread

2 cups flour
1 cup sugar plus
   2 tablespoons
1½ teaspoons baking powder
½ teaspoon soda
1 teaspoon salt
¼ cup shortening
3/4 cup orange juice,
   fresh or frozen
   (measure after diluting)

1 tablespoon grated
   orange rind
1 egg, well beaten
½ cup nuts
½ cup white raisins
   (optional)
2 cups cranberries,
   cut in halves

Sift together flour, sugar, baking powder, soda and salt. Cut in shortening until mixture resembles coarse corn meal. Combine orange juice and grated rind with well-beaten egg. Add to dry ingredients, mixing enough to dampen. Fold in cranberries and nuts. Put into greased loaf pan (9 x 5 x 3). Bake in 350 degree oven and cool on rack. Store overnight for easy slicing. Also good with powdered sugar frosting. Good for Christmas and can be toasted for breakfast.

Yield: one loaf
Frances Boyer

Harvest Loaf

1 3/4 cups flour
1 teaspoon soda
½ teaspoon salt
2 teaspoons pumpkin pie spice
½ cup butter

1 cup sugar
2 eggs
3/4 cup pumpkin
3/4 cup chocolate chips
3/4 cup walnuts

Cream butter, sugar, and pumpkin. Add remaining ingredients and mix. Grease only the bottom of a loaf pan and bake at 350 degrees for 65 to 70 minutes. Avoid overcooking.

Yield: 1 loaf
Mrs. George E. Edwards

Date Nut Bread

1 10-ounce package of
    dates, cut in thirds

2 cups hot water
2 teaspoons baking soda

Soak these three ingredients for ½ hour.

3 tablespoons butter
2 cups sugar
2 teaspoons vanilla
2 eggs, beaten

4 cups sifted flour
1 teaspoon salt
3/4 cup chopped nuts

Combine these ingredients and add to date mixture. Bake in greased tin can for 1 hour at 375 degrees. Cool slightly and shake cans carefully to remove bread.

Cans: Use large soup cans. Use four 1-pound 10-ounce cans or five 1-pound 3-ounce cans. Fill cans half full.

  Yield: four round loaves   *Mrs. Stanley Rheaume*

Crullers

3 eggs, lightly beaten
1/3 cup powdered sugar
3 tablespoons melted butter
2¼ cups cake flour
    (approximately)

1 teaspoon salt
1 teaspoon cinnamon

Add sugar and butter to eggs. Sift one cup of flour with salt and cinnamon. Add to egg mixture with enough additional flour to make dough stiff enough to roll. Roll out thin; cut into strips and fry in deep fat heated to 360 degrees until light brown. Drain on paper towels and dust with powdered sugar.

Mrs. Ed McGuire

Prune Bread

3/4 cup dried prunes
(measure whole)
1 tablespoon margarine
½ cup granulated sugar
½ teaspoon vanilla
1 egg
½ cup whole wheat flour

3/4 cup sifted cake flour
½ teaspoon soda
¼ teaspoon salt
1 teaspoon cinnamon
½ cup chopped walnuts
or pecans

Put prunes in hot water and let stand for a few minutes. Pit and grind or chop fine. Add 3/4 cup hot water to prunes and let stand while mixing remaining ingredients. Cream butter and sugar and eggs. Add vanilla and sifted dry ingredients. Blend in prunes and nuts. Beat a few quick strokes. Bake in oiled and floured loaf pan at 350 degrees about 45 minutes. Chill before making sandwiches with softened cream cheese. Cover and chill again.

Yield: one loaf
Helen K. Pachak

Banana Nut Bread

1/3 cup shortening
3/4 cup light brown sugar
1 cup mashed bananas (2-3)
2 eggs
1½ cups flour

1 teaspoon salt
1 teaspoon baking soda
½ cup milk
½ cup chopped walnuts
½ cup chopped black walnuts

Cream the shortening with sugar. Add the mashed bananas and eggs. Sift the flour with salt and soda. Add to the creamed mixture, alternating with the milk. Stir in the nuts. Bake in a greased loaf pan, 8½ x 4½ x 2½ inches, in a 350 degree oven for one hour. Turn out and cool on rack. Wrap in foil and refrigerate.

This bread is dark and heavy; it slices better after chilled. Freezes well.

Yield: 1 loaf
Ann Gardner

Easter Bread or Yellow Sweet Bread

1 dozen eggs
1 tablespoon sugar for
    every egg, or 3/4 cup
2 cakes yeast
½ cup oil
1 cup butter

1 teaspoon orange juice
1 teaspoon lemon juice
1 teaspoon anise seed
1 pinch salt
9 cups flour (approximately)
Warm milk, enough to dissolve
    yeast

Beat eggs; add juices, yeast and milk and beat slightly. Mix flour, sugar, salt and anise. Now add to liquid mixture and mix until well-blended. Let rise in bowl until nearly double in size. Punch down. Let rise again. Shape into four loaves. Place in greased pans. Let rise and bake for 20-30 minutes at 350 degrees.

Yield: 4 loaves

Mrs. Jennie Quirico

Gum Drop Bread

1 cup pitted dates
1 cup water
1 teaspoon soda
3/4 cup sugar
¼ cup shortening
2 beaten eggs

½ teaspoon salt
2 cups sifted flour
1 cup nuts
1 cup sliced gumdrops
¼ cup flour

Cook dates in water until mushy. Let cool and add soda. Cream sugar, shortening and add beaten eggs. Add salt and 2 cups flour. Flour nuts and gumdrops in the ¼ cup flour before adding to the mixture. Put in greased loaf pan.

Bake in 325 degree oven for one hour.

Yield: one loaf

Mrs. J. Sturgeon

Pineapple Bread

2 eggs
1/3 cup sugar
1/3 cup oil
2 cups flour

½ teaspoon salt
3 teaspoons baking powder
1 cup crushed pineapple
1 cup nuts

Beat eggs; add sugar and oil and mix well. Then add flour, salt and baking powder (which have been sifted together), pineapple (including juice) and nuts. Mix and bake in loaf pan for 1 hour at 350 degrees.

Yield: one loaf

Sylvia Jackson

Potica

Dough:
8-10 cups flour
1 pint warm milk
3/4 cup butter
3/4 cup sugar

1½ teaspoons salt
½ cup warm water
3 packages dry yeast
3 well-beaten eggs

Mix all dry ingredients together. Add milk, ½ of the butter, yeast and eggs. Knead dough, dipping hands in the other ½ of the butter, for 10 minutes. Let rise in warm place about one hour.

Filling:
2 pounds ground nuts
  (use meat grinder)
2 cups sugar
3/4 cup honey

1 13-ounce can condensed milk
1 teaspoon cinnamon
3/4 cup butter
3 eggs, well-beaten

Glaze:
1 beaten egg

Mix all these ingredients except egg for glaze and warm. When dough has risen, dump dough on large table covered with lightly floured sheet. Roll dough some; then pull dough until thin (easier to pull with two people.) Spread filling on dough and roll. Place dough on greased flour pans in the shape of an elongated backward "E." Brush glaze over all the dough. Let raise one-half hour. Bake one hour at 350 degrees.

Yield: 5 loaves

Barbara Comaianni

Cherry Potica

Dough:
8-10 cups flour
1 pint warm milk
3/4 cup butter
3/4 cup sugar
1½ teaspoons salt
1/3 cup warm water
3 packages dry yeast
3 eggs, well beaten

Filling:
3 cans cherry
  pie filling
2 cans *drained*
  pie cherries
1 cup sugar
1 cup honey (optional)
¼ teaspoon almond extract
  or 1 teaspoon cinnamon
2-4 cups chopped nuts (almonds, walnuts, or mixed)
½ cup butter

Mix all dry ingredients together. Add milk, ½ of the butter, yeast and eggs. Knead dough about 10 minutes, dipping hands in butter as needed. Let rise in warm place about one hour.

Mix all the filling ingredients and warm. Spread thinly over very thinly rolled dough. Roll up into loaves, patching ends with left-over dough. Place in greased floured pans or well-greased angel food cake pan. Brush tops with beaten egg to glaze and let rise ½ hour. Bake at 325 degrees for one hour.

Yield: 5 loaves   *Leah Rae Puleo*

Carrot Bread

1 cup sugar, half
  brown and half white
3/4 cup cooking oil
1½ cups flour
1 teaspoon baking soda
1 teaspoon cinnamon

½ teaspoon salt
1 cup grated carrots
2 egg yolks
2 egg whites
1 cup raisins

Beat egg whites until stiff. Set aside. Combine the rest of the ingredients folding in the beaten egg whites last. Bake at 350 degrees for about 50 minutes, in a greased loaf pan.

Yield: one loaf   *Sally Zimdahl*

Apple Nut Bread

1½ cups oil
2 cups sugar
4 eggs
3 cups flour
1 teaspoon cinnamon
½ teaspoon salt

1 teaspoon baking soda
1 teaspoon vanilla
3 cups delicious apples,
  peeled and sliced
1 cup walnuts, large pieces

Beat together the oil, sugar and eggs. Sift together the dry ingredients and add to the egg mixture. Add the remaining ingredients.

Bake in 2 greased bread pans for 1 hour and 20 minutes at 325 degrees.

Yield: 2 loaves   *Suzie Bornt*

Pumpkin Bread

2/3 cup shortening
4 eggs beaten
2/3 cup water
2 teaspoons soda, dissolved
  in 1 teaspoon water
1½ teaspoons salt
1 teaspoon cinnamon

2½ cups sugar
1 number 303 can pumpkin
3 1/3 cups flour
1 teaspoon cloves
½ teaspoon baking powder
2/3 cup raisins and nuts

Cream sugar and shortening. Add eggs, water, and pumpkin. Blend in remaining ingredients. Pour into 3 greased 1-pound coffee cans; fill 3/4 full. Bake 65 minutes at 350 degrees. Serve in round slices. Especially good hot.

Yield: 3 1-pound loaves   *Mrs. Doug Brown*

Apple Strudel

Dough:

2 cups flour	1 teaspoon salt
1/3 cup oil	½ cup warm water

Filling:

8-10 tart apples (thinly sliced)	1 cup sugar and 2 tablespoons cinnamon, mixed together
1 cube melted butter	½ cup ground graham crackers

Mix dough ingredients and knead this dough at least 20 minutes. Slap the dough down hard on the board frequently; work until it is elastic and silky-smooth. Cover with a warm bowl and let rest at least one hour. While dough is resting prepare apple filling. Place the ball of dough in the center of the cloth; roll with a warm rolling pin as thin as possible. Then stretch dough using your hands palm-side down under dough. Work carefully, stretching from the center outward. Work gently and stretch as thin as possible moving around the table; dough should be paper thin. Brush entire surface with melted butter. Place thinly sliced apples over 2/3 of dough; sprinkle with sugar-cinnamon mixture. Sprinkle graham crackers over apples. Roll as for jelly-roll until all dough is used up. Brush with melted butter.

Bake at 375 degrees for 1 hour.

Sprinkle with confectioners' sugar, or make a light glaze with confectioners' sugar and water, and brush over hot strudel. Serve warm.

Serves 10-12   *Mrs. Mickey Giarrantano*

Sour Cream Coffee Cake

¼ pound butter
1 cup sugar
2 eggs
1 cup sour cream

1 teaspoon baking soda
1 tablespoon vanilla
1½ cups cake flour
1½ teaspoons baking powder

Cinnamon Mixture:
1½ teaspoons cinnamon (or
   more, depending on taste)

½ cup chopped pecans
   or walnuts
½ cup sugar

Cream butter and sugar in mixer. Add eggs, one at a time. Add sour cream, soda and vanilla, a little at a time, alternating with flour and baking powder. Pour half the batter into greased and floured 8 x 8 cake pan. Sprinkle half the cinnamon mixture over batter. Pour the rest of the batter and top it with the rest of the cinnamon mixture.

Bake at 350 degrees for 35 minutes.

Sandy Stein

Brown Sugar Crumb Coffee Cake

2 cups flour
2 cups brown sugar
¼ pound margarine, melted
¼ teaspoon salt
1 teaspoon soda

1 cup buttermilk
1 egg
1 teaspoon vanilla
½ cup chocolate chips
½ cup chopped nuts

Mix the first four ingredients to a crumb stage. Save ½ cup of this for the cake topping. Add the remaining ingredients to the crumb mixture. Pour into an 8" x 13" pan and sprinkle with ½ cup chocolate chips, ½ cup chopped nuts and the saved crumbs. Bake 30 minutes at 350 degrees.

Jean Longmore

Danish Coffee Cake

4 cups flour
½ teaspoon salt
½ cup sugar

1 pound butter (half
   margarine if desired)
2 cakes or packages yeast
1 1/3 cups lukewarm water

Icing:
1½ cups powdered sugar
Milk

1 teaspoon vanilla
½ teaspoon almond extract

Avoid trying to roll out this recipe during hot, humid weather. Cut one cube butter into flour, salt, and sugar until fine. Soften the yeast cakes (or dry yeast) in water. Add to flour mixture. Mix well. Turn onto floured board—knead well. Roll out into large circle. Spread with one cube butter or margarine. Fold sides over each other and ends in, then roll out again. Repeat this procedure two more times, spreading the dough each time with a cube of butter. Finally, cut rolled out circle into long fourths. Spread each strip with different flavors of jams or jellies (grape, apple, blackberry, brown sugar and cinnamon.) Slash each side of each strip every inch or so and in about three-quarters of an inch. Fold each segment over opposite segment, alternating sides braid fashion. Place in greased pans. Let rise 2 hours or until light and fluffy looking.

Bake at 375 degrees 10-12 minutes until light golden brown.

Prepare icing: Combine powdered sugar, extracts and enough milk to make a liquid. Drizzle over the tops of the baked coffee cake. This has been used in my husband's family for many years, with minor variations.

Yield: 2-3 dozen pieces

Mary Beth Stjernholm

Believe it or Not Coffee Cake

1 pound pork sausage (raw)
1½ cups brown sugar
1½ cups white sugar
2 eggs
3 cups flour
½ teaspoon ginger
½ teaspoon cinnamon
1 teaspoon baking soda
1 cup cold coffee
1 cup raisins
1 cup chopped nuts
1 teaspoon baking powder
1 teaspoon allspice

Combine meat and sugars. Add eggs. Stir soda into coffee. Combine all other dry ingredients including spices. Alternate coffee mixture with flour mixture and add to meat mixture. Pour boiling water over raisins. Let stand 5 minutes; drain and add with nuts. Bake in well-greased tube pan. Bake at 350 degrees for 1½ hours.

This keeps indefinitely in the refrigerator, but serve well-warmed.

Judy Caldwell

Coffee Cake

½ cup butter
3/4 cup sugar
1 egg
1½ cups flour
1 teaspoon baking powder
Salt, pinch
½ cup milk
1 teaspoon vanilla

Topping:
½ cup brown sugar
2 tablespoons flour
2 teaspoons cinnamon
2 tablespoons melted butter
½ cup chopped nuts

Cream butter and sugar. Add remaining ingredients, and mix well. Batter will be thick. Grease a 9-inch square pan. Spread half of batter in pan and sprinkle with half of topping. Repeat layers. Bake for 30 minutes at 350 degrees.

Marilyn Hunter

Hungarian Coffee Cake

1½ cups scalded milk
½ cup butter
2 teaspoons salt
2/3 cup sugar
3 beaten eggs
1 package yeast

½ cup warm water
7-7½ cups flour
1 cup melted butter, cooled
1½ cups brown sugar
2 teaspoons cinnamon
1 cup walnuts, ground fine

Frosting:
3/4 cup powdered sugar
½ teaspoon vanilla

Dash salt
Milk

Add hot milk to the butter, salt and 2/3 cup sugar. Cool mixture. Beat in eggs. Dissolve yeast in warm water. Add to milk mixture. Stir in flour. Let dough rise 2 times.

Mix brown sugar, cinnamon and walnuts together.

Grease 2 10-inch tube pans.

Shape dough into golf-sized balls; dip balls into melted butter, then into sugar mixture. Let rise until double in size about one hour, in slightly warm oven.

Bake at 375 degrees 35-40 minutes. Turn out onto plate immediately. If wanted drizzle frosting over tops and sides.

For frosting: Mix powdered sugar, vanilla, salt with enough milk to make spreading consistency.

Yield: 2 tube pans of rolls   *Rita Benzmiller*

Kolache

Filling:
1 pound prunes
1 cup water
¼ teaspoon allspice

½ cup sugar
1 tablespoon lemon juice
1 tablespoon grated lemon peel

Pastry:
1½ cups flour
½ teaspoon baking powder
1 cup butter
1 tablespoon sugar

1 egg yolk
1 8-ounce package cream cheese
1 tablespoon milk

Simmer prunes and water for 30 minutes until tender. Chop finely and add allspice, sugar, lemon and peel. Set aside.

Mix flour and baking powder. Cream butter, cheese, milk and sugar. Add egg yolk. Add flour mixture. Chill thoroughly. Roll dough ¼ -inch thick and cut into 2-inch rounds with biscuit or cookie cutter. Place on ungreased cookie pan and make depression in center of each round. Place 1½ teaspoons of prune mixture in center.

Bake at 400 degrees for 10 minutes until golden. Sprinkle with powdered sugar.

Other fruits can be used, such as apricots or pineapple, instead of the prunes.

Yield: Two dozen

Lana Hunter

Sour Cream Coffee Ring

1 stick margarine	½ teaspoon soda
1 cup sugar	2 eggs
1 cup sour cream	1 teaspoon vanilla
2 cups flour	1 teaspoon cinnamon
1 teaspoon baking powder	½ cup sugar
½ teaspoon salt	Walnuts

Cream together margarine and sugar; add sour cream; beat well and add eggs, vanilla. Sift together flour, baking powder, salt and soda, and add to above. Mix together cinnamon and sugar and set aside. Put half of batter in greased angel pan, sprinkle with half of sugar and cinnamon. Add remaining batter, then sprinkle over remaining cinnamon on top. Poke in pieces of walnuts on top. Bake at 350 degrees for about 40 minutes.

Judy Cully

231

Carmel Crown Rolls

2 cups scalded milk
½ cup shortening or margarine (melted and cool)
1 cup sugar
2 teaspoons salt
4 cakes or 4 ounces yeast

½ cup lukewarm water
4 eggs slightly beaten
8-10 cups flour
3 cups cinnamon and sugar (approximately)

Topping PER pan:
½ cup brown sugar, packed
¼ cup white sugar

1 tablespoon melted margarine

Soften yeast in lukewarm water. Scald milk and cool to lukewarm. Add shortening, sugar, salt and eggs to milk. Add softened yeast. Gradually add flour, mixing on low speed until a soft dough consistency. Let dough rise double. Place brown sugar, white sugar and melted margarine in the bottom of a well-greased angel food tube pan. Pinch off 1½-inch balls of dough and roll in melted margarine and then cinnamon sugar. Place balls into pans until ½ full. Let rise until double. Bake at 375 degrees for approximately 35 minutes. Immediately upon removing from the oven, turn out onto serving plate.

Yield: 3 angel food cake pans   *Helen Pachak*

German Stollen

6 packages yeast
1 teaspoon sugar

1 tablespoon flour

Add enough warm milk to above ingredients to make thin dough. Let rest 5 to 10 minutes.

Dough:
Yeast mixture
12 cups flour
1½ teaspoons salt
1½ cups sugar
1 pound butter

2/3 cup rum
1 lemon peel
1½ to 2 cups milk
4 eggs

232

Knead it well. Let rest 20 minutes and add following ingredients:

1 3/4 cups raisins
2½ cups almonds,
   chopped (thin slices)

12 ounces citron
   (candied peel), chopped
6 ounces candied
   orange peel, chopped

Let double in bulk and form 4 stollen. Place on greased cookie sheet and let rise again. Bake at 325 degrees for one hour.

While stollen is still hot, baste with 1 stick butter and sprinkle with powdered sugar.

Yield: 4 stollen
Mrs. George Pardee

Hungarian Walnut Roll

½ cup milk
4 tablespoons sugar
1 cake yeast, crumbled
4 cups flour
½ teaspoon salt
3/4 pound butter (3 sticks)

4 eggs
1 pound ground walnuts
1½ cups sugar
1 teaspoon vanilla
Powdered sugar

Separate eggs. Set aside. Scald milk and cool to lukewarm. Add 4 tablespoons sugar and crumbled yeast and 4 egg yolks, slightly beaten. Let stand until yeast is dissolved and mixture is bubbly. Combine flour, butter, and salt as for pie crust. Add milk mixture to flour mixture, blending well. Divide dough into four parts; chill, well covered. Beat egg whites until stiff but not dry. Add 1½ cups sugar gradually; fold in nuts and vanilla. Roll dough between waxed paper. Spread ¼ of filling on each rectangle of dough, leaving a one-inch margin on all sides. Roll lengthwise as for jelly roll, lifting paper to help roll easily. Seal edges. Bake 20-30 minutes at 375 degrees. Cut into 1½ inch widths and serve. Sprinkle with powdered sugar.

Yield: 4 rolls
Rose Pluss

Penny Rolls

1 package active dry yeast
½ cup warm water
¼ cup sugar
1 tablespoon salad oil

½ teaspoon salt
½ cup hot water
1 egg
3-3¼ cup sifted flour

Soften yeast in warm water. In large mixer bowl, combine sugar, salad oil, salt and hot water. Cool to lukewarm. Stir in egg and yeast mixture. Add 2 cups of the flour and beat at medium speed for 2 minutes. Stir in remaining flour with a spoon. (For lighter rolls, use 3 cups flour). Beat vigorously with spoon for 3 minutes until dough is smooth. Scrape down sides of bowl, cover, and let rise in warm place until double (time being 1-1¼ hours). Punch down, cover tightly and refrigerate overnight. Turn out on floured board and shape into 1¼ inch balls; or roll out dough, dot with butter and sprinkle with cinnamon and sugar, roll up and cut into 1¼ inch sections. Put balls or cinnamon rolls into 2 round greased cake pans. Cover and let rise until double (45-60 minutes). Bake at 375 degrees for 10 minutes.

Connie Estep

Pecan Tea Ring

3/4 cup firmly packed
   light brown sugar
3/4 cup chopped pecans
1/3 cup butter or margarine

2 tablespoons water
2 cans (8 ounces each) refrigerated buttermilk biscuits

Combine brown sugar, pecans, margarine and water in medium saucepan. Stir over low heat until butter melts. Set aside. Separate each can of biscuit dough into 10 biscuits. Cut each into quarters and stir into sugar mixture until all pieces are well coated. Spread in generously greased 9-inch tube pan. Bake at 400 degrees for 20 to 30 minutes, until golden brown. Set aside 3 minutes. Invert pan to remove ring. To serve, pull apart. Serve warm.

Reheat, loosely-wrapped in foil, at 400 degrees for 10-12 minutes, until warm. To make ahead: Prepare, cover and refrigerate up to 2 hours before baking. Bake as directed. May add more sugar or some cinnamon.

Yield: 8-10 servings

Ann Bramer

mosaíco
culínarío
de recetas

(culínary mosaíc of recipes)

Neither oven nor range
is required in the familiar southwestern
pepper-drying process, for the arid climate
provides the final touch in the preserving
of the brightly-colored strings.

Tomato Quiche Lorraine

Crust:

1 cup flour
3/4 teaspoon salt
¼ cup vegetable oil
2 tablespoons milk

8 slices bacon, fried and
  crumbled
¼ cup finely chopped onion
10 ounces Swiss cheese, grated
4 eggs, beaten
1 8-ounce can tomato sauce
1 tablespoon flour
½ teaspoon salt
1/8 teaspoon dry mustard

Make 9-inch pie crust with crust ingredients or use frozen shell or crust mix. Line a 9-inch pie tin with pastry. Prick crust. Cover with foil and weight with another pie pan. Bake in 400 degree oven for 12 minutes. Remove foil. Arrange bacon, onion, and cheese in pastry shell. Beat remaining ingredients, and pour over cheese, bacon and onion. Bake until center is set . . . 325 degrees for 50 minutes. Garnish with chopped parsley.

Serve for luncheon with salad and hot rolls.

Serves 6   *Kay Abbot*

Hawaiian Chicken Casserole

2 cups chopped cooked chicken
2-3 cups cooked instant rice
2 bananas (sliced)
2 cups crushed pineapple
1 can concentrated orange juice

½ cup shredded coconut
½ cup slivered almonds
½ cup chopped fresh parsley
½ teaspoon ginger
Cherries (garnish)

Prepare rice according to package directions, but use orange juice as a portion of the water needed. Add parsley and ginger to the cooked rice, and mix well. Add chicken, bananas, and pineapple to rice and mix. Spoon into casserole dish and bake 15 minutes at 350 degrees. Remove from oven, and sprinkle coconut, and almonds over top. Bake another 15 minutes at 350 degrees. Remove from oven and place parsley and cherries on top, if desired.

Serves 8   *Patsy Kenyon*

Chicken Spaghetti Casserole

4 cups tomatoes (canned)
2 cups chicken broth
1 large onion, chopped
1 clove garlic, minced
1 tablespoon Worcestershire
  sauce
2 teaspoons salt
Basil and thyme (pinch)
1 can sliced mushrooms (small)
2 tablespoons butter
  or margarine
2 tablespoons flour

1 cup light cream
1 teaspoon salt
¼ teaspoon pepper
½ pound Cheddar cheese
½ cup ripe olives, sliced
4 cups chicken, cooked
½ pound spaghetti (cooked)

Simmer tomatoes and chicken broth until liquid is reduced in half. Season with onion, garlic, Worcestershire sauce, salt, basil and thyme. Sauté mushrooms in butter until golden brown. Remove mushrooms and to the butter, add flour and blend. Add cream, salt, pepper, and half of Cheddar cheese, grated. Mix tomato mixture, sauce, mushrooms, sliced ripe olives, chicken (cut up) and cooked spaghetti. Turn into casserole dish and top with remaining grated Cheddar cheese. Bake 45 minutes at 325 degrees.

Serves 12

Mary Green

Chicken Casserole

1 tablespoon margarine (melted)
½ cup cornflake crumbs
1 can cream of mushroom soup
1 cup mayonnaise
1 teaspoon lemon juice

½ teaspoon curry powder
2 packages (10-ounce) frozen
  broccoli (thawed)
2½ cups cubed, cooked chicken
½ teaspoon garlic salt

Mix margarine and crumbs. Heat soup, remove from heat, and add mayonnaise, lemon juice and curry powder. Cut broccoli stalks in half lengthwise. Place broccoli in bottom of a 2-quart casserole. Spread chicken over broccoli and add sauce. Top with buttered crumbs. Bake in pre-heated oven for 30 minutes at 350 degrees.

Serves 6

Mrs. Joel Zais

238

Last Minute Chicken Rice Casserole

3/4 pound sliced mushrooms
  (or 1 can)
¼ cup diced green pepper
1 tablespoon chopped onion
¼ teaspoon lemon pepper
2 tablespoons butter
1 can cream of celery soup
Parmesan cheese (grated)

1 cup water
1 cup instant rice
½ teaspoon salt
1 whole canned chicken
1 can green beans
  (French style)

Sauté mushrooms, pepper, onion and lemon pepper in butter. Add soup and water, and bring to a boil. Bone chicken and cut into bite sized pieces. Pour half the sauce into casserole. Layer chicken, rice (dry from the box) and beans and pour remaining sauce on top. Sprinkle with grated cheese. Bake covered at 375 degrees for 20-25 minutes. Slice through with sharp knife after first 10 minutes of baking.

Serves 4
Ann Gardner

Spicy Sweet Sour Casserole

1 cup brown sugar
5 tablespoons cornstarch
½ to 1 teaspoon chili powder
1 teaspoon salt
3/4 cup red wine
1½ tablespoons Worcestershire
  sauce
1/3 cup vinegar
2/3 cup catsup
Chinese noodles or rice

½ cup water
1 can pineapple tidbits (13 ounce)
2 slices lemon
1 clove garlic
2 onions, cubed
1 green pepper, cubed
1 can water chestnuts, sliced
2-3 cups cooked, cubed ham
  Pork or beef may be used

Mix together in saucepan the brown sugar, cornstarch, chili powder, salt, wine, soy sauce, Worcestershire sauce, vinegar, catsup, water, the juice from the pineapple, lemon, and garlic. Simmer gently for 45 minutes; then add the pineapple, onions, green pepper, and water chestnuts. Simmer gently for 10 - 15 minutes. The vegetables should be crisp . . . do not overcook. Add the meat of your choice last, and serve hot over heated chinese noodles or rice.

Rene Holden

Ham Asparagus Casserole

1 box frozen asparagus
2 cups chopped ham
3/4 cup shredded Cheddar
cheese
3 tablespoons tapioca
2 tablespoons chopped onion
1 tablespoon chopped parsley
1 tablespoon lemon juice

3 hard-cooked eggs (sliced)
½ cup half & half
1 can cream of mushroon soup
1 small can drained mushrooms
½ cup buttered bread crumbs

Cook the asparagus, but do not add salt. Place cooked asparagus in buttered 7-inch x 11-inch baking dish. Cover with ham mixture, then egg slices. Combine soup, cream and mushrooms and pour over all. Top with bread crumbs. Bake at 375 degrees for 30 minutes.

Sue Mastro

Goodbye Turkey Casserole

5 tablespoons flour
1 teaspoon salt
¼ teaspoon onion salt
¼ cup melted butter
2¼ cups milk
1 and 1/3 cups minute rice

1½ cups turkey or chicken broth
½ cup grated American cheese
1½ cups cooked asparagus
or peas
2 cups sliced or diced
turkey
2 tablespoons toasted
slivered almonds

Make white sauce; stir flour and half the salt, and onion salt into the butter. Stir in milk (cook over hot water), stirring occasionally until thickened. Directly from the box, pour rice into a 1-quart shallow baking dish. Combine broth and remaining salt, and pour over rice. Sprinkle half of cheese over rice; top with asparagus, then turkey, and pour white sauce over top. Sprinkle with remaining cheese, and a little paprika on top. Top with almonds after baking. Bake at 375 degrees—20 minutes.

Fran Tate

Corned Beef Casserole

1 8-ounce package noodles
1 12-ounce can corned
   beef, diced (or fresh)
¼ pound American cheese,
   diced

1 can condensed cream
   of chicken soup
1 cup milk
½ cup chopped onion
3/4 cup buttered crumbs

Cook noodles in boiling salted water until tender; drain. Add corned beef, cheese, soup, milk and onion. Pour into greased 2-quart casserole. Top with buttered crumbs. Bake in moderate oven (350 degrees) 45 minutes.

When using fresh corned beef, boil according to directions. Use remainder for sandwiches.

Serves 8-10   *Pat Pumphrey*

Mad Mod Mostaccioli

1 pound ground beef
½ cup chopped onions
½ cup chopped green peppers
1 package Italian style spaghetti
   sauce mix (packaged)
2 cups tomatoes (1 pound can)
1 can tomato paste (6-ounce can)

3/4 cup water
8 ounces Mostaccioli noodles,
   cooked (4 cups)
2 cups sharp natural Cheddar
   cheese (shredded, 8 ounces)
Salt and pepper to taste

Brown meat, add onions and green peppers, cook until tender. Stir sauce mix, tomatoes, tomato paste and water into meat mixture. Simmer 5 minutes. Combine meat sauce and noodles; mix lightly. Using a 2-quart casserole, layer half of the noodle mixture and cheese. Repeat layers.

Bake 30 minutes—350 degrees.

Serves 6-8   *Mrs. Claude Davis*

Meat Ball Casserole

1 pound ground beef
½ cup pork sausage
½ cup bread crumbs
1/3 cup evaporated milk
2 tablespoons onion, chopped
1 teaspoon chili powder

Sauce:
1 can mushroom soup
1 can cream of celery soup
1 cup evaporated milk
½ cup water
Biscuits (may use refrigerator type)

Combine beef, sausage, bread crumbs, milk, onion, and chili powder and mix well. Shape into meat balls; brown, cover and cook 10 minutes. Place in casserole. Combine four sauce ingredients and heat until steaming. Pour over meat balls. Top with biscuits and bake. 400 degrees — 20-25 minutes. *Rita Thompson*

Pork Chop Casserole

Pork chops
Onion
Rice (uncooked)

Tomato juice
Salt, pepper to taste

Brown pork chops . . . salt, and place in a 9x12 inch pan. Put 1 slice of onion on each pork chop, 1 teaspoon uncooked rice, and cover with tomato juice.

Cook slowly, covered for 1½ hours at 350 degrees.

Marie Pumphrey

Scalloped Corn and Oyster Casserole

1 can cream style corn
1 can frozen oyster stew, thawed
1 cup soda cracker crumbs
1 cup milk
¼ cup celery, diced

1 egg, slightly beaten
1 tablespoon pimiento, diced
¼ teaspoon salt
Pepper, dash
2 tablespoons margarine
½ cup cracker crumbs

Combine corn, oyster stew, 1 cup cracker crumbs, milk, celery, egg, pimiento, salt and pepper. Pour into a greased 1½ quart casserole. Combine melted margarine or butter, and ½ cup crumbs; sprinkle over corn mixture. Bake at 350 degrees for 45 minutes. Done when knife comes out clean.

Serves 6-8

Betty Johnson

242

Moravian Rice

1 pound ground beef
1 cup onion, chopped
1 cup celery, chopped
1 can chicken rice soup
1 can chicken noodle soup
Chow mein noodles and
    cashew nuts

1 can mushroom soup
1 can peas
½ cup raw rice
3 tablespoons soy sauce

Mix all ingredients except noodles and nuts in a baking dish; Bake 1 hour, 15 minutes — 350 degrees.

Sprinkle with chow mein noodles, and nuts; bake fifteen minutes longer. Water may be added if too dry.

Serves 8-10   *Rheuanna Kelly*

Manicotta Shells and Filling

Shells:
3 eggs
1 cup flour
Salt (pinch)
3/4 cup water

Tomato sauce

Filling:
1 pound ricotta cheese
½ piece of round Mozzarella
    cheese
2 eggs
½ teaspoon sugar
Salt, pepper to taste
Parsley, chopped
Grated cheese

Shells: To every 3 eggs, add listed amounts of flour, salt and water, making amount of batter desired. Grease grill once, and heat. Pour as for hot cakes, but very thin, and cook only on one side as batter will bubble, and cook without turning. Stack while preparing filling.

Filling: Grate Mozzarella cheese and mix all filling ingredients together. Place in shells (above), and roll. Top with tomato sauce. Bake in moderate oven (350 degrees) for 25 minutes.

Fran Posa

243

Grandma's Spaghetti Pancakes

8 cups spaghetti and
   sauce (left-over)
4 eggs

2 tablespoons vegetable oil
Salt and pepper to taste

Add 1 tablespoon oil to large round skillet, and heat to 350 degrees. Break the eggs into bowl of left-over spaghetti, stir to distribute eggs evenly. Pour spaghetti into skillet and spread evenly. Cover, and cook 10 minutes, or until browned and crisp. Loosen edges with a spatula; place large round plate (same size as pancake) over spaghetti and carefully remove from pan. Add 1 tablespoon oil to skillet, let it heat and then carefully slide spaghetti pancake from plate (uncooked side down) onto skillet. Cover, and brown until crisp. Cut into pie-shaped wedges, and serve. When preparing spaghetti, we always make extra so that we can look forward to this recipe the next day.

Serves 6
Mrs. Charles Battiste

Fried Spaghetti Cake

1 pound long thin spaghetti
6 eggs, beaten
2 tablespoons oil

Mozzarella cheese
Grating cheese
Salami, sausage or pepperoni

Add eggs to cooked spaghetti. In frying pan, to which oil has been added, arrange half the spaghetti, mozzarella cheese, grating cheese, and salami, sausage, or pepperoni. Top with remaining half of spaghetti. Fry slowly until brown. Turn all at once with the help of a plate and fry on the other side.

This may be made plain without any of the middle ingredients or any combination. May be a side dish or use more meat and cheese for a main dish.

Fran Posa

Spaghetti Roma

8 ounces spaghetti	½ teaspoon salt
¼ cup olive oil	3 eggs (hard cooked)
¼ cup butter	1 can tuna fish (drained)
1 teaspoon garlic salt	½ cup parsley
½ teaspoon oregano	Parmesan cheese

Combine olive oil, butter, garlic salt, oregano and salt. Heat over low heat for about 10 minutes. Boil spaghetti and drain. Pour sauce over spaghetti, mixing well. Add chopped eggs and tuna fish, and mix again. Sprinkle with cheese and parsley.

Margie Hyde

Mozette

1 pound ground beef	1 can tomato soup
1 pound ground pork	1 package broad noodles,
3 large onions, diced	8 ounces
1 can tomatoes, large	Grated cheese
2 green peppers, diced	1 bud garlic
Salt and pepper to taste	1 can corn (optional)

Sauté beef and pork, onions and pepper. Heat tomatoes and tomato soup together with bud of garlic. Remove garlic later. Cook noodles, mix all together in large bowl and top with grated cheese.

Bake at 350 degrees until bubbly.

Serves 8-10

Ruth Gast

Sloppy Joes

1 pound hamburger	1 tablespoon mustard
1 onion, finely chopped	1 can chicken gumbo soup
Celery, finely chopped	½ to 1 cup water
1 tablespoon catsup	1 teaspoon Worcestershire
	sauce

Brown first three ingredients and add remaining ingredients. Simmer 30 minutes. Serve over hamburger buns.

Serves 6-8

Anita Currier

Maid Rite Hamburger or Sloppy Joe

Maid Rite Sloppy Joe:
1 pound ground beef
1 can tomato sauce (8 ounce)
1 tablespoon sugar
½ teaspoon salt
1/8 teaspoon ground
    black pepper
1 teaspoon onion salt
1½ teaspoons Worcestershire
    sauce
1 teaspoon mustard (prepared)
1 tablespoon vinegar

Spaghetti Sauce:
1 can tomato paste (8 ounce)
Fill 4 of paste cans with water
1 tablespoon sugar
½ teaspoon salt
¼ teaspoon black pepper
Garlic salt (dash)
1 teaspoon onion salt
3/4 teaspoon ground oregano
2 bay leaves

In heavy skillet over high heat brown the ground meat until crumbly and well browned. Add the remainder of ingredients. Rinse the tomato paste can with at least ¼ cup water, and add to the meat mixture. Simmer mixture over low heat for at least 30 minutes. Serve on warmed hamburger buns.

This recipe can be tripled and the hamburger mixture used several days later for an easy spaghetti dinner. Make a recipe of above spaghetti sauce, add the hamburger mix to this, and let sauce and meat simmer together for 1 hour. Cook spaghetti or favorite form of macaroni. Drain the spaghetti when done and stir the sauce meat mixture and spaghetti together, and serve hot with grated cheese over top.

Mix all spaghetti sauce ingredients together, and simmer until thickens.

Pauline Genova

Open Face Sandwich

For each sandwich: 1 slice of bread. On top of this, 1 slice of boiled ham, 4 cooked asparagus spears. Place 1 slice of tomato next, and top with 1 slice of American cheese. Place under broiler until cheese is slightly melted.

Ange Jagger

Gourmet Sandwich

2 slices white bread
  (per sandwich)
Sliced ham
Sliced Swiss cheese
  or Monterey Jack

Fresh mushrooms, sliced
  and sautéed in butter
French toast batter
Hollandaise (see
  Blender Hollandaise)

On one slice of bread, place a slice of ham, a slice of cheese, a layer of the sautéed mushrooms, and another slice of ham. Top with second slice of bread. Trim crusts. (Eat trimmings!) Dip in French toast batter. Fry in butter until brown on both sides. Place on a flat pan. Put Hollandaise on top of each sandwich. Run under broiler just to brown. Serve immediately.

Option: May add can green chilies to inside of sandwich.

Kay Abbot

Tuna Coneys

1 can tuna
1 hard boiled egg
½ cup mayonnaise or
  salad dressing

¼ cup chopped onions
¼ cup chopped pickles (dill)
½ cup shredded cheese
Salt and pepper to taste

Pile mixture in hamburger buns and warm in 300 degree oven 15-20 minutes. Additional seasoning may be added, if desired, such as celery salt, etc.

Serves 4

Mrs. Don Peaker

Tuna Rolls

2 cans tuna fish
1 can water chestnuts, sliced
½ cup salad dressing
2 tablespoons minced onion

1 tablespoon lemon juice
2 tablespoons soy sauce
1 teaspoon curry powder
6 grinder buns

Mix all ingredients together until well blended. Cut grinder buns in fourths, and spread with mixture. Broil until lightly browned. Garnish with slice or two of avocado and serve.

Good with a tossed salad, and white wine.

Helen Berry

247

Cheese Strata

12 slices bread
1½ cups shredded,
   sharp Cheddar cheese
2 cups diced ham
6 eggs

3½ cups milk
1 teaspoon salt
¼ teaspoon dry mustard
2 tablespoons onion (minced)

Cut donuts from bread, remove crusts from scraps, and place in bottom of 9 x 13 inch pan. Place cheese in a layer over bread; add layer of ham. Arrange donuts and centers on top. Combine ingredients. Pour over bread, cover, and refrigerate overnight. Bake uncovered in a slow oven (325 degrees) for 1 hour and 15 minutes.

Let this set about 5 minutes before cutting into squares for serving.

Jennie Hunkins

Tomato Delight

1 cube margarine
1 cup brown sugar
2 cups bread cubes (4 slices)

1 can tomato puree (10½ -ounce)
¼ cup water
¼ teaspoon salt

Melt butter, and pour over bread and toss. Heat tomato puree with salt, sugar and water. Pour over bread and toss. Bake covered for 45 minutes at 325 degrees. Serve with turkey or ham.

Serves 8

Kendall Abbott

Simple Cheese Soufflé

6 slices white bread (not too soft)
½ cup melted butter*
1½ cups sharp cheese (grated)

4 large eggs
2 cups milk
½ teaspoon nutmeg

Remove crust from bread, and cut into cubes. Place 1/3 of this into a greased 1½ quart casserole. Sprinkle 1/3 of melted butter and grated cheese over bread. Repeat 3 times. Beat eggs with milk and nutmeg; pour over bread layers. Cover, and let stand for 3 hours. Bake in preheated 350 degree oven, covered, for 30 minutes. Uncover, and bake 15 minutes longer. May be served with mushroom sauce.

*Herb uses a little less butter.

Serves 6-8

Herb Casebeer

Turkey Soufflé

8 slices bread (day old)
2 cups cooked turkey (diced)
1 medium onion (chopped)
1 cup celery (diced)
½ cup mayonnaise
4 eggs (beaten)

3 cups milk
1 can mushroom soup
1 cup Cheddar cheese
Paprika
Salt to taste

Put half of bread cubes (crusts removed) into buttered baking dish 9x15x2. Mix turkey, celery, onion and mayonnaise. Spread over bread. Put remaining bread cubes over top. Beat eggs and mix with milk. Pour over mixture, and let stand overnight in refrigerator. When ready to prepare, put into 325 degree oven for 15 minutes. Remove and pour undiluted soup over top. Top with cheese and paprika. Return to oven and bake for 1 hour or until knife comes out clean.

Good for turkey leftovers.

Serves 12 ladies

Mary Beth Jensen

Cheese Fondue Casserole

8 slices bread (stale)
1 pound Cheddar cheese
  (grated)
4 eggs (slightly beaten)
2½ cups half and half
  (milk, cream)
1 teaspoon brown sugar
¼ teaspoon paprika

½ teaspoon dry mustard
1 green onion (minced)
½ teaspoon salt
½ teaspoon Worcestershire
  sauce
Pepper, cayenne (dash)

Cube and butter bread well. In buttered flat casserole (1½ quart) alternate two layers each of bread and cheese. Blend remaining ingredients and pour over top layer of bread and cheese. Cover and refrigerate 24 hours. Remove from refrigerator at least one hour before cooking. Add enough milk or cream just to show around edges. Bake 300 degrees at least 1¼ hours until puffy and set. May hold in warm oven before serving. Do not put in pan of water!

Serves 8

Mrs. Harry S. Petersen

Spiced Pineapple

1 can (number 2) sliced pineapple
  (with juice)
2/3 cup vinegar
1 stick cinnamon

1 cup sugar
8 whole cloves
¼ teaspoon mace

Put pineapple juice in sauce pan. Add spices and bring to a boil. Add pineapple and bring to a boil again. Remove from heat and let stand overnight.

Obviously this is very simple, but it does make a nice change from spiced peaches and apples.

Vera McDermid

Pepper Relish

6 red bell peppers
6 green peppers
6 large onions
Vinegar

2 tablespoons salt
1 tablespoon pepper
1 tablespoon celery salt
½ cup sugar

Grind together peppers and onions. Scald by pouring boiling water over them, and drain. Bring to a boil in vinegar enough to cover, season with salt and pepper, celery salt, and sugar. Boil 5 minutes, pack in pint jars and seal. Good with beans or on sandwiches.

Mrs. Kenneth Casey

Sauerkraut Relish

1 quart fresh bulk sauerkraut
2 cups celery, chopped
2/3 cup onion
1 or more green peppers

Bring to boil:
2 cups sugar
2/3 cup vinegar

Drain all juice from sauerkraut. Cool sugar and vinegar and put over kraut, mix with above ingredients. May add celery seed, and small jar of diced pimiento. Good after 24 hours.

Mrs. Hubert Glover

special desserts and sauces

The side-by-side "stove" and oven was the latest thing in the twenties and permitted for the first time the luxury of letting the pot boil while pursuing other kitchen activities.

Apple Fritters

1 cup flour
1 teaspoon baking powder
1 tablespoon sugar
1 teaspoon vanilla
¼ teaspoon salt
1 egg
¼ cup milk

Mix flour, baking powder, and sugar. Add milk to well beaten egg, then stir in dry ingredients; add apples. The more apples the better. Fry in deep fat.

Mrs. Dennis Feister

Apple Roll

½ cup melted shortening
1 3/4 cups flour
2 teaspoons baking powder
½ teaspoon salt
½ cup milk
1 egg
1 quart tart apples (about 6), chopped fine
Cinnamon
3 cups water
1½ cups sugar
2 tablespoons butter
1 teaspoon cinnamon

Mix shortening, flour, baking powder, salt, milk and egg. Roll dough to 1/8 inch thickness. Spread apples over dough, sprinkle with cinnamon. Roll like jelly roll, cut in ½ inch slices and place on sheet pan in hot sauce made from water and sugar. Brush tops with melted butter and sprinkle with cinnamon. Bake 45 minutes at 350 degrees. Serve warm sauce over top. Serve as a dessert in sauce dishes.

Sauce:
5 cups water
1¼ cups sugar
2 tablespoons lemon juice
1 tablespoon butter
6 tablespoons cornstarch

Mrs. Harry Amick

Company Apple Dessert

12 cups apples
1½ cups sugar
1 teaspoon cinnamon
Dash nutmeg
Dash salt

2½ cups flour
½ teaspoon salt
1 cup shortening
2 tablespoons sugar
2 eggs, separated

Mix apples, sugar, cinnamon, nutmeg and salt; set aside while preparing dough. Mix flour, salt, shortening and sugar. In measuring cup, beat egg yolks; add milk to equal 2/3 cup. Add to dough mixture. Roll dough on floured paper. Put half of dough in jelly roll pan. Spread apples over dough. (If apples are juicy, add 1 cup crushed corn flakes.) Top with dough. Beat egg whites until stiff and spread over top. Bake at 400 degrees 45-50 minutes. Make glaze of powdered sugar, almond flavoring, margarine and milk.

Betty Ludlow

Apple Torte

1 egg, slightly beaten
3/4 cup sugar
3/4 cup sliced apples
½ cup flour

1 teaspoon baking powder
Salt (dash)
1 teaspoon almond flavoring
¼ cup nuts

Bake in greased pie tin at 325 degrees for 30 to 40 minutes, until brown and crisp.

Cut in pie-shaped wedges and serve with ice cream as you would pie ala-mode.

Mrs. Richard I. Lyles, Jr.

254

Coffee Crunch Surprise

3 cups ice cream,
   coffee flavored
2 chocolate-covered hard
   toffee candy bars,
   chopped coarsely

½ cup liqueur such as
   Kahlua or Creme de Cacao

For each dessert, scoop 3/4 cup ice cream into a serving dish, sprinkle with 2 tablespoons chopped toffee and pour over 1½ tablespoons liqueur. Serve immediately.

Serves 4

Jean Whitaker

Bananas Foster

1 tablespoon butter
2 tablespoons brown sugar
1 ripe banana, peeled and
   sliced lengthwise

Dash cinnamon
½ ounce banana liqueur
1 ounce white rum

Melt butter in chafing dish. Add brown sugar and blend well. Add banana and sauté. Sprinkle with cinnamon. Pour over banana liqueur and rum, ignite, basting banana with flaming liquid. Serve when flame dies out.

Serves 1

Barbara Henry

Tutti Frutti

1 13½-ounce can
   pineapple chunks
1 10-ounce can
   Mandarin oranges
1 cup shredded coconut
   (optional)
½ cup miniature marshmallows

1 cup dairy sour cream
2 bananas
¼ cup almonds

Drain fruits well Combine all ingredients except last two and chill in refrigerator for 24 hours. Add bananas and nuts just before serving.

Serves 6

Beth Thatcher

Cape Cod Blueberry Grunt

2 cups blueberries, fresh
   or frozen
½ cup sugar
1 cup water

1 cup sifted flour
2 teaspoon baking powder
¼ teaspoon salt
½ cup milk

In a large saucepan, heat blueberries, sugar and water. Cover for 10 minutes or until berries thaw and sugar dissolves. Sift flour, baking powder and salt together into a bowl. Add milk and stir quickly to form a dough. Drop from spoon like small dumplings into the boiling sauce. Cook 10 minutes with cover off; then 10 minutes covered. Serve with cream, hard sauce, brandy sauce or ice cream. This is a popular dessert with blueberry pickers in Martha's Vineyard, Massachusetts. It's rather filling, hence the term "grunt."

Serves 4

Mrs. Kenneth McCabe

Empanadas de Camote Con Fina
(Sweet Potato Dessert Turnovers)

1 3-ounce package
   cream cheese
1 cube butter
1 cup sifted flour
½ cup mashed sweet potatoes
   (may be canned)

¼ cup drained crushed
   pineapple
¼ cup sugar
¼ teaspoon salt
¼ cup flaked coconut

Mix cream cheese, butter and flour until it holds together. Divide dough in half (works easier if chilled) and roll to regular thinness. Cut into 3-inch circles. Mix remaining ingredients together well. Put a teaspoon of filling on half of pastry circle. Fold pastry over to make a half-moon. Press edges together with tines of fork. Bake on cookie sheet 15 minutes in a 375 degree oven.

Excellent for teas, coffees or hand eaten dessert. Tastes like pineapple apricot filling. Especially good with spiced tea in the fall.

Yield: 20 turnovers

Punky Robbe

Sherry Dessert

1 cup sherry
1 10-ounce package
  marshmallows

2 cups vanilla wafers,
  crushed
½ pint whipping cream,
  whipped

Cover bottom of 7½ x 11½ inch pan with vanilla wafers. In double boiler melt marshmallows and sherry. Cool until thick; fold in whipped cream. Pour over wafer crumbs; sprinkle a few crumbs over top. Serve with a dot of whipped cream. Very rich—make small servings.

Serves 10-15   *Terry Fonda*

Hot Curried Fruit

1 can pears
1 small jar maraschino
  cherries
1 can peaches
1 can apricots
2 cans pineapple chunks

1 can Mandarin oranges
½ cup melted butter
3/4 cup dark brown sugar
4 scant teaspoons
  curry powder

Drain fruit (liquid makes good jello with lemon, orange or lime). Put in Dutch oven. Cover with mixture of butter, brown sugar, and curry powder. Bake uncovered at 325 degrees for 30 minutes. Serve in place of vegetable.

Mrs. Frank Beattie

Frozen Fruit

2 cups sugar
1 cup water
2 boxes frozen strawberries

1 large can
  crushed pineapple
4 bananas, diced
4 cups apricot nectar

Boil sugar and water and let cool slightly. Put strawberries, pineapple, bananas in large bowl. Mix and add additional fruit such as peaches, blueberries, if desired. Add apricot nectar. Freeze in cups. Use plastic old fashioned glasses, sauce dishes or parfait glasses.

Yield: 15-20 servings   *Virginia Ann Porr*

257

Quick and Easy Fruit Flan
(Modified French)

1 package frozen sugar cookie mix, thawed
4 tablespoons apricot preserves, mixed with 2 tablespoons water
1 package vanilla pudding mix
Pinch mace
2 bananas, thinly sliced
1 cup blueberries, canned or frozen, or
   1 cup raspberries, canned or frozen, well drained
1 cup green grapes, fresh or canned, well drained
1 cup peaches, sliced, canned or frozen, well drained
2 tablespoons Cointreau or Triple Sec

Cook vanilla pudding mix according to instructions. Chill. Generously grease a flan pan or 9-inch cake pan having straight sides. Roll out the cookie mix and pat into pan, making sure the mix reaches the rim evenly. Bake according to instructions. Cool and carefully remove from pan. The success of this crust depends on how thick you have made it and how crusty it is. Keep it on the soft side of crisp. Using a pastry brush, generously brush on apricot mix, both inside and out, on the shell. Add the cooled vanilla pudding. Decorate with the various fruits. Brush again with apricot mix and dash on Cointreau. Chill for at least one hour.

When decorating this flan, you can let your imagination go wild and use the different colors of the fruits in different patterns. I prefer stripes, putting the bananas down the middle and then going out either side with different fruits. The French touch here is using the apricot preserves, since this is a favorite trick of French pastry cooks. If you want to make it more sophisticated, add a touch more Cointreau or if you use orange slices, a touch of Grand Marnier.

Serves 8   *Mrs. Jack Wolther*

Lemon Schaum Torte

5 egg whites, beaten stiff
¼ teaspoon cream of tartar
¼ teaspoon salt
1½ cups fine sugar
1½ teaspoons vanilla
1 cup sugar

1/8 teaspoon salt
2 tablespoons butter
6 egg yolks
Juice of 2 lemons
2 teaspoons grated
   lemon rind
1 cup heavy cream, whipped

Beat egg whites stiff, add cream of tartar and salt. Beat in 1½ cups sugar, a little at a time; add vanilla. Spread in well-greased 8 x 12 inch pan. Preheat oven to 425 degrees for 20 minutes. Put pan in oven, *shut off heat* immediately, *do not open oven* for 10 hours (overnight).

For filling, beat egg yolks; add sugar, salt, lemon juice, lemon rind and butter. Cook in double boiler until very thick. Cool. Fold in whipped cream. Spread over torte. Refrigerate for 12 hours. Can be frozen. Great to make ahead for bridge club.

Jan Messman

Fresh Frozen Lemon Tarts

3 eggs, separated
¼ cup fresh lemon juice,
   strained
2/3 cup sugar
¼ teaspoon salt

1 teaspoon grated lemon rind
1 teaspoon vanilla
½ cup finely crushed vanilla
   wafer crumbs
1 cup heavy cream, whipped

In a double boiler combine well beaten egg yolks, lemon juice, sugar and salt. Cook over hot, not boiling, water until custard coats a metal spoon. Chill. Stir in rind and vanilla. Beat egg whites until stiff, fold into custard. Fold in whipped cream. Place #5 fluted paper baking cups in 2½ inch muffin tins. Sprinkle bottom of each cup with 1 teaspoon crumbs, fill with custard mixture, sprinkle remaining crumbs over top. Freeze until firm. Remove from paper cups before serving.

Yield: 12-16 tarts

Rheuanna Kelly

Lemon Soufflé

8 eggs
2 cups sugar

2 lemons
¼ teaspoon salt

Separate eggs; beat yolks until thick and lemon-colored. Add sugar slowly. Add salt to egg whites and beat until stiff, but not dry. Add juice of lemons and rind of one lemon to yolks. Fold in whites and put in a 3-quart casserole, ungreased. Place casserole in a pan of hot water and bake at 325 degrees for 60 minutes. Top with whipped cream.

Serves 10

Addie Cole

Lemon Cream Mold

1 package lemon
  flavored gelatin (3-ounce)
½ teaspoon plain gelatin
½ cup sugar
1/8 teaspoon salt

1 6-ounce can frozen
  lemonade concentrate
1 cup heavy cream

(Seasonal fruit such as watermelon or cantaloupe balls, strawberries, etc. may be used if desired.)

Blend gelatin, sugar and salt in mixing bowl. Add boiling water and stir until dissolved. Stir in lemonade concentrate. Chill until jelly-like consistency. In a chilled bowl, whip cream until soft peaks form. Blend into lemon mixture until color and taste of lemon gets through whipped cream (I use a hand mixer to blend together). Pour into 1 quart mold that has been rinsed with cold water. Unmold on chilled tray. Fill center with fruit. Garnish with parsley or mint.

Sherry Clarkin

Lemon Custard

1 cup sugar
4 tablespoons flour
1/8 teaspoon salt
2 tablespoons butter

3 egg yolks, well beaten
1½ cups milk
3 egg whites, stiffly beaten
5 tablespoons lemon juice

Combine sugar, flour, salt, butter and lemon juice. Add to egg yolks and milk. Mix well. Fold in egg whites and put into buttered custard cups. Set cups in pan of hot water and bake 45 minutes at 325 degrees.

Debi Robbe

Vanilla Wafer Dessert

3/4 pound vanilla wafers
½ cup butter
2 eggs, beaten
1 cup powdered sugar, sifted
½ pint whipping cream

1 cup crushed pineapple
   pineapple, drained
½ cup chopped
   walnuts or pecans
Non-dairy whipped cream
Maraschino cherries

Roll vanilla wafers in plastic bag until fine. Spread half of crumbs in a buttered and floured pyrex baking dish about 6 x 8 inches in size. Cream butter and powdered sugar, add eggs. Spread mixture over wafers. Whip cream and fold in well-drained crushed pineapple. Spread on top of other mixture and cover with remaining half of wafers. Sprinkle top with chopped nuts and refrigerate overnight. Cut in squares and serve with whipped cream topping and maraschino cherry.

Serves 12

Bev Hurley

Pots de Creme

3/4 cup milk,
   scalded to boiling
1 package semi-sweet
   chocolate bits

1 egg
1 tablespoon sugar
1 teaspoon vanilla
Pinch of salt

Heat milk to boiling. Put all other ingredients in blender, add hot milk. Blend on low speed for 1 minute. Pour into cremes and and chill several hours. Top with whipped cream, if desired.

Serves 6

Petie Pryor

Dreamy Dessert

2 cups graham
  cracker crumbs
¼ cup powdered sugar
¼ pound butter, melted
1 package whipped topping,
  prepared according
  to directions

8-ounce package
  cream cheese
3/4 cup powdered sugar
½ cup nuts, crushed
1 can cherry pie filling

Mix cracker crumbs, powdered sugar and butter. Pat down hard into well buttered 8 x10 inch glass pan. Combine softened cream cheese with 3/4 cup powdered sugar until creamy. Add whipped topping and mix well; spread over graham crumbs. Pour powdered nuts (crush with rolling pin) evenly over mixture. Spread cherry pie filling over nuts. Cover with saran wrap, refrigerate for 12 hours. Keep in refrigerator until last minute before serving.

June Ebbert

Pineapple Lady Finger Frozen Dessert

3 egg yolks
Dash salt
½ cup sugar
9-ounce can crushed pineapple
2 tablespoons lemon juice

3 egg whites
2 tablespoons sugar
1 cup whipping cream, whipped
2 cups lady fingers
  or vanilla wafers

Beat egg yolks, salt and sugar together; add juice from drained pineapple and the lemon juice; cook over hot water until mixture coats spoon. Add crushed pineapple and let mixture cool. Beat egg whites and sugar until stiff and fold into whipped cream; fold mixture into custard. Line pan with lady fingers (crumbs) and add custard. Top with sprinkling of crumbs. Freeze.

Mrs. George Pardee

Chocolate Delight

1 6-ounce package
  chocolate bits
4 eggs, well beaten
1 cup whipping cream,
  whipped

1 teaspoon vanilla
3/4 cup nuts
Angel food cake

Melt and cool chocolate bits. Mix with eggs. Fold in cream, add vanilla and nuts. Tear cake into pieces and place in loaf cake pan. Pour sauce over cake, making sure all pieces are covered. Chill several hours.

Sue Wager

Dutch Chocolate Roll

6 eggs, separated
½ teaspoon cream of tartar
1 cup sugar
¼ teaspoon salt
4 tablespoons sifted flour

4 tablespoons
  Dutch chocolate
½ teaspoon vanilla
½ teaspoon almond extract
Powdered sugar
Whipped cream

Beat egg whites and cream of tartar until stiff. Gradually add ½ cup sugar. Beat egg yolks until lemon-colored and add to them ½ cup sugar. Sift together the salt, flour and chocolate and add to egg yolk mixture. Stir in vanilla and almond flavoring and mix. Carefully fold into egg white mixture. Bake in 10 x 15 inch pan lined with greased waxpaper at 350 degrees until done. Immediately turn upside down onto a towel sprinkled with powdered sugar. Remove waxpaper. Roll as for jelly roll and chill. Several hours later, gently unroll and fill with unsweetened whipped cream and chill again. Slice two ½ inch slices for each serving and face inward, butterfly fashion.

Eleanor Evans

Steamed Cranberry Pudding

1½ cups flour
¼ teaspoon salt
½ teaspoon baking powder
1 teaspoon soda

1 heaping cup cranberries,
   uncooked, cut in half
½ cup molasses
½ cup water

Mix dry ingredients and cranberries. Add liquids and steam in covered dish 1½ hours at 375 degrees.

Butter sauce:
½ cup butter
1 cup sugar

½ cup light cream

Melt together and serve hot over the pudding.

Mrs. B. Lenz

Cranberry Pudding with Sauce

2 cups cranberries, cut in half
1 1/3 cups flour
1 egg
2 teaspoons soda dissolved in
   1/3 cup boiling water

½ cup dark molasses
½ teaspoon vanilla
½ teaspoon salt

Mix well and place in well-oiled mold or two #2 cans. Steam 1½ hours. Must be served with plenty of sauce.

Sauce:
2 cups sugar
4 tablespoons flour
½ cup butter

1 cup cream
1 cup milk

Cook in double boiler until slightly thick. Always heat sauce before serving.

Rachel K. Curless

264

Angel Pudding

1 pint whipping cream
1 package lemon jello (3-ounce)
1 tablespoon lemon juice
1 pint milk
1 cup sugar
2 egg yolks

2 egg whites
Angel food cake
½ cup crushed pineapple
¼ cup maraschino cherries
½ cup nuts

Heat milk, egg yolks and sugar in double boiler until mixture coats a spoon. Stir in dry jello and lemon juice. Cool in refrigerator until set; beat.

Beat 2 egg whites and fold into mixture. Whip cream and fold in. Break cake into pieces; place in 9x13 pan. Top with pineapple, cherries and nuts. Pour custard mixture over cake. Refrigerate.

Serves 10-12   *Punky Robbe*

Suet Date Pudding
(Old Fashioned Christmas Pudding)

1 cup ground suet (ask butcher, usually free)
1 cup sour milk
2/3 cup sugar
1 teaspoon soda

½ teaspoon salt
2 cups flour
1 pound dates, cut
1 cup nuts (walnuts are best)

Mix all ingredients together in a large bowl. Pour into a 2-quart mold and steam 3 hours. Serve hot or cold slice topped with hard sauce.

Hard sauce:
½ cube butter
Confectioners' sugar
2 egg whites

1 jigger rum or bourbon
Nutmeg

Cream butter, work in as much sugar as it will take. Beat egg whites and add rum or bourbon. Sprinkle top with nutmeg. Serve at room temperature. Keeps for days.

Mary Ellen Rutledge

Cherry Pudding

1 egg, well beaten
1 cup sugar
1 tablespoon butter, melted
½ cup milk
1 cup flour, sifted

1 teaspoon baking powder
3 cups *sour* cherries
1 cup sugar
1 cup boiling water
Butter

Sift together flour and baking powder; add egg, sugar, butter and milk. Pour into buttered baking dish. Pour over this, cherries and sugar. Dot with pieces of butter. Pour boiling water over pudding. Bake at 325 degrees 30-35 minutes.

Mrs. Whitney Newton

Farley's Plum Pudding

½ pound beef suet, grated
¼ ounce jar
    candied citron
1 4-ounce jar
    candied lemon peel
1 4-ounce jar
    candied orange peel
2½ cups pared,
    chopped apples
5 egg yolks, beaten
1 1/3 cups sugar
1 cup light molasses
1 tablespoon grated
    lemon peel
3/4 cup dark raisins,
    chopped
3/4 cup currants
2½ cups sifted cake flour
2 cups sifted all-purpose flour

¼ cup cinnamon
1 tablespoon ground cloves
1 tablespoon ground ginger
1 tablespoon salt
3/4 teaspoon mace
3/4 teaspoon nutmeg
Dash allspice
3/4 teaspoon baking soda
4 cups fresh white
    bread crumbs
3/4 cup dark brown
    sugar, packed
½ cup milk
2 tablespoons lemon juice
6 tablespoons brandy

Grease well two 2-quart pudding molds with tight fitting covers. In very large bowl, combine suet, raisins, currants, the peels and citron. Mix well. Sift flour with baking soda and spices. Add to fruit mixture along with bread crumbs; toss to mix well. With rotary beater beat eggs until foamy. Beat in sugar, milk, lemon juice and ¼ cup brandy. Add egg mixture to fruit mixture; beat hard with wooden spoon to mix thoroughly, about 5 minutes. Turn into molds and cover tightly. Place each mold on a trivet in a large kettle. Pour in enough boiling water to come halfway up sides of molds. Cover kettle and boil gently 4 hours, adding water as needed. Remove molds and cool on wire rack 10 minutes. Let stand overnight. Return puddings to molds and sprinkle tops with 2 tablespoons brandy. Cover, return to kettle and re-steam for 3 hours. Remove molds to wire rack. Let puddings age in refrigerator for several weeks with an occasional addition of brandy. Resteam for two hours and serve warm with brandy hard sauce. Just before serving, sprinkle with brandy and serve flaming.

Brandy hard sauce:

1/3 cup soft butter	1 cup unsifted confectioners'
4 tablespoons brandy	sugar

In small bowl, cream butter until light with electric mixer. Add brandy and sugar. Beat until fluffy and smooth.

Yield: 40 servings   *Mrs. Tom Farley*

Date Pudding

1 cup nuts, chopped	1½ teaspoons baking powder
1 cup dates, chopped	½ cup milk
1 cup sugar	2 egg whites, whipped stiff
¼ cup flour	

Mix all dry ingredients, add milk, fold in eggs. Pour into greased 8 x 10 inch baking dish. Set in pan of water (just a little in bottom of pan to keep pudding from burning.) Bake 50 minutes at 350 degrees. Take out of water for last 10 minutes. Serve with whipped cream topping.

Good for Thanksgiving or Christmas—very, very rich.

Mrs. Nora Carlisle

Pineapple and Orange Pudding

3/4 cup frozen orange
   juice concentrate
¼ cup water
1 cup pineapple juice

40-50 large marshmallows
1 pint whipping cream,
   whipped

Heat juices and water. Pour over marshmallows. Melt marshmallows completely; let stand until jellied. Fold in half of the whipped cream and put in mold. Chill. Frost with remaining sweetened whipped cream. Decorate with fruit, fresh or frozen (do not used pineapple). If peaches are used to decorate, crush some additional fruit and add a little sugar and Cointreau and pass as a sauce. Same can be done with strawberries. The taste and texture are improved if pudding is frozen before it is iced with whipped cream, then served semi-frozen.

Mrs. Whitney Newton

Apple Pudding Dessert

½ cup margarine
1 cup sugar
1 egg
2½ cups apples, peeled
   and chopped
1¼ cup sifted flour

1 teaspoon cinnamon
1 teaspoon nutmeg
1 teaspoon soda
Dash salt
½ cup nuts, chopped

Combine margarine, sugar and egg; beat until fluffy. Add remaining ingredients. Bake in greased 8 x 8 inch square pan for 45 minutes in 350 degree oven. Serve with lemon sauce or whipped cream.

Mrs. Clyde Green

Cherries Jubilee

1 small can bing cherries
1½ ounces brandy
1½ ounces Kirsch

3/4 ounce Cointreau
  or Triple Sec
Vanilla ice cream

Drain 3/4 of the juice from cherries and discard. Put the cherries and remaining juice in a bowl and add brandy, Kirsch and Cointreau. Allow to marinate 3-4 hours.

Just before serving, warm the cherries and the marinade. Serve large individual scoops of ice cream in deep dishes (these can be kept in freezer). Put 1-ounce of brandy in a spoon (not silver), warm it, light it and ignite the cherry mixture. Mix while blazing and ladle cherries and juice over ice cream.

Mary Ann Sturgeon

Creme de Menthe Ice Cream

½ gallon vanilla ice cream
6 jiggers creme de menthe

3 jiggers creme de cacao
2 jiggers bourbon

Soften ice cream 45-60 minutes. Mix ingredients with electric mixer to taste. Freeze in plastic cups or dishes and do not remove from freezer until ready to serve.

Yield: about 21 3-ounce servings   *Dagmar Borkowitz*

Fresh Peach Ice Cream

8 large, ripe peaches
4 lemons

4 cups sugar
1 quart half and half
  (heavier cream if desired)

Peel peaches, put through blender. Pour into large bowl, squeeze juice from lemons and add to peaches. Add sugar and stir until sugar is dissolved. Refrigerate until ready to make ice cream. Pour peach mixture into freezer, add half and half, let freezer run 2 minutes before adding ice. Then add layer of ice, layer of salt, repeat until motor labors. Drain all water and pack with ice and salt until ready to serve.

Yield: 1 gallon   *Jeanette Dincler*

Fresh Lemon Ice Cream

1 cup whipping cream
1 egg
1½ cups sugar
1/3 cup lemon juice

2¼ teaspoons lemon peel
Dash salt
1 1/3 cups milk

In a large bowl combine whipping cream and egg, beating until blended. Add sugar slowly as you continue to beat until mixture is almost stiff. Beat lemon juice, lemon peel and salt into mixture. Stir in milk and immediately turn into large refrigerator tray or 8-inch square pan.

Freeze overnight or at least 5 hours. Melts fast.

Delicious topped with blueberries.

Serves 8

Jean Whitaker

Homemade Ice Cream

1 quart half and half
3/4 cup sugar

Dash salt
2 tablespoons vanilla

Place ingredients in ice cream freezer and let mix about 20-25 minutes or until the mixer's motor seems to labor. Remove paddle.

Serves 6

Marie Longfield

Mincemeat Ice Cream Dessert

11½ cups graham
  cracker crumbs
1/3 cup sugar
½ cup melted butter

1 cup mincemeat
1 quart vanilla ice cream

Mix together cracker crumbs, sugar and butter. Press firmly into greased 9-inch pie pan. Chill for 45 minutes.

Stir mincement into softened ice cream. Place mixture in freezer until almost firm and remove and place in pie shell. Wrap in foil and freeze. Remove from freezer 15 minutes before serving.

6-8 servings

Gwen Redwine

270

Almond Sauce

1 cube butter
1 cup sugar
½ cup whipping cream

1 tablespoon almond extract
1 tablespoon Karo

Melt butter in top of double boiler. Add sugar and whipping cream and cook until sugar dissolves. Add almond extract and Karo. Serve hot over cake and add almonds just before serving.

Slivered almonds can be toasted.

Mu Anton

Berry Sauce

1 cup berries (blue, black, raspberry)
½ cup water
1/3 cup sugar

1 teaspoon cornstarch
1 teaspoon butter
2 tablespoons lemon juice
1/8 teaspoon salt

Boil half the berries in the water for several minutes (3-4). Mix sugar, cornstarch, and salt together and stir into hot berries. Cook and stir until thick and clear. Add the rest of the berries and simmer a few minutes. Stir in butter and lemon juice. Serve warm or cold over pancakes, ice cream or sponge cake.

Note: May be frozen and brought out in early evening before guests arrive and warmed slightly before serving.

Pat Siemsen

Hot Fudge Sauce

1 cup chocolate chips
   (1 6-ounce package)
2 cups sifted powdered sugar

1 teaspoon vanilla
½ cup butter
1 1/3 cups evaporated milk

Melt chocolate chips and butter. Add sugar and milk, blending well. Stirring constantly, bring to a boil and cook about 8 minutes. Add vanilla. Serve sauce warm.

Yield 2 2/3 cups

Colleen Von Bermuth

271

Hot Fudge Sauce

1 cup sugar
1/3 cup cocoa
2 tablespoons flour
1/4 teaspoon salt

1 cup boiling water
1 tablespoon butter or
   margarine
1/2 teaspoon vanilla

Place first four ingredients in sauce pan—mix. Add next two ingredients, stir and place over low heat stirring until thickened. Remove from heat. Add vanilla and stir.

Serve hot—store covered in refrigerator—reheat to use but also is delicious served cold.

This is a great last-minute dessert—can be fixed in a jiffy while finishing dinner. Also good for company in fancy parfait glass served with cookies. This old recipe, some 50 years old, is going around the world by giving it to friends and acquaintances.

Serves 8 generously   *Nancy T. Bunce*

Creamy Chocolate Sauce

1 cup sugar
2 cups boiling water
5 tablespoons cocoa

Dash of salt
1 teaspoon vanilla
3 tablespoons butter
   or margarine

Mix well in large pan: sugar, boiling water, cocoa and salt. Cook over medium high heat for 15 minutes, stirring frequently. (If thinner sauce is desired, reduce cooking time by 2 or 3 minutes). Remove from heat, add vanilla and butter. Stir well. Sauce may be served either hot or cold over ice cream, angel food cake, etc.

Recipe is original and may be doubled if desired and sauce can be stored in refrigerator in covered container.

                                   Mrs. F. B. Fimple

Chocolate Fondue Sauce

6 squares unsweetened
   chocolate
1 cup light cream
1½ cups sugar

½ cup butter
1/8 teaspoon salt
2 teaspoons vanilla

Heat all ingredients, except vanilla, stirring occasionally until melted. Continue cooking until thickened. Add vanilla.

Many foods may be used to dip into fondue. Here are my favorites:

Mandarin oranges
Bananas
Pears
Pineapple
Dates
Large salted nuts

Popcorn
Small marshmallows
Angel food cake
Sponge cake
Pound cake (best cake to dip)
Mini cream puffs
Mini donuts or holes

I usually have a dish of powdered sugar and chopped nuts to roll food in after dipping in chocolate.

Punky Robbe

cakes and frostings

The thirties and forties saw the advent of improved gas ranges which surely delighted the cake maker, for cakes demand especially perfect results, whether for birthday party or favorite dessert.

Apple Walnut Pan Cake

1 cup apple pie filling
2 cups flour
1 cup sugar
1½ teaspoons soda
1 teaspoon salt
2 eggs, beaten
1 teaspoon vanilla
2/3 cup oil
3/4 cup walnuts

Sour Cream Topping:
1 cup sugar
½ cup sour cream
½ teaspoon soda

Spread pie filling in bottom of 9 x 13-inch pan. Combine flour, sugar, soda and salt and sprinkle over pie filling. In a bowl combine eggs, vanilla, oil and ½ cup of nuts. Mix well. Pour over ingredients in pan; stir only until blended. Bake at 350 degrees for 40 to 45 minutes, until it springs back in center when lightly touched. Prick warm cake with fork and pour hot topping over. Sprinkle with rest of nuts. Serve warm or cold.

To prepare topping, combine sugar, sour cream and soda in a saucepan. Bring to a boil, stirring constantly.

Lora Smith

Angel Food Cake

1 cup sifted flour
1 cup sugar less 1½ teaspoons
1 3/4 cups egg whites
1½ teaspoons cream of tartar
½ teaspoon salt
½ cup sugar
½ teaspoon vanilla
½ teaspoon almond extract

Have egg whites at room temperature. Beat egg whites and salt until frothy. Add cream of tartar and continue beating until whites come to a peak. Add sugar, a tablespoon at a time, beating with a whip until all the sugar is used up. (1 cup less 1½ teaspoons). Next, sift flour and ½ cup sugar together four times. Fold lightly into egg white mixture. Add vanilla and almond extract. Pour into cold, ungreased angel cake pan. Bake for 30 to 35 minutes in pre-heated 375 degree oven. Cool upside-down.

Angie Jersin

Applecake and Sauce

2 cups sugar
2 eggs
1¼ cups vegetable oil
3 cups flour
3 large apples, chopped fine
1 teaspoon salt
1 teaspoon soda
1 teaspoon vanilla
1 teaspoon cinnamon

Sauce:
½ cup butter
½ cup evaporated milk
½ cup brown sugar
½ cup white sugar

Beat together sugar, oil, eggs and vanilla. Add sifted dry ingredients. Stir in apples. (Dough is quite stiff). Bake in 9 x 13-inch pan, 45 to 50 minutes at 350 degrees. Serve warm with the sauce poured over. Prepare sauce in top of double boiler, cooking until slightly thick. This cake may be frozen before adding sauce.

Nancy Bonforte

Banana Cupcakes

2 cups flour
1 teaspoon salt
1 teaspoon baking powder
1 teaspoon soda
1 cube butter
1 cup brown sugar
  (firmly packed)

1 teaspoon vanilla
2 eggs
4 small or 3 large
  overripe bananas
¼ cup buttermilk
¼ cup chopped nuts (optional)

Sift together the flour, salt, baking powder and soda. Cream the butter, brown sugar and vanilla. Add eggs and beat until light and fluffy. Add bananas, mashed well, and buttermilk. Add dry ingredients and mix well; add nuts if desired. If teflon cupcake pans are used, grease lightly; if aluminum, grease and dust with flour. Fill 2/3 full and bake for 25 minutes at 350 degrees. Frost with favorite icing.

Yield: 18 cupcakes

Clare May Myers

Macaroon Cupcakes

6 tablespoons sifted
  cake flour
½ teaspoon baking powder
1 3/4 cups cookie coconut
2/3 cup sugar
2 large egg whites
½ teaspoon almond extract

Glaze:
1 cup sifted powdered sugar
2 teaspoons lemon juice
1/8 teaspoon grated
  lemon rind
2-4 teaspoons milk

Sift flour and baking powder together onto waxed paper. In top of double boiler combine coconut, 1/3 cup sugar and 1 egg white. Place over boiling water and stir until heated—about 5 minutes. Remove from hot water; add flour and extract and mix well. In a small mixing bowl, beat the remaining egg white until foamy. Gradually beat in remaining 1/3 cup sugar; continue beating until mixture forms peaks that tilt. Fold into coconut mixture. Pour into 8 medium or 15 small baking cups, filling each to the top. (Paper cups may be used in muffin tins if foil cups cannot be found.) Place on cookie sheet and bake at 325 degrees for about 25 minutes.

To prepare glaze, combine all ingredients and beat until right consistency to spread thinly.

Jane Robbe

Crow's Nest Surprise

1 can fruit cocktail
  (number 303 size)
1 cup sugar
1½ cups flour
1 teaspoon soda

½ teaspoon salt
1 egg
½ cup brown sugar
½ cup chopped pecans

Mix together the fruit cocktail, sugar, flour, soda, salt and egg. Pour into greased and floured 9 by 13½-inch pan. Spread brown sugar and pecans over top. Bake for 25 minutes at 350 degrees, reduce heat to 310 degrees and bake for 15 minutes longer. Serve with whipped cream or ice cream.

Helen C. White

Strawberry Glaze for Cheesecake

2 to 3 cups fresh or
    frozen strawberries
1 cup water

1½ teaspoons cornstarch
½ cup sugar

Crush 1 cup berries; add water and cook for 2 minutes. Mix cornstarch with sugar and stir into hot berry mixture. Cook gently until clear, stirring constantly. Cool slightly. Place remaining berries on top of cheese cake and pour glaze over.

Marie Peake

Cheesecake

Crust:

1 cup flour
¼ cup sugar
1 teaspoon grated lemon peel

½ cup butter
1 egg yolk
½ teaspoon vanilla

Combine flour, sugar and lemon peel. Cut in butter until mixture is crumbly. Blend egg yolk and vanilla. Pat 1/3 of dough on bottom of 9-inch springform pan, sides removed. Bake at 400 degrees about 6 minutes. Cool sides of pan and attach to bottom. Pat remaining dough evenly on sides 2 inches high.

Cheese Filling:

5 8-ounce packages
    cream cheese
1 3/4 cups sugar
3 tablespoons flour
Grated rind of one lemon

Grated rind of ½ orange
5 whole eggs
2 egg yolks
¼ cup heavy cream

With ingredients at room temperature, beat cheese until fluffy. Mix sugar and flour; gradually mix into cheese. Add grated rinds. Add eggs and egg yolks one at a time, beating well after each. Fold in cream. Turn into crust and bake in 500 degree oven for 8 minutes. Reduce heat to 200 degrees and bake one hour longer. Remove from oven and cool away from drafts. Refrigerate until cold; remove sides of pan and place on serving plate. Top with thickened, glazed fruit.

Lana Hunter

Cheese Cake

1½ cups graham cracker crumbs (plain or cinnamon)
¼ cup melted butter or margarine
1 8-ounce package cream cheese
½ cup sugar
1 tablespoon lemon juice
½ teaspoon vanilla
2 eggs
Dash of salt

Combine crumbs and melted butter; press into 8-inch pie plate. In mixer, beat the cream cheese until fluffy. Gradually blend in sugar, lemon juice, vanilla and salt. Add eggs, one at a time, beating well after each. Pour filling into crust and bake at 325 degrees for 25 to 30 minutes or until set.

Topping:
1 cup dairy sour cream
2 tablespoons sugar
½ teaspoon vanilla

Combine and spoon over top of pie. Chill several hours. Garnish with fresh strawberries.

Double recipe if using a 10-inch pie plate or springform pan.

Catherine Burick

Spice Cake

3 cups cake flour
1½ teaspoons soda
1 teaspoon baking powder
½ teaspoon cloves
¼ teaspoon ginger
2 teaspoons nutmeg
1 teaspoon cinnamon
2 cups brown sugar
1 cup shortening
1¼ cups buttermilk
1¼ cups hot (not boiling) water
3 eggs

Cream shortening and sugar. Sift dry ingredients together until thoroughly mixed, then add buttermilk, hot water and eggs. Mix all together and pour into greased 9 by 13-inch pan or two 9-inch pans. Bake at 350 degrees for 40 minutes.

LeAnn Long

Graham Cracker Cake

3 egg yolks
1 cup sugar
1 cup coconut
1 cup pecans
1 teaspoon vanilla
Pinch of salt

½ cup margarine
  or butter
24 graham crackers
  (2 cups crumbs)
1 cup milk
1 teaspoon baking powder
3 egg whites

Crush crackers fine and add dry ingredients. Add remaining ingredients except egg whites and mix well. Beat egg whites and fold into mixture. Pour into greased, floured 9 by 13-inch pan. Bake at 350 degrees for 35 to 40 minutes.

Icing:
½ cup brown sugar
3 tablespoons corn syrup
1 or 2 tablespoons butter

1 cup sugar
½ cup cream

Cook about 1½ to 2 minutes after icing starts to boil. Let cool and beat until thick. Spread over top of cake.

Mrs. James Utt

Williams' Family Fruitcake

3½ cups sugar
3/4 pound butter
10 eggs
1½ quarts self-rising flour
2 tablespoons vanilla
½ tablespoon cinnamon
1 large can sliced pineapple,
  drained and diced (save juice)
1 pound dates, diced
1 pound prunes, diced

1½ quarts pecans, walnuts
  and Brazil nuts
2 pounds raisins
¼ pound shredded coconut
½ pound Maraschino
  cherries, diced
1 small package figs, diced
2 cups flour
1 cup bourbon
Pineapple juice

Dredge fruit and nuts in 2 cups flour. Mix all ingredients in roaster or large pan, adding pineapple juice until mixture is liquid. Because the recipe is old, the baker needs to judge this liquid addition. If batter is too stiff, the cake isn't moist. Bake at 300 degrees for 3 to 4 hours. A pan of water set in the oven facilitates even baking. Remove from pans; wrap in cheesecloth and soak in rum or bourbon. Best made early in November—these keep six months or more.

Note: Do not substitute! Makes an elegant, moist, dark cake.

Makes 2 large tube pans plus 1 loaf   *Mrs. Henry Williams*

Oatmeal Cake

1¼ cups boiling water	2 eggs
1 cup quick oatmeal	1½ cups flour
½ cup soft butter	1 teaspoon soda
1 cup granulated sugar	½ teaspoon salt
1 cup brown sugar, packed	3/4 teaspoon cinnamon
1 teaspoon vanilla	¼ teaspoon nutmeg

Pour boiling water over oatmeal and let stand 20 minutes. Beat butter until creamy. Gradually add sugars, beating until fluffy. Blend in vanilla and eggs; stir in oatmeal. Sift flour, soda, salt and spices together and add, mixing well. Pour into greased and floured 9-inch square pan. Bake at 350 degrees for 50 to 55 minutes. Do not remove from pan.

Icing:

¼ cup melted butter or margarine	1/3 cup chopped nuts
½ cup brown sugar	3/4 cup coconut
3 tablespoons half and half	

Mix and spread over cake. Place under broiler until it bubbles.

Mo Shomaker

Prune Cake

Icing:

4 eggs, well beaten
2 cups sugar
1 cup oil
1 teaspoon soda
1 cup buttermilk
2 cups sifted flour
1 teaspoon cloves
1 teaspoon nutmeg
1 teaspoon cinnamon
Dash of salt
1 cup cooked prunes,
   chopped fine
1 cup pecans

½ cup buttermilk
¼ teaspoon soda
1 cup sugar
½ cube butter
2 teaspoons vanilla

Dissolve soda in buttermilk; combine with well beaten eggs, sugar and oil. Sift dry ingredients and add, mixing well. Stir in chopped prunes and pecans. Bake in tube or loaf pan at 325 degrees for one hour.

To prepare icing, boil ingredients for one minute. Spread on cool cake, cutting slits in cake so frosting can soak in.

Jeanette Fredregill

Mud Pie Cake

1½ cups sifted flour
3 tablespoons cocoa
1 teaspoon soda
1 cup sugar
½ teaspoon salt

5 tablespoons cooking oil
1 tablespoon vinegar
1 teaspoon vanilla
1 cup water

Put all dry ingredients into sifter (flour, cocoa, soda, sugar and salt) and sift directly into greased square pan. Make three grooves or holes. Into one pour the oil, into the next the vinegar, and into the last the vanilla. Over all of it pour the water. Don't you feel ridiculous now? Don't panic! Just stir until it's nearly smooth and you can't see the flour. Bake at 350 degrees for 30 minutes.

Note: Great for the kids to bake.

Louise Wertz

Carrot Cake

3 cups grated carrots*
2 cups sifted flour
2 cups sugar
2 teaspoons soda
4 eggs
1¼ cups vegetable oil
1 teaspoon salt
3 teaspoons cinnamon

Icing:
1 8-ounce package cream cheese
1 cube margarine
1 box powdered sugar
2 teaspoons vanilla
1 cup chopped pecans

Beat together eggs, sugar and oil. Add carrots. *(These may be grated in blender or meat grinder.) Add flour, soda, salt and cinnamon. Beat well. Bake in 350 degree oven for 40 to 45 minutes.

To prepare icing, cream together cream cheese and margarine. Add remaining ingredients and beat until fluffy. This is enough frosting for a layer cake; half a recipe will frost a sheet cake.

Isabel Peryatel

Pumpkin Cake

½ cup shortening
1¼ cups sugar
2 eggs or 2 yolks and 1 egg
    (save 2 whites for frosting)
2 cups sifted flour
3 teaspoons baking powder
½ teaspoon salt

½ teaspoon cinnamon
½ teaspoon nutmeg
½ teaspoon ginger
3/4 cup milk
½ teaspoon soda
½ cup nuts
1 cup pumpkin

Mix dry ingredients. Cream shortening; add sugar and eggs. Mix milk, pumpkin and soda. Add alternately with dry ingredients. Stir in nuts. Bake at 350 degrees for 35 minutes.

Frosting:
½ cup white sugar
1 cup brown sugar
2 egg whites
3 tablespoons cold water

Combine in top of double boiler and cook for 10 minutes, beating constantly.

Mrs. Hilda Giordano

Potica Cake

Dough:
1 cup margarine
½ cup milk
2 packages dry yeast
¼ cup lukewarm water
2 tablespoons sugar
2½ cups flour
¼ teaspoon salt
3 egg yolks

Filling:
½ cup ground nuts
½ cup chopped dates
3 tablespoons sugar
1 teaspoon vanilla
¼ cup milk
2 tablespoons honey
3 egg whites
1 cup sugar

Melt margarine in milk and cool. Mix yeast in water. Sift flour, sugar and salt together. Stir egg yolks into milk mixture. Add to flour mixture; add yeast mixture. Beat well. Cover and refrigerate overnight. Dough will be sticky.

Mix nuts, dates, sugar, vanilla, milk and honey to a paste over low heat. Cool. Beat egg whites until stiff; then gradually add one cup of sugar. Fold into paste mixture. Roll half of dough into a 20-inch square on a well-floured cloth. Spread half of filling over dough and roll as for jelly roll. Place in a well-greased angel food cake pan. Roll other half of dough and proceed as above. Place over first roll in pan. Bake at 350 degrees for 1 hour and 5 minutes. May be sprinkled with powdered sugar or spread with confectioners' frosting when cool.

Mrs. Mel Tekavec

Pound Cake

½ pound butter
½ cup shortening
3 cups sugar
5 large eggs

3 cups flour
1 teaspoon baking powder
2 teaspoons vanilla
1 cup milk

Cream shortening and add sugar. Beat in eggs, one at a time. Mix vanilla and milk. Sift dry ingredients together. Add to creamed mixture alternately with milk, adding flour last. Bake in two greased loaf pans at 350 degrees for 1 hour or until done.

Esther Donegan

Potica Cake

3/4 cup shortening
4 eggs
1½ teaspoons baking powder
1 pint sour cream
1½ cups sugar
2 cups flour
1½ teaspoons baking soda
1½ teaspoons vanilla

Filling:
¼ cup finely chopped nuts
¼ cup brown sugar
2 tablespoons flour
1 teaspoon cinnamon

Work shortening with spoon until fluffy and creamy. Add sugar gradually and beat each time until light. Add eggs one at a time and mix well. Sift dry ingredients three times and add to egg mixture, alternating with sour cream. Beat after each addition until smooth. Add vanilla last. Combine filling ingredients. Into an ungreased 9-inch tube pan, alternate layers of batter and filling. When finished, cut through with knife. Bake at 350 degrees for one hour and 15 minutes, or until done. Invert pan and cool cake thoroughly before removing.

Gwen Redwine

Gentleman's Delight

1 cup raisins
1 cup chopped pecans
2 cups boiling water
2 teaspoons soda
2 cups sugar
2 cups sifted flour
1 teaspoon allspice

1 teaspoon nutmeg
1 teaspoon salt
1 teaspoon cinnamon
4 tablespoons sweet chocolate
1 cup oil
2 eggs

Combine raisins, nuts, boiling water and soda and set aside. In a large bowl mix sugar, flour, spices and chocolate. Add blended oil and eggs and mix well. Stir in raisin and nut mixture. Pour into a 9 by 13-inch pan and bake at 350 degrees for 30 minutes.

This cake stays moist and may be frozen. You may frost with chocolate fudge icing if desired. We like it without the icing.

Frances Hensen

Orange Teacakes

2 cups and 1 tablespoon
 flour
¼ cup brown sugar
1 teaspoon cinnamon
¼ cup grated orange peel
2 teaspoons baking powder
1 teaspoon salt

¼ teaspoon soda
½ cup sugar
2/3 cup orange juice
½ cup and 1 tablespoon
 melted butter
2 eggs, unbeaten
½ cup nuts

Mix one tablespoon flour, brown sugar and cinnamon; set aside. Combine flour, baking powder, soda, salt, sugar and grated orange peel. Stir in, all at once, the orange juice, margarine, nuts and eggs. Spoon into well-greased muffin tins. Add one tablespoon of margarine to the brown sugar mixture; mix well. Sprinkle on top of each filled muffin tin. Bake at 350 degrees for 15 to 20 minutes.

Makes one dozen

Beth Thatcher

Orange Date Cake

1½ cups sugar
3/4 cup margarine
3 eggs
1 cup sour milk
1½ teaspoons soda

3 cups flour
1 cup chopped dates
1 cup chopped nuts
Grated rind of 2 oranges
Juice of 2 oranges
 and 1 cup sugar

Cream margarine and sugar; add orange rind. Add eggs one at a time and beat well. Add sifted dry ingredients alternately with sour milk. Stir in dates and nuts after dusting with flour. Pour into a greased and floured tube cake pan. Bake at 375 degrees for one hour. Mix juice and 1 cup sugar. Let stand while cake bakes, stirring occasionally. When cake is removed from oven, while still hot and in pan, spread with orange juice mixture. Using one-third at a time, rub in with spoon. Allow to cool in pan. Cake is better if allowed to stand for a day or two.

Lois Le Baron

Petite Orange Fruit Cakes

1 cup white sugar
½ cup butter or margarine
2 eggs
2 cups sifted flour
1 teaspoon soda
1 cup broken pecans
1 package dates, chopped
2/3 cup buttermilk
1 grated orange rind

Topping:
3/4 cup sugar
½ cup orange juice
1 tablespoon grated
   orange rind

Cream shortening and sugar until light. Add eggs one at a time and mix. Sift dry ingredients together; add dates and nuts to this. Alternate dry mixture with buttermilk while adding to egg mixture. Blend in orange rind. Grease miniature muffin tins and fill two-thirds full. Bake at 375 degrees for 15 to 20 minutes. While cakes are baking, bring sugar, orange juice and rind to a boil for topping. Pour slowly over cakes while they are still hot.

Makes 5 dozen   *Rheuanna Kelly*

Cinnamon Bundt Cake

1 1-pound, 3-ounce package
   yellow or white
   cake mix
1 package instant
   vanilla pudding
4 eggs

1 cup water
½ cup vegetable oil
1 teaspoon vanilla extract
¼ cup sugar
1 teaspoon cinnamon
Confectioners' sugar

Combine cake mix, pudding, eggs, water, shortening and vanilla in large mixing bowl. Beat at medium speed of electric mixer for 10 minutes. Pour into greased 10-inch tube pan or bundt pan. Combine sugar and cinnamon and sprinkle over batter. Cut through batter with a spatula or knife. Bake in 350 degree oven for 45 minutes to 1 hour or until done. Cool in pan for 10 minutes. Remove from pan and sprinkle with confectioners' sugar just before serving.

Note: Be sure to make high altitude changes recommended on box.

Mrs. Richard I. Lyle

Choco-Mock Angel Cake

1 chocolate or white
    angel food cake
2 ounces unsweetened
    chocolate
2/3 cup coffee cream
1 1/3 cups coffee
4 egg yolks
1 whole egg
3 teaspoons cornstarch

2 tablespoons cold coffee
1 cup powdered sugar
2 teaspoons rum or
    1 teaspoon vanilla
1½ cups whipping cream
1 cup powdered sugar
2 teaspoons rum
Grated sweet chocolate

Slice cake in three layers. Put chocolate, cream and coffee in top of double boiler and heat until chocolate melts. Stir until smooth. Add beaten egg and egg yolks, cornstarch, cold coffee and powdered sugar. Cook, stirring constantly, until thick enough to spread. Cool and add rum or vanilla. Spread between layers and over top and sides of cake. Whip cream; add sugar and rum and spread over cake. Sprinkle grated chocolate over top and sides. Grated nuts may be added if desired.

Mu Anton

Children's Favorite Devils Food Cake

1 cup sugar
3 squares chocolate
2 egg yolks
¼ cup milk
1 tablespoon soda
1 cup sugar minus 2
    tablespoons
3/4 cup butter minus
    1 teaspoon

2 egg yolks
2 cups sifted cake flour
1¼ cups plus 3 tablespoons
    milk
1 teaspoon vanilla
3 egg whites

In a saucepan combine 1 cup sugar, chocolate, 2 egg yolks and ¼ cup milk. Cook slowly until custard is formed. Remove from stove and add soda. Set aside to cool. Cream 1 cup minus 2 tablespoons sugar, butter and 2 egg yolks. Add alternately the sifted flour and milk. Add vanilla and custard mixture; mix well. Fold in egg whites beaten stiff but not dry. Pour into two 9 by 9-inch pans. Bake at 375 degrees for 30 minutes. Frost.

Rose Pluss

Hottenholler Whiskey Cake

½ cup butter
1 cup sugar
3 beaten eggs
1 cup flour
½ teaspoon baking powder
¼ teaspoon salt
½ teaspoon nutmeg

¼ cup milk
½ cup molasses
¼ teaspoon soda
1 pound seedless raisins
2 cups chopped pecans
¼ cup bourbon

Cream butter with sugar; add beaten eggs. Mix together flour, baking powder, salt and nutmeg, add add to butter mixture. Add milk. Next mix soda into molasses and add to batter. Stir in raisins, nuts and whiskey. Pour into greased, floured loaf pan and bake for 2 hours at 275 degrees.

Lorraine Sheets

Mary Lou's Chocolate Cake

2 cups sugar
2 cups plus 2 tablespoons
   flour
1 cube butter
1¼ cups water
½ cup oil
4 tablespoons cocoa
2 eggs
1 teaspoon soda
½ cup buttermilk
1 teaspoon cinnamon
1 teaspoon salt
1 teaspoon vanilla

Frosting:
1 cube butter
4 tablespoons cocoa
6 tablespoons milk
1 cup nuts, chopped
1 box powdered sugar
1 teaspoon vanilla

Sift flour and sugar together. In pan bring to boil butter, water, cocoa and oil. Pour over dry ingredients, stir well. Add slightly beaten eggs, soda, buttermilk, cinnamon, salt and vanilla. Mix well and pour into well-greased cookie sheet (approximately 11 x 17 x 1 inch). Preheat oven to 425 degrees, reduce to 400 degrees and bake for 20 minutes. While cake is baking, make frosting. Bring to boil butter, cocoa and milk. Remove from heat. Add powdered sugar, mix well. Add vanilla and nuts. Pour hot frosting over hot cake.

Sally Boucher

Chocolate Chip Cake

1 cup chopped dates
1 cup plus 2 tablespoons
   boiling water
1 cup margarine
3/4 cup sugar
2 eggs
1 tablespoon vanilla

1 3/4 cups sifted flour
2 tablespoons cocoa
2 teaspoons soda
½ teaspoon salt
1 cup chopped nuts
1 6-ounce package
   chocolate chips

Cover chopped dates with boiling water and let stand. Cream margarine, sugar, eggs and vanilla. Add dry ingredients, then date mixture. Pour into greased 9 x 13-inch pan. Sprinkle nuts and chocolate chips over top. Bake at 350 degrees for 30 to 35 minutes.

Joan Clementi

Spicy Apple Cake

3¼ cups sifted flour
2½ cups sugar
3/4 cup butter or margarine
3 eggs
2 teaspoons baking soda

1¼ teaspoons salt
½ teaspoon ground nutmeg
½ teaspoon cinnamon
5 cups pared, chopped apples
1½ cups chopped walnuts

Heat oven to 350 degrees. Combine flour, sugar, shortening, eggs, soda, salt, nutmeg and cinnamon in large mixing bowl. Mix at low speed until thoroughly blended (mixture is very dry). Add apples, a cup at a time, mixing well after each addition. Stir in nuts. Turn into a greased and floured bundt pan or 10-inch tube pan. Bake for 1 hour and 15 minutes. Cool in pan at least 15 minutes before removing. Spoon orange syrup* over hot or cool cake and dust with powdered sugar. Serve with whipped cream if desired.

Orange Syrup:
2 teaspoons grated orange rind   ¼ cup sugar
½ cup orange juice   ¼ cup water

Combine ingredients in saucepan; bring to boil and cook 10 minutes. Makes about ½ cup.

Serves 20 to 24

Gloria Burch

White Chocolate Cake

¼ pound white chocolate
½ cup hot water
1 cup solid shortening
1 cup sugar
1 teaspoon imitation
butter flavoring
4 large eggs, separated
1 teaspoon vanilla

2 3/4 cups sifted cake flour
1 teaspoon soda
¼ teaspoon salt
1 cup plus 2 tablespoons
buttermilk
½ to 1 cup chopped pecans
1 cup flaked coconut

Melt white chocolate in water; cool to room temperature. Cream together shortening, sugar and butter flavoring until fluffy. Add egg yolks, one at a time, beating after each addition. Blend in chocolate mixture and vanilla. Sift together twice the flour, soda and salt. Add dry ingredients alternately with buttermilk to shortening mixture. Blend in nuts and coconut. Beat egg whites until stiff and fold into batter. Pour into three greased and floured 9-inch cake pans. Bake in pre-heated 375 degree oven for about 25 minutes. Allow to cool in pans.

Courtesy Nettie's Candies

White Chocolate Icing

3/4 cup solid shortening
4 cups powdered sugar
2 egg whites, unbeaten
½ teaspoon imitation
butter flavoring
¼ cup milk

½ teaspoon almond flavoring
½ teaspoon lemon flavoring
¼ pound grated or finely
chopped white chocolate

Mix until smooth the shortening, one cup of the sugar and egg whites. Blend in flavorings and white chocolate. Gradually add remaining sugar and enough milk for spreading consistency. Tint with food coloring if desired.

Courtesy Nettie's Candies

20-Minute Chocolate Cake

2 cups sugar
2 cups flour
1 teaspoon soda
2 eggs
½ cup buttermilk
½ cup shortening
1 cube margarine
1 cup water
4 tablespoons cocoa
1 teaspoon vanilla

Frosting:
1 cube margarine
1/3 cup milk
4 tablespoons cocoa
1 pound box powdered sugar
1 cup nuts
1 teaspoon vanilla

Sift and mix sugar, flour and soda. In a saucepan, mix and bring to a boil shortening, margarine, water and cocoa. Pour over sugar and flour mixture while hot. Stir in milk, eggs and vanilla. Pour into greased 12 by 18 by 1-inch cookie sheet. Bake at 400 degrees for 20 minutes. Start preparing frosting during last 5 minutes of baking. In a saucepan mix margarine, milk and cocoa and bring to a boil. Stir in powdered sugar, nuts and vanilla. Spread on cake while it is still hot.

Serves 24

Mrs. Aletha Roberts

Angel Icing

3 tablespoons butter
3 tablespoons cornstarch
   or flour
1 cup milk
1/8 teaspoon salt

½ cup white vegetable
   shortening
½ cup and 2 tablespoons
   sugar
1 teaspoon vanilla

1. Melt butter in large sauce pan. Stir in cornstarch or flour, milk and salt. Cook as a white sauce over low heat until thickened. Cool.

2. Cream vegetable shortening and sugar until fluffy. Add vanilla.

Whip mix 2 into cooled mix 1.

Liberally frosts 2 9-inch layers or large sheet cake or large angel sponge cake.

Nancy Bunce

Caramel Topping for Cinnamon Rolls

4 cups brown sugar
2 cups cream or half and
   half or condensed milk

¼ cup butter or margarine
20 marshmallows

Cook on low heat until all ingredients are melted. Pour over cinnamon rolls before putting in oven . . . ½ cup topping for each pan of 12 rolls.

Yield: 1 quart

Esther Donegan

Butter Cream Icing

3/4 cup shortening
¼ cup butter
4 tablespoons canned milk
2 teaspoons flavoring

4 tablespoons chocolate
(for chocolate icing)
1 pound powdered sugar,
sifted

Mix all above ingredients at high speed for about 5 minutes. Add one egg. If you desire pure white frosting, add two egg whites and no yolk. Mix again for 3 to 5 minutes. Makes enough for 24 cupcakes or two layer cakes.

Can be refrigerated for 5 - 7 days. If covered tightly, will not harden.

Leah Rae Puleo

Quick Boiled Frosting

1 cup sugar
5 tablespoons water

1 tablespoon vinegar
2 egg whites

Combine sugar, water and vinegar and bring to soft-ball stage. Add to stiffly beaten egg whites, slowly until of spreading consistency.

Mrs. Frank Beattie

Fluffy White Frosting

In pan:
1/3 cup water
1 tablespoon light corn syrup

1 cup sugar
½ teaspoon salt

Stir until sugar melts over heat (must come to a full boil).

Put 1 egg white in mixer. Beat until frothy, then increase speed. Add hot mixture *very slowly,* thread like. Add 1 teaspoon vanilla or almond flavoring.

Rose Pluss

296

Mocha Chocolate Frosting

6 tablespoons cocoa
6 tablespoons hot coffee
6 tablespoons butter
  or margarine

1 teaspoon vanilla
3 cups confectioners' sugar
  (1 box)
1 egg yolk (optional)*

Combine cocoa and coffee. Add butter and vanilla. Beat until smooth. Add sugar gradually and stir until of spreading consistency.

*If you add the egg yolk, the frosting will stay fresh and soft longer.

Gay McCabe

Lemon Frosting

2 3/4 cups confectioners'
  sugar
½ teaspoon salt
1 egg
1 tablespoon light
  corn syrup

½ cup shortening
1 teaspoon vanilla
2 tablespoons lemon juice
1 tablespoon grated lemon
  peel

Mix confectioners' sugar, salt, egg. Blend in syrup. Add shortening, vanilla, lemon juice and peel. Mix until smooth and creamy.

Mrs. Dennis Feister

cookíes and candy

The "flameless" electric range brought
new possibilities to the art of cooking.
Candy-making with the advantage of electric
thermostatic control and cookies baked
with dependably even browning were
features extolled to the homemaker.

Butterhorns

2 cups sifted flour
½ pound butter
1 egg yolk
3/4 cup sour cream

1 teaspoon cinnamon
3/4 cup sugar
1 cup chopped nuts
Powdered sugar

Cut butter into flour with fingertips. Add egg yolk and sour cream. Shape into a ball and sprinkle with flour. Wrap well in waxed paper and chill several hours or overnight. Sprinkle board lightly with flour; divide dough into three parts. Roll one portion at a time, making a circle about 1/8-inch thick. Mix cinnamon, sugar and nuts together and sprinkle over top. Cut into 12 wedge-shaped sections and roll up, starting with the widest part. Place on a greased cookie sheet and bake at 370 degrees for 25 minutes. Roll in powdered sugar.

Yield: 3 dozen
Leah Rae Puleo

Brownies

4 eggs
½ cup milk
4 squares chocolate
1 cup flour
1 cup chopped dates
   (optional)

2 cups sugar
1 cube butter or margarine
1 teaspoon vanilla
Nuts

Beat eggs at high speed until very light and foamy. Gradually add sugar and beat well. Melt chocolate, shortening and milk in saucepan. Allow to cool, then add to beaten eggs and sugar. Lastly fold in nuts, flour and vanilla (and dates) and beat well. Bake for 30 minutes at 350 degrees in a 9 x 13 inch pan. Cool. Dust top with powdered sugar and cut into squares. These brownies are like cake and are very good served ala mode.

Rose Pluss

301

Banana Drop Cookies

1½ cups butter
1½ cups brown sugar
2 eggs, beaten
4 ripe bananas, mashed

3½ to 4 cups flour
2 teaspoons baking soda
1½ teaspoons baking powder

Cream butter and sugar. Add remaining ingredients, beating well after each addition. Drop by teaspoonfuls on lightly greased cookie sheet. Bake 10 minutes at 350 degrees.

Icing:
6 tablespoons brown sugar
4 tablespoons cream or whole milk
Powdered sugar

4 tablespoons butter
1½ teaspoons vanilla

Bring all ingredients to a boil in a saucepan. Add enough powdered sugar to make it frosting consistency. Spread on cooled cookies.

Helen Clayton

Banana Oatmeal Cookies

1 cup sugar
2/3 cup shortening
2 medium eggs
½ teaspoon vanilla
½ teaspoon lemon extract
3/4 cup mashed ripe bananas
½ cup semisweet chocolate bits

1½ cups quick-cooking rolled oats
2 cups sifted flour
3/4 teaspoon soda
1½ teaspoon salt
1 teaspoon baking powder
½ cup chopped nuts

Cream sugar, shortening and eggs until fluffy. Add flavoring, bananas and rolled oats. Sift dry ingredients together and add to creamed mixture. Stir in nuts and chocolate chips. Drop by tablespoonfuls onto a well greased baking sheet. Bake in a moderate oven (350 degrees) for 15 to 18 minutes.

Makes 3 dozen cookies

Pauline Genova

Brown Edge Cookies

2 cubes margarine
1½ cup sugar
Dash of salt
2 well beaten eggs

1 tablespoon vanilla
1 tablespoon almond extract
2 cups flour

Mix all ingredients, adding flour last. Stir well. Roll into marble-size balls and place on a greased or teflon cookie sheet. Press down with finger or the bottom of a glass dipped in cold water. Bake at 350 degrees about 10 or 12 minutes until edges are brown.

Edna Snyder

Carrot Cookies

1 cup shortening
1 cup sugar
2 cups flour
1 egg
1 teaspoon vanilla

1 teaspoon baking powder
½ teaspoon salt
Nuts, if desired
1 cup cooked carrots, drained well and mashed

Mix all ingredients, adding carrots last. Stir well and drop by teaspoon on greased cookie sheet. Bake at 350 degrees, not too hard.

Icing:
3 tablespoons orange juice
Grated rind of one orange

1 tablespoon margarine
1 tablespoon powdered sugar

Mix together and spread on cookies while warm.

Mrs. Nora Carlisle

Chocolate Candy Cookies

½ cup butter or
  margarine
2 cups sugar
½ cup milk
1 teaspoon vanilla
Dash salt

1½ cups oatmeal
1½ cups coconut
5 tablespoons cocoa
½ cup chopped nuts

Boil butter, sugar and milk on high for one minute, stirring constantly. Remove from stove and add all remaining ingredients. Drop by teaspoonfuls on waxed paper and cool.

Marie Peake

Chocolate Fudge Cake Brownies

1 cube butter or
   margarine
1 cup sugar
3 tablespoons cocoa

1 cup flour
2 eggs, well beaten
1 cup chopped nuts
½ teaspoon vanilla

Melt butter, add sugar and mix well. Add cocoa, flour and eggs, mixing well. Add vanilla, and nuts. Bake in a square, greased 8 by 8-inch pan at 350 degrees for 30 to 40 minutes, until straw or toothpick comes out clean. Do not overbake. Cut into squares. Roll in powdered sugar, if desired.

Mrs. F. R. Rouch

Chocolate Chip Meringues

3/4 cup sugar
2 egg whites
1/8 teaspoon salt
1/8 teaspoon cream of tartar

1 teaspoon vanilla
1 package mint chocolate
   chips
¼ cup chopped nuts

Beat egg whites, salt and cream of tartar until they form a soft peak. Add sugar gradually, continue beating until peaks are stiff. Add chips and nuts. Drop by teaspoonfuls on brown paper sack and bake in 300 degree oven for 25 minutes.

Betty Lenz

Cinnamon Raisin Bars

1 egg
2/3 cup brown sugar
1/3 cup melted butter
1 teaspoon vanilla
1 cup sifted flour
½ teaspoon baking powder
¼ teaspoon salt
2/3 cup seedless raisins

Topping:
2 tablespoons sugar
2/3 teaspoon cinnamon
1/3 cup walnuts,
   chopped fine (optional)

Beat egg. Add brown sugar, melted butter and vanilla. Sift together and add dry ingredients and raisins. Spread in greased 9 by 9 inch pan and sprinkle with topping. Bake at 350 degrees for 20 minutes. Cut in squares or bars.

Yield: 24 bars

Bev Brill

Devil's Food Drop Cookies

½ cup butter
1 cup brown sugar
1 egg
1 teaspoon vanilla
2 squares semi-sweet
  chocolate

2 cups sifted flour
½ teaspoon soda
¼ teaspoon salt
3/4 cup sour cream
½ cup chopped walnuts

Cream butter and sugar. Beat in egg, vanilla, and melted, cooled chocolate. Sift together dry ingredients; add to chocolate mixture alternately with sour cream. Mix well. Stir in nuts. Drop from teaspoon, 2 inches apart, on greased sheet. Bake 10 minutes or until done at 350 degrees.

Frosting:
¼ cup soft butter
2 tablespoons cocoa
2 teaspoons instant coffee
Dash of salt

1 cup confectioners' sugar
2 cups powdered sugar
3 tablespoons milk
1½ teaspoons vanilla

Cream butter, cocoa, instant coffee and salt. Slowly add confectioners' sugar and remaining ingredients. Beat until smooth.

Makes 4½ dozen   *Punky Robbe*

English Dainties

1 cup sifted flour
¼ pound butter

1 tablespoon sugar

Mix until crumbly and press into 9-inch square pan; bake at 370 degrees for 10 minutes.

Topping:
1 cup brown sugar
1 cup chopped nuts
½ cup coconut
½ teaspoon baking powder

2 tablespoons flour
2 eggs
3/4 teaspoon vanilla

Mix all together and spread on top of crust. Bake at 375 degrees for 20 minutes. Cool and ice with:

1 cup confectioners' sugar
2 tablespoons butter

Juice of ½ lemon

Cut into squares when cool.

Mary Frances Brummett

Italian Honey Cookies

2½ tablespoons butter
  or margarine
6 large eggs
½ cup sugar
1½ teaspoons vanilla
3 cups flour

2 teaspoons baking powder
¼ teaspoon salt
2 cups honey
Powdered sugar

Melt shortening; cool. Add well beaten eggs, sugar and vanilla; mix well. Sift the dry ingredients together into a large bowl. Make a well in the flour and pour in liquid. Knead dough until smooth. If sticky, add more flour. Divide dough into 3 parts. Roll each into a circular shape about 1/8-inch thick. (Keep other portions covered while working). Cut into strips 3 inches long and 1 inch wide. Place two strips together, twist and press ends with finger tips like a doughnut. Fry in hot deep fat. Remove and drain. Hand dip each cookie in heated honey and sprinkle with powdered sugar. (Cookies may be stored in a covered container for several weeks before dipping).

Makes 4 dozen   *Mrs. Vera Puleo*

Frosted Cashew Clusters

½ cup butter
1 cup brown sugar
1 egg
½ teaspoon vanilla
2 cups sifted flour

3/4 teaspoon baking powder
3/4 teaspoon soda
¼ teaspoon salt
1/3 cup sour cream
1 3/4 cups salted
  whole cashews

Cream butter and sugar until light. Beat in egg and vanilla. Add sifted dry ingredients alternately with sour cream. Drop by teaspoon onto greased sheets. Bake at 400 degrees for 10 minutes.

Golden Butter Icing:
½ cup butter
3 tablespoons cream

¼ teaspoon vanilla
3 cups sifted confectioners'
  sugar

Lightly brown butter, then add remaining ingredients.

Yield: 4½ dozen   *Bev Brill*

306

Spicy Ginger Snaps

3/4 cup soft shortening
1 cup sugar
1 egg
¼ cup molasses
2 cups sifted flour

2 teaspoons soda
¼ teaspoon salt
1 tablespoon cinnamon
3/4 tablespoon cloves
3/4 tablespoon ginger

Cream sugar and shortening; add next two ingredients. Sift dry ingredients together and add. Mix well. Form into balls and flatten with fork. Bake 10 to 12 minutes at 375 degrees.

Makes 4 dozen   *Angie Jersin*

Kifflins
(Gourmet Christmas Cookies)

3½ cubes unsalted butter
  or margarine
2/3 cup sifted powdered
  sugar
3/4 cup ground blanched
  almonds

4 cups all-purpose flour
Vanilla bean
1½ cups powdered sugar

Cream butter with 2/3 cup powdered sugar and almonds. Knead in the flour. Roll out on floured surface to ½ inch thickness and cut in crescent shapes. Bake in 375 degree oven just until very light tan. Watch closely. When cool enough to handle, dip in 1½ cups powdered sugar in which ground vanilla bean has been mixed.

Doris Flutcher

Gum Drop Cookies

1 cup shortening
1 cup brown sugar
1 cup white sugar
2 cups flour
1 teaspoon baking powder
1 teaspoon soda

2 eggs, beaten
1 cup coconut, flaked
1 cup gum drops, cut fine
  (remove black ones)
2 cups quick oatmeal
1½ teaspoons vanilla
Nuts (optional)

Cream shortening and sugar. Add remaining ingredients and mix well. Form into balls and flatten with fork. Brush with milk. Bake at 350 degrees for 12 minutes.

Mrs. Anthony Clementi

Grandmother's Molasses Cookies

2 cups light molasses
1 cup butter
1 teaspoon salt
2 teaspoons ginger

2 teaspoons cinnamon
1 cup sour milk or
  buttermilk
3 teaspoons soda
6 cups flour

Mix ingredients in order given, creaming molasses and butter. Sift dry ingredients together and add alternately with milk. Must stand overnight in cool place or refrigerator. Roll out on floured surface to ¼ inch thickness. Cut with 2½ inch cookie cutter. Bake in preheated oven at 325 degrees for 20 minutes. Add more flour if necessary after baking a test cookie.

Her grandmother used to make these up the night before and serve them hot for breakfast. These are supposed to be soft cookies.

Tory Thatcher

Lemon Snowdrops

Filling:

1 cup butter or margarine
½ cup sifted powdered sugar
1 teaspoon lemon extract
2 cups flour
¼ teaspoon salt

1 egg
1 lemon rind, grated
2/3 cup sugar
3 tablespoons lemon juice
1½ tablespoons soft butter

Heat oven to 400 degrees. Cream butter and sugar. Add lemon extract, flour and salt and mix well. Chill awhile. Measure level teaspoon of dough, round up and form like a vanilla wafer. Place about one inch apart on cookie sheet and bake 8 to 10 minutes, or until very lightly browned. Cool and put two together with lemon butter filling. Roll in powdered sugar.

For filling, blend one egg, slightly beaten, and remaining ingredients in top of double boiler. Cook over hot water until thick. Cool before filling cookies.

Makes 4 dozen

Mrs. Dennis Feister

Oatmeal Date Bars
(No Shortening)

½ cup sifted flour
½ cup sugar
½ teaspoon salt
1 teaspoon baking powder

½ cup quick oatmeal
16 dates, pitted and chopped
4 teaspoons milk
2 eggs, separated

Sift dry ingredients together, stir in oatmeal and add chopped dates. Add milk to beaten egg yolks and stir into dry ingredients. Fold in stiffly beaten egg whites. Turn into an 8-inch square pan, lightly greased and floured. Bake for 25 minutes in 325 degree oven. Dust with powdered sugar and cut into bars.

Mrs. Gordon Allott

Oatmeal Crispies

1 cup shortening
1 cup brown sugar
1 cup white sugar
2 well beaten eggs
1 teaspoon vanilla

1½ cups flour
1 teaspoon salt
1 teaspoon soda
3 cups quick oatmeal
Nuts, raisins, chocolate
 or butterscotch bits

Cream shortening and sugars, add eggs and vanilla. Sift dry ingredients together and add to creamed mixture. Add oatmeal and nuts and/or raisins, chocolate bits or butterscotch bits. Mix well and drop by teaspoon on greased cookie sheets. Bake at 350 degrees for 10 to 12 minutes.

Makes 6 to 8 dozen
Mrs. R. E. Staats

Orange Balls

1 pound vanilla wafers,
 crushed fine
1 soft stick butter
1 pound powdered sugar

1 6-ounce can frozen
 orange juice
Flake coconut

Mix crushed wafers, butter, powdered sugar and orange juice concentrate. Roll into small balls, then roll in coconut. Store in covered container or in refrigerator if weather is warm. Much better when stored for a day or two.

Makes approximately 100
Mrs. Anthony Clementi

Pireshkies
(Fruit-filled cookies dipped in honey)

Dough:
6½ cups sifted flour
3 eggs
2 teaspoons baking powder
½ cup and 2 tablespoons
   Crisco
3/4 cup peanut oil
½ cup orange juice
1½ tablespoons poppy seeds
¼ cup sugar
1/8 cup honey
1¼ cups water

Filling:
1½ cups plum jelly
¼ cup apricot jelly
8 ounces dried apricots,
   ground
1½ cups chopped walnuts
Lemon juice to taste

Blend dry ingredients and Crisco with pastry blender. Add oil, eggs, sugar, juice, water and honey and mix well. Refrigerate overnight. Next day, divide dough into four equal parts and roll out on lightly floured board. Cut into strips two inches wide. Place a small amount of filling in corner of strip, fold over three times cornerwise, and cut. Continue until one strip is finished, then proceed to others. Place on well greased baking sheet about ¼ inch apart. Bake at 375 degrees for 15 to 20 minutes, or until lightly browned.

Honeying Process:
2 cups honey
Small amount of water

2 jiggers whiskey
2 pinches flour

Mix and bring to a rapid boil, then cook for 15 or 20 minutes. Place pireshkies in mixture, a few at a time; cook for 3 to 5 minutes. Remove and place on shiny side of freezer paper to prevent sticking. Work fast with these or they will get too well done. You may decorate slightly cooled pireshkies with coconut or poppy seeds if desired.

Makes 5 dozen

Mrs. Philip Hilvitz

Orange Pecan Cookies

½ cup shortening
1 cup brown sugar, packed
1 egg
1 tablespoon grated
  orange rind
½ teaspoon vanilla

1 3/4 cups flour, sifted
¼ teaspoon salt
½ teaspoon soda
½ cup chopped pecans

Mix shortening, sugar, egg, orange rind and vanilla. Stir into dry ingredients which have been sifted together. Stir in pecans and form into rolls 2½ inches in diameter. Wrap in waxed paper and chill until firm. Slice 1/8 inch thick and place on ungreased baking sheet. Bake for 8 to 10 minutes at 400 degrees.

Makes 5 dozen   *Mrs. Claude Davis*

Pumpkin Cookies

1 cup butter or shortening
1 cup sugar
1 cup pumpkin
1 egg
1 teaspoon vanilla
2 cups flour
1 teaspoon baking powder
1 teaspoon soda
1 teaspoon cinnamon
½ teaspoon salt
½ cup dates or raisins
  (optional)
½ cup nuts (optional)

Icing:
½ cup brown sugar
¼ cup milk
3 tablespoons butter
3/4 teaspoon vanilla
1 cup confectioners' sugar

Work butter until creamy. Gradually blend in sugar until smooth. Add pumpkin, egg and vanilla and mix well. Sift dry ingredients together and add. Stir in raisins and dates or nuts if desired. Drop by teaspoon onto cookie sheet and bake for 10 to 15 minutes at 375 degrees, or until golden brown. Cool on rack.

To prepare icing, combine brown sugar, milk and butter in saucepan and cook for two minutes. Remove from heat and stir in vanilla and confectioners' sugar to spreading consistency.

Makes 50   *Pat Siemsen*

Geneva's Cookies

½ cup brown sugar
1 cup flour
½ cup butter
2 eggs
1 cup brown sugar

½ teaspoon vanilla
3/4 cup coconut
½ cup chopped nuts
½ teaspoon baking powder

Cream butter and ½ cup sugar; add flour. Press into 8 x 9 inch pan and bake 10 minutes at 350 degrees. Mix remaining ingredients together and spread on first mixture. Bake for 20 minutes at 350 degrees. Cut into squares and remove from pan.

Mrs. Fred Mattoon

Toffee Coffee Squares

2 cubes butter
   (*not* margarine)
1 cup brown sugar
1 egg yolk (cream)
1 teaspoon vanilla

2 cups flour
8 Hershey bars
Chopped pecans

Spread cookie mixture with hands on cookie sheet. Bake for 15 minutes at 375 degrees, or until brown. Lay broken Hershey bars on top, allow to soften and spread. Sprinkle nuts over top. Cut into squares while hot.

Yield: 1½ to 2 dozen 2 inch squares. *Wanda Glover*

Aunt Daisy's Scotch Shortbread

1 pound butter
   (no substitution)

1 cup sugar
4 cups flour

Cream sugar and butter. Sift flour into mixture and work in with hands until smooth. Shape into a round, or use an 8 by 12 inch pan, and shape to pan size. Perforate all over with fork at ½ inch intervals. Bake at 375 degrees for about one hour or until shortbread is light golden brown. Cut into size desired while very hot.

Makes about 20 pieces. *Mrs. Don Vickery*

Almond Bark Candy

2 pound package almond
    bark candy
9½ cups rice crispies

5 1/3 ounces packaged
    walnut pieces

Melt almond bark in heavy pan at 150 degrees on top of stove (low heat). Then mix in rice crispies and walnuts. Drop on wax paper in globs to cool.

Yield: 90 *Gloria Sudduth*

Brazil Nut Crunch

1 pound butter (*must* be *butter*)
2 cups finely chopped Brazil nuts (walnuts may be substituted)
2 6 ounce packages semi-sweet chocolate morsels
2 cups sugar

Butter a shallow pan (about 10 by 15 inches). Sprinkle evenly with 1 cup nuts, then scatter 1 cup of the morsels over the nuts.

Melt butter in 2½ quart sauce pan over low heat. Add sugar. Put candy thermometer in pan. Stir over moderate heat until mixture becomes a pale caramel color and candy thermometer reaches 300 degrees. (This takes 20 minutes or more at this altitude.)

Remove from heat; spoon the sugar mixture evenly over the nuts and chocolate. Scatter the remaining chocolate morsels over the hot mixture. The heat of the candy will melt the morsels. As soon as they are soft, spread over the entire surface. Sprinkle with remaining nuts. Chill until chocolate is firm. Break into pieces.

If you place Brazil nuts in freezer for 12 hours, shelling is much easier.

Makes 3¼ pounds *Mae Vinci*

313

Butter Crunch Candy

1 cup butter
1 cup sugar
2 tablespoons water

1 tablespoon light Karo syrup
3/4 cup finely chopped nuts
½ package chocolate chips

Melt butter in heavy pan over low heat. Remove from heat, add sugar and stir until blended. Return to low heat and stir rapidly until it starts to bubble. Add water and syrup. Cook over low heat and stir to hard crack stage (290). Test in cold water and when a hard ball will crack against the side of a cup, it is ready. Remove and stir in nuts. Pour on well-buttered cookie sheet and spread ¼ inch thick. Keep pushing candy back from edges with spatula until it is cool enough so it will not run. When cold, melt chocolate chips and spread on top. When chocolate gets hard, cut and store in cold place.

Mrs. Gordon Green

Candy Coconut Chocolate Balls

1 stick margarine
1 pound pecans
1 can sweetened
    condensed milk
1 pound coconut

1½ boxes powdered sugar
1 teaspoon vanilla
12 ounces chocolate chips
¼ pound paraffin

Melt margarine and pour over pecans. Add sweetened condensed milk, coconut, powdered sugar, and vanilla. Mix well, make balls, and refrigerate. Melt chocolate chips and paraffin in top of double boiler. Dip chilled balls into mixture with toothpicks. Refrigerate overnight.

Do not eat these the same day you dip them as they will still taste of paraffin.
Yield: 100

Connie Estep

314

Peanut Brittle

In an electric skillet:

2 cups sugar
1 cup water
1 cup white Karo syrup

2 cups raw peanuts
2 tablespoons butter
2 teaspoons soda
1 teaspoon vanilla

Set skillet at 400 degrees and bring mixture of first three ingredients to a boil. Cook until it spins threads - do not undercook. Add raw peanuts and butter and cook until a golden yellow. Disconnect skillet. Add soda and vanilla. Pour on buttered cookie sheet.

Mrs. Allene Baldwin

Praline Confections

20-24 graham crackers
1 cup butter or margarine

1cup light brown sugar
1 cup chopped pecans

Line jelly roll pan (15 x 10) with whole graham crackers. Bring butter and sugar to boil (rolling) and boil for 2 minutes. Remove from heat. When bubbling has stopped, add nuts. Spread over crackers.

Bake in moderate oven 350 degrees for 10 minutes. Cool slightly, cut into 1 inch squares.

Put on several thicknesses of paper toweling to absorb excess butter.

Pauline Genova

Stuffed Dates

Combine:

3 ounce package softened
   cream cheese

¼ cup finely cut
   up marshmallows
½ cup chopped walnuts

Cut slits in dates - stuff, then roll in powdered sugar. Refrigerate.

Mrs. Hilda Giordano

315

Marshmallow Fudge

Mix in 2 quart saucepan:

2 cups sugar
2/3 cup evaporated milk
12 to 15 regular marshmallows
½ cup margarine
Few grains of salt

1½ packages chocolate
  chips (6 ounce)
1½ cups pecans
1 teaspoon vanilla

Cook and stir constantly over medium heat until it comes to a boil. (Mixture will bubble all over top). Boil and stir for 5 minutes. Remove from heat and stir until dissolved 1½ 6 ounce packages of chocolate chips. Add: 1½ cups pecans and 1 teaspoon vanilla. Stir and pour into buttered pan. This fudge is firm and creamy. Put in icebox until cool and slightly hard.

Mrs. Dennis Feister

Peanut Butter Fudge

2 cups sugar
½ cup canned milk
¼ cup water
2 tablespoons Karo syrup
  (light or dark)

1 tablespoon butter
½ teaspoon vanilla
2 tablespoons peanut
  butter (heaping)

Mix first five ingredients and stir until mixture reaches boiling point. Lower heat and boil until a small amount dropped in cold water can be formed into a ball (not hard). Remove from heat, add vanilla, cool and beat for a few minutes, add peanut butter and continue to beat until it is ready to pour into buttered pan.

Mrs. Ed McGuire

pies

"As American as apple pie" is a
part of the national vocabulary, because
pies are all-time favorites. A welcome treat
for the pie baker is contemporary kitchen design
offering wall ovens and perfected temperature/time
controls which add to the enjoyment of baking.

Almond Toffee Pie

2 eggs, separated
2 teaspoons vanilla
½ cup light brown sugar, packed
½ cup milk
½ pint heavy cream, whipped
1 cup ground Almond Rocca or Heath bars, plus ground almonds
1 9 or 10-inch graham cracker pie shell, baked

Combine egg yolks, 1 teaspoon vanilla and sugar. Add milk. Cook over medium heat, stirring constantly until mixture thickens and coats spoon. Cool thoroughly. Beat egg whites until stiff; whip cream separately. Fold together egg whites, whipped cream and 1 teaspoon vanilla. Add 3/4 cup ground candy to cooled egg yolk mixture, then fold into egg white-cream mixture. Pour into crust. Top with remaining ground toffee and freeze. Remove from freezer about 15 minutes before serving. Pie should be cold but not frozen.

Serves 6 to 8   *Mary Ann Sturgeon*

Apple Cobbler

Filling:
3/4 cup sugar
2 tablespoons flour
½ teaspoon cinnamon
¼ teaspoon salt
5 cups sliced apples
¼ cup water
1 tablespoon butter

Topping:
1 cup flour
1 tablespoon sugar
1½ teaspoons baking powder
½ teaspoon salt
3 tablespoons shortening
½ cup milk

Combine filling ingredients in baking pan. Cover with foil and bake for 15 minutes at 400 degrees. To prepare topping, sift dry ingredients together, cut in shortening and stir in milk. Drop by spoonfuls onto hot apple mixture. Bake uncovered for 25 to 35 minutes at 400 degrees.

Serves 6   *Mrs. A. C. Jones*

Brownie Pie

3/4 cup chocolate wafer
   crumbs
½ cup chopped pecans
3 egg whites
Few grains salt
3/4 cup sugar
½ teaspoon vanilla

Topping:
1 cup chilled whipping
   cream
2 tablespoons powdered
   sugar
Unsweetened chocolate
   shavings

Beat egg whites and salt until frothy. Add sugar gradually, beating well after each addition. Continue beating until stiff peaks are formed and egg whites do not slide when bowl is partially inverted. Blend in vanilla. Gently fold in wafer crumbs and pecans. Turn into well-greased 9-inch pie pan. Spread evenly, covering sides also. Bake at 325 degrees for 35 to 40 minutes.

To prepare topping, whip cream and add powdered sugar. Spread over cooled pie and garnish with chocolate shavings. Chill 3 to 4 hours before serving.

Sue Mastro

Butterscotch Pie

1 cup brown sugar
3 rounded tablespoons flour
¼ cup melted butter
3 egg yolks
1 pint hot milk
1 teaspoon vanilla

Meringue:
3 egg whites, beaten stiff
6 tablespoons sugar
     or
Whipped cream, sweetened
   to taste

Combine sugar and flour; add butter and egg yolks. Stir into hot milk and cook until thick. Add vanilla and pour into baked pie shell.* Cover with meringue and bake in slow oven until brown.

*For deluxe pie, sprinkle chopped nuts over filling before topping with meringue or whipped cream.

Mrs. N. E. Backlund

Charlotte Russe Pie

1 tablespoon gelatin
1 cup milk
2 egg yolks, beaten
1 cup sugar
2 egg whites, beaten stiff

1 pint whipped crean
Dash salt
½ teaspoon vanilla
Crushed graham crackers
Graham cracker pie shell

Heat milk and gelatin in top of double boiler. In a bowl, beat egg yolks and add sugar. Pour milk and gelatin into egg and sugar mixture. Return to double boiler and cook 5 minutes, stirring constantly. When cool and about the consistency of liquid hand cream, fold in stiffly beaten egg whites and whipped cream. Add salt and vanilla. Pour into graham cracker pie shell and sprinkle a few crumbs over top. Chill at least 5 hours before serving.

Mrs. Norval Anderson

Cherry Tarts

3/4 cup graham cracker
  crumbs
2 tablespoons melted butter
2 tablespoons sugar
½ pound cream cheese
½ cup powdered sugar
1 egg
1 teaspoon vanilla

Topping:
Cherry pie filling
1½ teaspoons almond extract

Mix together crumbs, butter and sugar. Press a few tablespoons of mixture in paper muffin cups (in muffin tins) with bottom of juice glass. Cream cheese, powdered sugar, egg and vanilla in electric mixer. Place a heaping tablespoon on crust in each muffin cup. Bake for 10 minutes at 350 degrees. Cool. Cover cooled tarts with cherry pie filling mixed with almond extract.

Yield: 10 tarts

Alysmai Ward

Cranberries and Cream Pie

Pastry:
1 cup sifted flour
1 cup coarsely ground nuts
1 teaspoon salt
½ cup oil
1 tablespoon cold water

Filling:
1 3-ounce package raspberry
  gelatin
1 cup hot water
1 #1 can whole cranberry
  sauce
1 cup sour cream
3-ounce package cream cheese
1 cup heavy cream
¼ cup sugar

Prepare pastry and press firmly into bottom and sides of a 9-inch pie plate. Bake at 400 degrees for 15 to 20 minutes. Dissolve gelatin in hot water; then cool until it begins to thicken. Stir in cranberry sauce and sour cream. Pour into pastry shell and chill until firm. Soften cream cheese, slowly add cream and sugar, stirring until blended. Chill for 4 hours, then whip and spread over pie. (If sweeter pie is desired, you may add six quartered marshmallows to topping before it is chilled).

Mrs. John Sturgeon

Grasshopper Pie

Crust:
1½ cups chocolate wafer
  crumbs
¼ cup sugar
1/3 cup melted margarine

Filling:
½ cup milk
20 marshmallows
1 cup whipping cream*
1½ ounces creme de menthe
1½ ounces creme de cacao

Melt margarine in 8-inch pie pan. Add crumbs and sugar; mix well. Press onto bottom and sides with fork. Cool. In double boiler, heat milk and marshmallows until marshmallows melt. Cool. Whip cream and fold in liqueurs. Add to cooled marshmallow mixture and pour crust. Refrigerate for 24 hours before serving.

*One cup prepared whipped topping may be substituted. Add liqueurs to your personal taste—I prefer an extra ounce of the creme de cacao.

Serves 8

Beth Thatcher

Honey Pumpkin Pie

1 1-pound can pumpkin
1 teaspoon pie spice
1 teaspoon salt
4 eggs, beaten

½ cup milk
½ cup light cream
1 cup honey
Unbaked pie shell

Blend pumpkin, spice and salt. Beat in remaining ingredients and pour into shell. Bake for 30 minutes at 400 degrees. Reduce heat to 375 degrees and bake 10 minutes longer, or until firm. Cool and serve with whipped cream.

Jonna Ussery

Rhubarb Pie

3 tablespoons flour
1 cup sugar
1 egg, beaten

3 to 4 cups rhubarb, cut small
Pie dough for 2-crust pie

Sift flour and sugar together. Add egg and beat thoroughly. Stir in rhubarb. Pour into unbaked pie shell and cover with top crust. Sprinkle with sugar or sugar-cinnamon mixture. Bake at 425 degrees for 10 minutes, reduce heat to 350 degrees and continue baking 35 minutes longer, or until golden brown.

Mrs. R. E. Staats

Sister Lizzies Shaker Sugar Pie

¼ cup soft butter
1 cup brown sugar
1/3 cup flour
1 3/4 cups light cream

½ teaspoon vanilla
Grated nutmeg
9-inch unbaked pie shell

Mix flour and sugar and place in bottom of pie shell. Add cream, vanilla and soft butter in small pieces. Sprinkle nutmeg over top. Bake in 350 degree oven for 40 to 45 minutes, or until knife inserted in center comes out clean. Let stand for 30 to 60 minutes before serving (needs to set up like a custard).

Note: This recipe was used by the Shaker women when their fruit bins ran dry before the new crops were harvested.

B. Henry

323

Merry Berry Pie

1 baked 9-inch pie shell
1 3-ounce package cream
  cheese
2 tablespoons milk
2 boxes fresh strawberries
1 box frozen strawberries,
  thawed

1 cup sugar
3 tablespoons cornstarch
1/3 cup water
1 cup heavy cream

Mix cream cheese with milk until smooth; spread over bottom of pie crust. Arrange washed and hulled fresh strawberries on cheese. Put frozen berries in blender until pureed. Strain juice and discard pulp. Bring juice to boil and stir in sugar until dissolved. Blend cornstarch with water and add to strawberry mixture. Cook slowly, stirring occasionally until thickened. Watch carefully to prevent scorching. Cool and pour over berries. Chill thoroughly. Top with whipped cream, sweetened to taste, before serving

Beth Thatcher

Karo-Nut Pie

3 eggs
½ cup sugar
1 tablespoon flour
¼ cup butter
3/4 cup dark Karo
¼ cup light Karo

½ teaspoon nutmeg
½ teaspoon salt
1 teaspoon vanilla
Unbaked pie shell
1 cup pecan halves

Beat eggs until lemon-colored. Combine sugar and flour and add to eggs. Add melted butter, syrup, nutmeg, salt and vanilla. Cover pie shell with pecans and pour filling over. Bake in preheated 375 degree oven for 45 to 50 minutes, or until filling is set.

Mary Green

Sliced Lemon Pie

1½ cups sugar
3 tablespoons flour
¼ teaspoon salt
¼ cup melted butter
½ cup cold water

3 eggs, beaten
Grated rind of 1 lemon
2 lemons
1 unbaked 9-inch pie shell

Combine sugar, flour and salt. Add butter, water, eggs and grated rind. Peel and remove all white part of two lemons; slice very thin and add to first mixture. Turn into pie shell and bake at 400 degrees for 10 minutes. Lower heat to 375 degrees and bake 35 minutes longer.

Serves 6 to 8

Mrs. David W. Boyer

Lemon Tart

6 egg yolks
2 cans sweetened
   condensed milk
Juice of 4 lemons
1 pint whipping cream

½ teaspoon vanilla
Sugar to taste
1 7¼-ounce box vanilla wafers,
   crushed fine

Beat yolks; add milk and mix well. Stir in lemon juice. Place 3/4 of the wafer crumbs in a pan. Pour in custard. Whip cream with sugar and vanilla and spread over top. Sprinkle on remaining crumbs. Refrigerate at least 6 hours before serving.

Serves 12 to 14

Mrs. Thomas Broome

Sour Cream Raisin Pie

1 cup sugar
1 teaspoon cinnamon
¼ teaspoon ground cloves
2½ tablespoons flour
½ teaspoon salt

1½ cups sour cream
½ cup raisins
½ cup walnuts
3 egg yolks

In a saucepan combine dry ingredients. Add sour cream, raisins, nuts and egg yolks. Cook over medium heat, stirring constantly, until thick and dark. Pour into baked pie shell, top with meringue and bake at 375 degrees until golden brown.

Punky Robbe

French Mint Pie

1 cup powdered sugar
2 eggs
¼ teaspoon mint flavoring

1 cube butter
2 squares chocolate
Graham cracker crust

Dissolve chocolate over hot water; then cool. Cream butter and sugar. Add unbeaten eggs, one at a time, and beat until smooth. Add chocolate and mint flavoring. Pour into graham cracker crust and refrigerate overnight, covered with plastic wrap. Top with whipped cream before serving. This is a very rich pie and should be served in small slices.

Nancy Bonforte

French Silk Pie

Crust:
1¼ cups graham cracker crumbs
2 tablespoons sugar
¼ cup melted butter

Topping:
Sweetened whipped cream
Chopped nuts
Grated semi-sweet chocolate

Filling:
¼ pound soft butter
3/4 cup sugar
2 squares unsweetened choco-
    late, melted

2 teaspoons vanilla
2 eggs

Combine cracker crumbs, sugar and butter. Mix well and press into bottom and sides of pie pan. Bake at 400 degrees for 8 minutes. Chill. To prepare filling, cream butter, sugar, vanilla and melted chocolate. Add eggs one at a time, beating for 5 minutes at high speed after each. This is important! Pour into crust and refrigerate overnight. Spread with topping before serving.

Kay Stillman

Peach Parfait Pie

Crust:
1 cup quick oatmeal,
  uncooked
½ cup slivered almonds
½ cup brown sugar
1/3 cup melted margarine

Filling:
1 3-ounce package
  orange gelatin
1 cup hot water
1 pint vanilla ice cream,
  softened
2 cups sliced fresh peaches*

Spread oats in shallow baking pan; toast in oven pre-heated to 350 degrees for 5 minutes. Add almonds and toast 5 minutes longer. Blend brown sugar and melted butter with oat mixture, mixing well. Reserve ½ cup for garnish. Press remaining mixture onto bottom and sides of 9-inch pie plate. Chill. To prepare filling, pour hot water over gelatin, stirring until dissolved. Add softened ice cream and stir until smooth Fold in peaches and pour into chilled crust. Sprinkle reserved oat mixture around outside edge of pie. Chill until set (several hours) before serving.

*If peaches are too tart, mix them with a small amount of sugar before adding to the gelatin mixture).

Serves 6 to 7   *Mrs. Allen Griffith*

White Christmas Pie

1 can sweetened
  condensed milk

½ cup lemon juice
1 cup whipped cream

Stir lemon juice into milk slowly. Fold in whipped cream. Pour into pre-made graham cracker crumb shell. Top with grated chocolate or chocolate decorettes. Chill at least 3 hours before serving.

Lorraine Sheets

Fudge Pie

2 squares bitter chocolate
1 stick butter or margarine
2 eggs, beaten

1 cup sugar
2/3 cup pecans
1 teaspoon vanilla

Melt chocolate and margarine together. Combine and add beaten eggs and sugar. Stir in pecans and vanilla. Pour into a well-greased pie pan and bake at 350 degrees for 30 minutes. Serve with vanilla ice cream.

Mrs. Paula McEniry

Strawberry Ice Cream Pie

1½ cups fine graham cracker crumbs
½ cup chopped almonds
½ cup confectioners' sugar
½ cup butter or margarine, melted
1 12-ounce package frozen strawberries, thawed and drained
1½ pints strawberry ice cream, softened
1 cup heavy cream, whipped and sweetened (optional)

Combine graham cracker crumbs, almonds and sugar. Stir in melted butter and press into a 9-inch pie pan, reserving ¼ cup to sprinkle on top. Bake at 350 degrees for 8 minutes. Cool thoroughly. Spread strawberries evenly over bottom of pie shell. Quickly spread with softened ice cream. Top with sweetened whipped cream if desired. Sprinkle reserved crumb mixture over top. Freeze for 15 to 30 minutes before serving.

Mrs. J. Sturgeon

Winks Strawberry Meringue Pie

3 egg whites, stiffly beaten
1 cup sugar
½ teaspoon vanilla
¼ teaspoon baking powder
12 soda crackers, rolled fine
¼ cup pecans
1 pint fresh strawberries
Whipped cream

Add sugar gradually to stiffly beaten egg whites; continue to beat until well mixed. Fold in vanilla, baking powder, cracker crumbs and pecans. Pour into well greased 9-inch pie pan and bake at 325 degrees for 25 to 30 minutes. Place strawberries on meringue and top with whipped cream. Garnish with additional berries. Allow to set for several hours before serving.

Mrs. Robert Garvey

Strawberry Cheese Pie

Filling:
1 8-ounce package cream
   cheese
1/3 cup sugar
1 teaspoon grated orange peel
2 tablespoons orange juice
2 tablespoons light cream
3 cups fresh strawberrries

1 pie shell (deep dish works best)

Glaze:
3 cups fresh strawberries
1 cup sugar
2 tablespoons cornstarch

Topping:
Whipped cream

Combine softened cream cheese, sugar, orange peel and orange juice. Add cream and beat until light and fluffy. Pour into baked pie shell and arrange 3 cups fresh berries over top. To prepare glaze, crush 3 cups berries in saucepan; add sugar and cornstarch. Cook over low heat, stirring constantly, until mixture comes to boil, thickens and becomes transparent. Strain and cool. Pour cooled glaze over berries and chill for 3 hours. Spread whipped cream over top before serving.

Barbara Daney

Peach Pie

1 unbaked pie shell
½ cup flour
3/4 cup sugar

1/3 cube butter
½ teaspoon cinnamon
Fresh peach halves

Mix flour, sugar, butter and cinnamon until crumbly. Put half of this into pie shell. Arrange peach halves, face down. Sprinkle remaining half of mixture over top. Bake at 400 degrees for 40 to 45 minutes until crust is brown.

Allene Baldwin

Pecan Pie
Southern Style

1 stick butter, melted
1 cup light Karo syrup
1 cup sugar
3 tablespoons flour

Dash of salt
1 cup whole or chopped pecans
3 eggs, beaten

Combine all ingredients and pour into a chilled, unbaked 9-inch pie crust. Bake at 325 degrees for 1 hour to 1 hour, 15 minutes.

Gay Bulloch

Ice Cream Meringue Pie

1 baked 9-inch pastry
   shell, cooled
1 pint chocolate ice
   cream, softened
1 pint strawberry ice
   cream, softened

Meringue:
4 egg whites
½ teaspoon vanilla
½ cup sugar
¼ teaspoon cream of tartar

Spread chocolate ice cream in baked pie shell; cover with layer of strawberry ice cream. Place in freezer. To prepare meringue, beat egg whites with vanilla and cream of tartar. Gradually add sugar, beating until stiff and glossy. Spread over ice cream, carefully sealing to edge of pastry. Bake in 475 degree oven for 2 to 3 minutes until lightly browned. Freeze several hours or overnight. To serve, cut in wedges and drizzle with chocolate sauce if desired.

Chocolate sauce:
4 squares unsweetened
   chocolate
3/4 cup water

1 cup sugar
6 tablespoons butter
1 teaspoon vanilla

Heat chocolate and water in sauce pan. Stir constantly over low heat until smooth. Stir in sugar and salt; simmer until slightly thickened, (about 5 minutes). Remove from heat. Stir in butter and vanilla.

Susie Anton

330

Pie Crust

3 cups sifted flour
Dash salt
1 teaspoon baking powder

1 cup margarine
½ cup water

Sift dry ingredients together. Cut in shortening to crumble stage. (Be sure shortening is at room temperature). Add water all at once. Roll out on lightly floured board. This makes enough crust for two pies and will store well in refrigerator.

Mrs. George Pardee

Pie Crust

3 cups flour
1 teaspoon salt
½ teaspoon baking powder
1¼ cups shortening

1 egg slightly beaten
5 tablespoons water
1 tablespoon vinegar

Mix together flour, salt, baking powder and shortening. Add egg, water and vinegar. Roll out on floured board. Makes enough for one 2-crust pie.

Betty Lenz

Stir And Press Pie Crust

1½ cups flour
1 tablespoon sugar
½ teaspoon salt

½ cup oil
2 tablespoons milk

Sift flour, sugar and salt into pie pan. Whip oil and milk together until cloudy and pour over flour mixture. Stir until you can press the crust to fit the pie pan. Prick with fork and bake at 450 degrees for 12 to 15 minutes.

Punky Robbe

brunch

An increasing preference for
entertaining family and friends at brunch
has seen the creation of new dishes which
combine breakfast and luncheon favorites,
prepared with ease by the host or hostess
who works in a kitchen complete with modern
range, oven and labor-saving appliances.

Apple Butter

8 cups unsweetened apple sauce
4 cups sugar

1 tablespoon cinnamon
¼ teaspoon salt

Mix all ingredients in large saucepan. Place on stove at medium heat. Simmer for about 60 minutes. To prevent scorching place wire rack under sauce pan. Put in sterilized pint jars and seal.

Mrs. Dennis Feister

Apple Butter

1 peck apples

½ gallon sweet cider

Cook apples in cider as if to make applesauce.

To make sauce add:
6 cups sugar
1 tablespoon cinnamon

1 to 2 teaspoons ground cloves

Bake in covered roasting pan in 250 degree oven overnight; then bake to desired consistency the next day if necessary.

Jean Beattie

Sunday Brunch Scrambled Eggs

¼ cup margarine or butter
6 eggs, slightly beaten
¼ cup milk
¼ teaspoon salt
¼ teaspoon basil

Dash freshly ground pepper
1 3-ounce package cream cheese (cut in small pieces)
1 small can sliced mushrooms, drained
¼ cup pimiento, diced

Melt butter; whip eggs, milk, and seasonings and pour into butter. Cook over low heat stirring frequently, until eggs begin to set. Add remaining ingredients. Continue to cook, stirring until cheese is blended and eggs are cooked.

Serves 4

Betty Johnson

Sunday Morning Breakfast

Melt ½ cup butter in skillet
In bowl, mix until lumpy:

½ cup flour	2 eggs
½ cup milk	½ teaspoon cinnamon

Pour flour mixture into skillet with melted butter. Put in 425 degree oven for 15-20 minutes.

Remove—sprinkle with powdered sugar. Squeeze half a lemon on it and drop spoonfuls of jam over it. (or fruit or syrup)

Serve with sausage.

Serves 3-4

Beth Thatcher

Egg and Bacon Soufflé

¼ cup diced bacon	½ teaspoon salt
3 slices bread	¼ teaspoon dry mustard
3 slightly beaten eggs	¼ teaspoon paprika
1 cup milk	

Fry bacon until light brown. Brush bread with bacon drippings; cut slices in pieces to fit deep casserole. Arrange in layers, sprinkling each layer with bacon. Combine eggs, milk and seasonings and pour over bread. Bake in moderate oven (350 degrees) until puffy and knife comes out clean—about 45 minutes.

Serves 4

Ruth Stenmark

Potato Omelet

2 packages frozen, hash brown potatoes	3/4 pound grated Velveeta cheese
1 dozen eggs, beaten with a little milk	1 pound bacon, fried crisp and crumbled

Fry bacon and remove bacon and most of grease. Cook potatoes until defrosted and soft, then pat down in bottom of electric frying pan. Pour on eggs, cover with grated cheese, and top with crumbled bacon. Cover and cook until eggs are cooked and solid.

Kay Abbot

Quickie Sausage Casserole

12 link sausages	1 cup sifted flour
3 eggs	1 teaspoon salt
1 cup milk	Dash pepper

Cook sausages for about 10 minutes until they are well-browned. Pour off most of fat. Put sausages and a little fat into baking dish. Keep hot while preparing topping:

Blend the eggs, milk, flour and spices in blender at high speed until smooth. Pour over the sausages* and bake at 400 degrees for about 35 minutes or until top is puffed and brown. Cut in wedges and serve. Good with applesauce.

*Sometimes I cook a chopped onion with the sausage and sprinkle ½ cup shredded Cheddar cheese over the sausage before pouring the batter over. Bake the same way.

Rene Holden

Egg Crab Casserole

Eggs	Grated onion
Deviled ham	Mayonnaise
Mustard	Salt and pepper

Hard cook two eggs apiece and stuff with deviled ham, mustard, grated onion, mayonnaise, salt and pepper.

1 can mushroom soup	2 tablespoons sherry or
½ cup grated Cheddar cheese	sauterne (optional)
1 can (flat) crab meat	1 can mushroom buttons
½ teaspoon Worcestershire	1 small can stuffed
sauce	olives, sliced
Dash hot pepper sauce	Salt to taste

Mix soup, cheese, seasonings, mushrooms and olives and pour gently over stuffed eggs in buttered casserole. Bake in 400 degree oven for 30 minutes and then arrange in serving dish. Serve over toast points.

Serves 6

C. Petersen

German Pancakes

2 eggs
¼ cup flour
½ cup milk

2 tablespoons butter
Powdered sugar
Lemon juice

Melt butter in a 2-quart casserole. In the blender, beat eggs, flour and milk slightly. Bake 15 minutes at 425 degrees. When done, sprinkle top with powdered sugar and lemon juice to taste.

Serves 2   *Allene Baldwin*

Cottage Cheese-Sour Cream Pancakes

3/4 cup sour cream
2 eggs
1/3 cup cottage cheese

½ cup flour
½ teaspoon baking soda
½ teaspoon salt

Put all ingredients into an electric mixer or blender and mix until smooth. Bake on grill or in pan until done, turning once.

Yield: 8-10 pancakes   *Pat Siemsen*
        (18-20 dollar size)

Beer Pancakes

1½ cups sifted flour
3/4 teaspoon salt
1½ teaspoon double-action
    baking powder
1 tablespoon sugar
2 egg yolks, beaten

3 tablespoons melted butter
½ cup beer
2/3 cup milk
1 egg white

Sift flour, salt, baking powder, sugar into bowl. Stir in egg yolks, butter, beer and milk until smooth. Beat egg white until stiff, but not dry; fold into mixture. Drop onto lightly greased, heated griddle or skillet. Cook until bubbles cover top, turn and cook until browned. Serve with maple syrup, or heated corn syrup mixed with equal quantity of beer.

These have a slightly yeasty flavor. Let beer set for awhile until it loses most of its carbonation before using.

                                        Doris Neumeister

Orange Marmalade

2 oranges
  Juice—then cut rind *very*
  thin

1 lemon

For each cup of juice add 3 cups water. Let stand 24 hours. Boil 10 minutes—set aside for 24 hours.

Measure and add equal parts of sugar. Cook as you do for jelly. Set aside 24 hours. Stir and mix thoroughly; seal in glasses and wax tops.

Note: It is advisable to allow a short time to ripen fruit before starting. It is also advisable to use a porcelain container as it keeps it lighter in color. After adding the sugar, it is better to cook the mixture for a shorter time on two successive days, thus cooking it twice for the right thickness.

Mrs. George Pardee

Schmarren
(A German dish for breakfast)

3/4 cup flour
3 tablespoons sugar
1 teaspoon salt

2 eggs
½ cup milk
¼ cup shortening (melted)

Mix flour, sugar, and salt. Add eggs and milk; stir until well-mixed. In a size 5 cast iron skillet, melt shortening until hot. Pour in batter. Brown on both sides. Then chop until fine with a pancake turner. May be served plain, with sugar, or your favorite syrup.

Yield: 3-4 servings

Mrs. Dennis Feister

Sour Dough Waffles

Must be made at least 8 hours ahead of use. Can be saved and 1 cup makes a starter. Proceed with step 2 if using starter. The longer dough stands, the more "sour" it is.

1. ½ cup lukewarm water   1 package yeast

Put in large container or mixing bowl. Let stand 5 minutes. Add:

2. 2 cups lukewarm milk   1 teaspoon salt
   ½ cup melted butter or oil   ' tablespoons sugar

Beat in: 2 cups flour

Cover container; let stand in refrigerator at least 8 hours before using. When ready to use:

   Beat in 2 eggs and ¼ teaspoon baking soda

Note: In summer, serve blueberry pie filling over waffles; in winter, cider syrup.

Cider Syrup

1 cup cider   ½ cup sugar
1 stick cinnamon

Simmer 10 minutes; remove cinnamon when aroma pleases you.

Mrs. Henry Williams

Waffles

2 cups cake flour   2 eggs, separated
2 teaspoons baking powder   1½ cups milk
½ teaspoon salt   ½ cup vegetable oil
2 tablespoons sugar   ½ cup melted butter
                     or margarine

Combine dry ingredients. Beat egg yolks and milk. Add alternately with oil and butter to dry ingredients, stirring until smooth. Fold in stiffly beaten egg whites and bake in waffle iron.

Leftover batter may be stored, covered, in refrigerator. If too stiff when ready to bake, spread with spatula or thin with a little milk.

Pat Siemsen

Chicken Crepes

5 tablespoons butter
5 tablespoons flour
½ teaspoon salt
1/8 teaspoon pepper
1 cup cream
1 cup chicken broth
½ teaspoon Worcestershire
   sauce

2 tablespoons chopped
   parsley
1 cup grated Swiss cheese
3/4 cup sauterne
2 cups diced, cooked
   chicken
½ cup chopped ripe olives
Paprika

Melt butter; blend in flour, salt and pepper. Add cream, chicken broth, and Worcestershire. Cook, stirring constantly, until thick. Stir in parsley, 3/4 cup cheese, and wine. Place about 1 cup of sauce in bowl. To that, add chicken and olives. Keep remaining sauce warm in double boiler.

Crepes:

2 eggs well beaten
3/4 cup milk

3/4 cup flour
1/8 teaspoon salt

Mix eggs and milk. Add flour and salt and beat until smooth. Pour about 2 tablespoons of batter into a greased, hot 7-inch skillet. Tip skillet from side to side with a rolling motion so batter spreads very thin. Brown underneath but do not turn. Place a spoonful of chicken mixture on each pancake; roll up and place in baking dish. Pour over remaining sauce and sprinkle with remaining cheese and paprika. Bake at 375 degrees for 15 minutes.

Note: Can be prepared an hour in advance, covered with foil, then heated longer in oven until sauce is bubbly.

Serves 6   *Mrs Fred Foster*

Ham Apricot Crepes

1 egg
1 cup milk
1 tablespoon melted butter
  or margarine
1 cup sifted all-purpose flour
10 thin slices boiled ham
1 8-ounce can apricot
  halves (1 cup)

2/3 cup sugar
2 tablespoons cornstarch
Dash of salt
1 12-ounce can apricot
  nectar (1½ cups)
2 teaspoons lemon juice
2 tablespoons butter
  or margarine

Beat egg just enough to blend. Add the milk, melted butter and flour; beat smooth. Lightly grease a 6-inch skillet; heat. Remove from heat and add 2 tablespoons batter into skillet; quickly tilt pan from side to side only. Repeat with remaining batter to make a total of 10 crepes. Crepes may be made a day ahead and put in refrigerator with wax paper between crepes to keep from sticking together.

Drain apricots, reserving syrup. Place a ham slice on unbrowned side of each crepe; roll up with a ham slice inside. Place on chafing dish or skillet with apricot halves. Pour apricot sauce over all; cover and heat through. Keep warm till ready to serve.

Apricot Sauce:
Mix sugar, cornstarch and salt. Blend in reserved apricot syrup. Add nectar. Cook and stir until slightly thickened and clear. Remove from heat; add lemon juice. Stir in 2 tablespoons butter until melted.

Nice for a brunch.

Doris Hadley

microwave and crockpot

As microwaves and space age cooking methods are developed to meet a faster pace of living, good, wholesome food, prepared with care and skill, remains an ongoing southwestern tradition.

Microwave Hints

In order to convert conventional recipes to microwave, cut cooking time by ¼ the required time. If more time is required to complete cooking, add 30-second additional heatings until done.

Use the microwave to soften a variety of foods:

If honey has crystalized, put jar (no metal trim) in microwave and heat one minute or until crystals disappear.

Hard butter can be softened by heating for 25 seconds on low setting. Let stand for 15 seconds.

Hard raisins can be softened by pouring a little water over them and heating for 3 minutes, uncovered. Let stand for a couple of minutes.

Cream cheese, spreads, and frostings can be softened by heating for 2 minutes on low setting.

Soften stale marshmallows on low setting for 3 minutes in opened bag.

To soften brown sugar, place it in a bowl with a quarter of an apple or a slice of white bread; cover. Heat for 15 or 20 seconds.

Ice cream—to soften for serving, heat a 1-pint package for 15 seconds, a quart for 30 seconds.

Chocolate squares can be melted in the paper wrappers, seam side up. Heat 2 to 3 minutes per 1-ounce square.

To caramelize sugar—place ½ cup sugar in a bowl, cook for 3 minutes or until brown liquid is formed.

Frozen orange juice may be thawed right in the container (cardboard container). Just remove the top lid* and heat on low setting for about 1½ minutes. Pour in pitcher and add water. (*lower lid can remain on container).

Frozen vegetables may be cooked right in the box or pouch. Just make a slit in the top of the box and cook on high setting for 4 minutes. No need to add water. Remove from container and put in serving bowl.

Leftover coffee may be saved in refrigerator and then reheated in microwave for 1 to 2 minutes, depending on size of cup.

A tomato may be scalded in the microwave to remove skin by heating for 15 seconds; let stand for same amount of time, and then peel.

Baby foods—heat a 4-ounce baby bottle for 20 seconds, an 8-ounce bottle for 40 seconds. Heat a jar of baby food, cover removed, for 30 to 45 seconds.

Hot cereal—mix ½ cup quick cooking oats, ½ cup water, dash salt. Microwave 1 minute, 15 seconds—let stand for 3 minutes (covered).

Three paper cup cake liners nested together will hold batter without a pan.

To dry herbs (parsley, etc.)—Place herbs between paper towels to absorb the moisture. Microwave on high until herbs crumble. Store in a glass jar.

Hot dogs—put relish, mustard, catsup, etc., on bun. Add hot dog. Put small slit in center of hot dog. Wrap in napkin. Microwave 30 seconds per hot dog on high.

Cheese and Onion Appetizers

½ cup mayonnaise or salad
  dressing
¼ cup grated Parmesan cheese

2 green onions, finely chopped
24 crackers or toast rounds

Combine first three ingredients in small mixing bowl; mix well. Spread mixture on rounds. Place on glass baking dish or tray. Microwave for 40 to 45 seconds until just bubbly.

Patti Sweeney

Cheesy Taco Chips

Round taco-seasoned tortilla
  chips

Taco sauce
Sharp cheddar cheese

Arrange tortilla chips on paper plate. Spoon ½ teaspoon taco sauce on each chip. Place thin slice of cheese on sauce. Microwave 10 seconds, turn plate ¼ turn and cook 10 to 15 seconds more. Serve hot.

Lucy McBurney

Jalapeño Cheese Ball

1 6-ounce package Jalapeño
  cheese spread
2 3-ounce packages cream
  cheese
1 teaspoon Worcestershire
  sauce

1 cup (4 ounces) shredded
  sharp Cheddar cheese
⅓ cup chopped parsley
½ cup chopped pecans
Crackers

Unwrap cheeses. Place Jalapeño cheese in a glass casserole (1½ quarts). Microwave 1 minute. Add cream cheese and microwave 1 minute or until cheese can be mixed together. Add Worcestershire sauce, mix well. Add Cheddar and mix. (Cheddar cheese won't melt entirely. Mixture should remain golden-flecked). Refrigerate mixture one hour or until it can be formed into a ball. Roll into a ball or 1 log shape. Roll in parsley, then pecans. Refrigerate till set. Serve with crackers.

Kathy Hedrick

Hot Spicy Cider

1½ quarts apple cider
1 teaspoon whole cloves
1 teaspoon whole allspice

2 sticks cinnamon, about 3"
long
2 tablespoons red hots
(optional)

Combine cider, cloves, allspice and cinnamon sticks in large bowl or large Pyrex dish. Microwave until warm (4 to 5 minutes). Let stand 15 minutes. Strain into cups or punch bowl.

12 half-cup servings   *Kathy Hedrick*

Beef Vegetable Cups

1 beaten egg
¼ cup milk
⅓ cup cracker crumbs
½ envelope sloppy joe
seasoning mix (2
tablespoons)
1 pound ground beef
2 medium carrots, peeled and
thinly sliced (1 cup)

1 cup fresh or frozen peas
¼ cup chopped onion
½ teaspoon instant beef
bouillon granules
1 tablespoon all-purpose flour
½ cup shredded American
cheese

Mix first 4 ingredients. Add beef; mix well. On 4 squares waxed paper pat meat into 4 to 5" rounds. Shape each over inverted custard cup. Discard paper. Place inverted cups in 12x7x2-inch baking dish. Cover; set aside. In a 1-quart casserole, combine carrots, peas, onion, bouillon, ¾ cup water, and dash of pepper. Micro-cook about 10 minutes until tender, stirring once. Stir ¼ cup cold water into flour; blend into vegetables. Cook 1 minute until thickened. Stir in cheese till melted. Cover—set aside. Micro-cook meat cups, covered, 3 minutes; give dish a half turn. Cook till almost done, about 2 minutes more. Lift meat cups from custard cups; place on serving platter. Fill with vegetable sauce. Cook, uncovered, till sauce is hot (1 to 2 minutes).

Serves 4   *Bev Brill*

Barbequed Meatballs

2 pounds ground beef
2 teaspoons salt
1 cup milk
½ cup cracker crumbs

4 tablespoons minced onion
1¼ cup catsup
2 tablespoons brown sugar
⅓ cup vinegar

Mix meat, salt, milk, crumbs and 2 tablespoons onion. Form into 36 balls. Place in 2-quart casserole. Mix remaining ingredients, pour over meat balls. Cover and cook in microwave oven 16 minutes. Turn dish occasionally, and stir center meatballs to the outside.

Serves 8

Bev Brill

Green Chili-Onion Quiche

1 frozen 9-inch pie crust
1 cup grated mozzarella cheese
½ cup evaporated milk
3 eggs

1 4-ounce can diced green
  chilies (or 3 drops tabasco
  sauce, if prefered)
1 3-ounce can french fried
  onions

Spray glass pie dish with spray-on vegetable oil. Carefully remove frozen pie crust from aluminum pan and place in glass dish. Place in microwave and cook for 1 minute on high. Remove and shape crust to dish. Return to oven and cook 3 to 4 minutes on high turning once. Remove and sprinkle the grated cheese on the crust. Beat together in a separate bowl the eggs, milk, green chilies (or tabasco) and pour over the cheese. Cover top with the french fried onions. Cook on medium setting for 15 minutes, turning once or twice during the cooking. Let stand in microwave for 5 minutes before serving to complete cooking. Serve with a green salad or a fruit salad.

Variations: For a change, add chopped bacon or ham to the egg mixture in place of the green chilies or tabasco.

Serves 6 to 8

Rosie Marta

348

Sweet-Sour Chicken

Sauce:

1 cup water	3 tablespoons cornstarch
1 cup sugar	3 tablespoons soy sauce
1 cup vinegar	

Mix well in medium bowl. Cover bowl and cook 1 minute, remove and stir well. Return to oven and cook 6 minutes, removing and stirring well at 2-minute intervals, until thick and glossy. Remove and set aside.

Chicken:

1 2½ to 3 pound frying chicken, cut up	1 teaspoon salt
⅓ cup flour	¼ teaspoon pepper
	⅓ cup butter or margarine

Melt butter in 12x7-inch baking dish in microwave oven. Mix together flour, salt and pepper. Coat chicken pieces in flour mixture; roll each piece in melted butter and place each piece skin side up in dish. Cover with plastic wrap and cook 8 minutes. Remove from oven, turn each piece over. Remove all but ¼ cup drippings from baking dish. Pour sauce over all chicken, making sure each piece is well coated. Cover and return to oven and cook 4 minutes. Remove from oven, turn pieces skin side up, baste with sauce, and cook 6 minutes more, or until done. Remove from oven, baste, and serve.

Serves 4 to 5   *Lucy McBurney*

Hot Chicken Salad

4 cups cut up chicken, cooked
2 tablespoons lemon juice
⅔ cup finely chopped, toasted
   almonds
¾ cup mayonnaise
1 teaspoon salt
½ teaspoon seasoned salt

1 cup grated Cheddar cheese
2 cups chopped celery
¾ cup cream of chicken soup
1 teaspoon minced onion
1½ cups crushed potato chips
1 can slivered water chestnuts

Combine all ingredients except cheese, potato chips and almonds. Place in large rectangular dish. Let stand overnight in refrigerator. Cook in microwave for 6 to 8 minutes on high. Stir. Add cheese and almonds. Cook 5 minutes or until it is heated through. Add potato chips at last minute and heat for another minute.

Conventional oven: Put on topping of chips, cheese and almonds. Bake at 400 degrees for 20 to 25 minutes.

Serves 6   *Kay Stillman*

Shrimp Casserole

1 can (10½ ounce) cream of
   mushroom soup
2 tablespoons chopped green
   pepper
2 tablespoons chopped onion
1 tablespoon lemon juice
2 cups cooked rice
½ teaspoon Worcestershire
   sauce

½ teaspoon dry mustard
¼ teaspoon pepper
½ pound uncooked shrimp,
   cleaned
¼ cup bread crumbs
Butter
Paprika

Combine all ingredients except crumbs and butter; place in a 1½ quart casserole. Sprinkle casserole with bread crumbs; dot with butter. Sprinkle with paprika. Cover and bake in Radarange Oven 10 minutes; turn dish halfway through baking time. Remove lid for the last 2 minutes of cooking time.

Serves 6

Turkey-wiches

4 toasted hamburger buns
1¾ cups chopped cooked
   turkey
1 tablespoon instant minced
   onion
1 teaspoon instant minced
   parsley

¼ cup chopped dry roasted
   peanuts (optional)
1 chopped hard-cooked egg
⅔ cup mayonnaise
⅓ cup shredded Cheddar
   cheese
Salt, pepper

Place bottom half of buns on paper towel-lined plate. Combine remaining ingredients. Spread on buns. Add bun tops. Cook in microwave 3 to 3½ minutes. (Chicken may be substituted for turkey).

Serves 4

Bev Brill

Taco Salad

1 pound ground beef
¾ cup water
1 package taco seasoning mix
1 head lettuce
1 1-pound can ranch style
   beans or fresh cooked pinto
   beans
2 diced tomatoes

¾ cup bottled Italian dressing
2 cups small corn chips,
   crushed
1 pound Cheddar cheese,
   grated
1 onion, finely chopped
1 4-ounce can chopped green
   chilies

Microwave ground beef in large covered casserole until done; drain. Add seasoning mix, water, beans and cook in microwave 5 minutes; chill. Combine lettuce, tomatoes, onion, green chilies, cheese, and dressing; chill. Just before serving, combine both cooled mixtures with crushed corn chips, mix well and serve. Excellent to use as a main course for a meal.

Serves 8 to 10

Bobbie Reynolds

351

Baked Corn

1 16-ounce can whole kernel
  corn (undrained)
1 egg
2 tablespoons flour
2 tablespoons butter
1 tablespoon sugar

¼ cup diced cheese
2 tablespoons chopped green
  pepper
1 tablespoon chopped onion
Salt and pepper to taste

Soften butter 15 to 20 seconds in 1½-quart casserole dish. Add all ingredients and mix well. Bake 12 to 15 minutes, stirring and turning dish three times during baking.

Serves 4

Sue Landrum

Potato Puff

2 cups leftover mashed
  potatoes
1 tablespoon butter

1 egg
½ cup grated cheese

Separate egg. Add yolk to potatoes and butter. Beat together with a fork. Beat the egg white and fold into potato mixture. Put in buttered 1-quart dish. Sprinkle cheese on top. Microwave until warmed through — about 8 minutes.

Serves 4

Sue Landrum

Parsley Cream Sauce

1½ cups milk
3 tablespoons flour
1 tablespoon butter

1 tablespoon chopped fresh
  parsley
1 tablespoon onion, chopped
Salt and pepper to taste

Shake milk and flour together to avoid lumps. Add remaining ingredients in a 2-quart bowl. Cook 5 minutes; stir. Cook at least another 5 minutes, stirring after each minute. Spoon on top of fried meat, baked potatoes or other vegetables.

Serves 4

Dixie Lee Mauger

Carrot Cake with Cream Cheese Frosting

Cake:

1½ cups sugar
1 cup cooking oil
1 teaspoon vanilla
3 eggs
1½ cups unsifted flour

¾ teaspoon salt
1¼ teaspoons soda
2½ teaspoons cinnamon
2¼ cups raw grated carrots
½ cup chopped nuts

Blend sugar, oil, and vanilla—add eggs and beat well. Mix together the dry ingredients, and add them to sugar-egg mixture. Fold in carrots and nuts. Pour into a 12x8x2-inch dish greased on bottom only. Put dish in microwave and cook 13 to 15 minutes, turning dish ¼ turn every 4 minutes. Let stand on wood board to cool. Frost with cream cheese frosting.

Frosting:

2 cups powdered sugar
1 3-ounce package cream
  cheese

3 tablespoons margarine
1 teaspoon vanilla

Put sugar in a 1-quart dish. Place cream cheese, margarine, and vanilla on top. Cook 1 minute in microwave just until ingredients can be beaten. Mix in sugar.

Phyllis Gould

Bananas Royale

6 tablespoons margarine
6 tablespoons packed brown
  sugar
¼ teaspoon cinnamon
¼ teaspoon nutmeg

½ cup light cream
4 medium bananas
¼ cup brandy, rum, or
  flavored liqueur
½ teaspoon vanilla

Place butter in 9-inch glass dish and melt. Stir in brown sugar, cinnamon, nutmeg and cream. Slice bananas once lengthwise and once crosswise. Place in mixture, stirring to coat bananas. Cook in microwave for 4 minutes. Heat brandy 15 to 20 seconds or until warm. Pour over bananas and ignite. Serve immediately over ice cream.

Serves 4 to 6

Donna Houser

Cherries Jubilee

2 16-ounce cans dark cherries   ¾ cup sugar
3 tablespoons cornstarch   ½ cup brandy

Drain cherry syrup into a 2-quart casserole. Add cornstarch and sugar. Microwave 6 minutes, stirring after 3 minutes. When syrup begins to thicken, add cherries. Measure ½ cup of brandy, microwave ½ minute. Pour brandy over cherries, saving 1 tablespoon to ignite. Ignite brandy in the tablespoon and pour over cherries. When flame has subsided, serve over ice cream.

Serves 8 to 10   *Sue Haney*

Fruit-Filled Pineapple

1 medium fresh pineapple   ¾ cup maraschino cherries
1 cup shredded coconut   ½ cup orange marmalade
1 11-ounce can mandarin   ⅓ cup rum
    oranges, drained

Cut pineapple, including leafy crown, in half lengthwise. Cut out fruit, leaving outside shell intact. Remove woody core; cut remaining fruit in chunks. Mix together pineapple, coconut, mandarin oranges, cherries and marmalade. Fill pineapple with mixture. Place pineapple on a serving plate suitable for microwave and cook 8 to 10 minutes, checking for doneness. Place rum in glass measure. Microwave 15 seconds. Pour over pineapple, saving 1 tablespoon to use to ignite rum. Pour ignited rum over pineapple.

Suggestion: Serve in small bowl.

Serves 8   *Sue Haney*

Micro Walnut Fudge

1 1-pound box confectioners
  sugar
½ cup cocoa
¼ teaspoon salt
¼ cup milk

1 tablespoon vanilla extract
½ cup butter
1 cup coarsely chopped
  walnuts

Stir sugar, cocoa, salt, milk and vanilla together in 1½-quart casserole till partially blended. Put butter over top in center of dish. Cook in microwave 1 to 1½ minutes until milk feels warm on bottom of dish. Stir vigorously till smooth (butter may not be completely melted but will blend). Stir in nuts. Pour into buttered 8-inch dish or pan. Refrigerate till firm.

Bev Brill

Microwave Peanut Brittle

1 cup sugar
1 cup raw peanuts

½ cup white corn syrup

Mix in large glass bowl and microwave 4 minutes; stir. Cook 3 to 4 minutes more. Add and microwave 1½ to 2 minutes:

1 teaspoon butter
1 teaspoon vanilla

Add and stir in 1 heaping teaspoon baking soda. Spread on a greased cookie sheet as thinly as possible.

Marge Rabatin

Lemon Crumb Pie

1⅓ cups graham cracker
   crumbs
¼ cup butter or margarine
3 eggs
⅛ teaspoon salt

Grated rind and juice of 1½
   lemons
1 can (15-oz.) sweetened
   condensed milk

In a 9-inch glass pie plate, mix crumbs and butter until well blended. Set aside ¼ cup crumb mixture. Press crumb mixture firmly against bottom and sides of pie plate.

Separate eggs and beat yolks until very thick. Stir in lemon juice, grated rind, and condensed milk. Fold into stiffly beaten egg whites to which salt was added. Pour into unbaked pie shell and sprinkle reserved crumbs on top. Bake pie in Radarange Oven 5 minutes, turning dish at 1½ minute intervals during this time. Cool at room temperature and chill pie before serving.

Serves 6

Rocky Road Squares

1 12-ounce package semi-
   sweet chocolate morsels
1 14-ounce can sweetened
   condensed milk

2 tablespoons butter or
   margarine
2 cups dry roasted peanuts
1 10½-ounce package
   miniature marshmallows.

In 1½-quart glass dish put chocolate morsels, condensed milk, and butter. Microwave one minute, stir. Microwave one more minute until mixture is smooth. Combine nuts and marshmallows in large bowl. Fold in chocolate mixture. Spread in wax paper-lined or buttered 9x13-inch pan. Chill 2 hours or until firm. Cut into squares.

Patti Sweeney

Crockpot

Barbecued Short Ribs and Beans

1 pound pinto beans, rinsed
and picked over
6 cups water
4 pounds beef short ribs
2 tablespoons oil
4 medium onions, chopped
1 8-ounce can tomato sauce

¼ cup packed brown sugar
1 tablespoon cider vinegar
1 tablespoon Worcestershire
sauce
1 tablespoon prepared mustard
2 teaspoons salt
2 teaspoons chili powder

Use large cooker—at least 4½ quarts. Soak beans 24 hours in 6 cups water. Drain, reserving 1 cup liquid. In crockpot, combine beans, reserved liquid, and remaining ingredients, except ribs. Top with unbrowned ribs, cover and cook on low setting for 7 to 8 hours or until ribs and beans are tender.

Note: If there is time, brown the ribs and sauté the onions for enhanced flavor.

Serves 6 *Judy Pike*

Burgundy Beef

1½ to 2 pounds beef stew
meat, cut in bite-sized
pieces
1 tablespoon margarine
1 tablespoon olive oil
Salt and pepper
3 tablespoons tapioca
1 medium onion, chopped
1 2-ounce can sliced
mushrooms, undrained

½ teaspoon instant beef
bouillon (granulated)
2 tablespoons tomato sauce
(catsup may be substituted)
1 cup Burgundy wine
½ cup water
¼ teaspoon garlic powder
1 bay leaf

Brown meat in heavy skillet with margarine and oil. Salt and pepper to taste. Put meat in crockpot, sprinkle with tapioca, and add remaining ingredients. Mix well and cook 1 hour on high, then 5 to 6 hours on low. Serve with buttered rice or noodles.

Serves 4 to 6 *Phyllis Riesner*

Burrito Meat Casserole

4 pounds stew meat
2 tomatoes, diced
2 yellow or green chilies, diced
½ onion, diced

Garlic salt
1 can tomato sauce
1 large can pinto beans

Brown meat; place all ingredients in crockpot. Cook on high for 1 hour, then on low 8 to 10 hours. Serve with warm flour tortillas, and sour cream and guacamole if desired. Great for a buffet with tossed salad.

Serves 8   *Rosie Marta*

Chicken Continental

6 to 8 chicken breasts
6 to 8 bacon slices
1 package dried beef

1 can cream of mushroom
  soup
¼ cup sour cream mixed with
  ¼ cup flour

Arrange dried beef on bottom of greased crockpot. Wrap each piece of chicken with bacon and lay on top of beef. Mix soup and sour cream together; pour over chicken. Cover and cook on low 8 to 10 hours. Serve over hot buttered noodles.

Serves 6   *Kay Anderson*

Crockpot Chile

In skillet, brown 2 pounds hamburger with ½ cup diced onion. Cook till tender, and drain off grease. In crockpot, combine hamburger with:

2 1-pound 14-ounce cans chile
  beans
2 1-pound cans tomatoes

Mix well; cook on high 1 hour, then low 10 hours. Add chili powder or Tabasco to taste.

Serves 6   *Alice Bollinger*

Crockpot Meatloaf

1 pound ground beef
½ cup bread or cracker crumbs
1 egg
¼ cup milk

Grated onion, if desired
1 teaspoon garlic salt
1 tablespoon ketchup

Combine crumbs, egg, milk and onion. Add garlic salt (or regular salt) and ketchup, then crumble meat into the mixture and mix well. Shape into a mound just smaller than crockpot and place into the pot so no sides of the loaf are touching. Cover the top with ketchup or any tomato sauce if you wish. Cook for 30 minutes to 1 hour on high and then reduce to low. Cook another 5 to 6 hours.

Note: If extra lean beef is used, more liquid may need to be added to mixture.

Serves 4   *Candy Quigg*

Crockpot Surprise

2 pounds beef stew meat, cut
   into 1-inch pieces
1 envelope dry onion soup mix
½ cup red wine

1 can cream of mushroom
   soup
½ pound fresh mushrooms,
   sliced

Sauté mushrooms in 1 tablespoon butter. Remove from pan and lightly brown meat. Combine all ingredients in pot. Mix well. Cover and cook on high 1 hour. Turn to low, cook 10 hours. Serve over rice or noodles.

Serves 6   *Alice Bollinger*

Swiss Bliss

2 pounds chuck steak, 1½-inch thick
1 1-pound can tomatoes
1 envelope dry onion soup mix
1 tablespoon steak sauce
1 4-ounce can sliced mushrooms, drained
1 tablespoon cornstarch
1 tablespoon chopped parsley

Cut steak into bite-sized pieces and arrange in crockpot. Drain tomatoes, reserving juice. Place tomatoes over steak. Sprinkle soup mix and mushrooms over tomatoes. Combine reserved juice with remaining ingredients and pour over all. Cover and cook on low 6 to 8 hours. Serve with rice.

Serves 6   *Helen Murley*

The Clark's Rump Roast

1 pound rump roast (fat removed)

Roll roast in flour seasoned with:

A little garlic salt
½ teaspoon salt
¼ teaspoon seasoned salt
Freshly ground black pepper

Brown roast in sauté pan, using 1 tablespoon margarine. While roast is browning, warm crockpot on high temperature. Place roast in pot and pour ⅓ cup red or pink wine over it (no water needed). Cook 1 hour, 15 minutes on high, turn to low and cook 1 hour (a larger roast, 3½ to 4 pounds, should cook in approximately 3 to 4 hours). Vegetables may be added, such as carrots, potatoes, celery, etc. Carrots should be cut in half or quartered and placed in bottom of pan.

Serves 2 to 3   *Eunice S. Clark*

natural flavors

In an era where getting
back to the basics is popular,
an exciting new world of possibilities is
offered by the ever-increasing emphasis on
natural foods and their preparation.
What could be more natural than
utilizing the hot rays of the sun
to dry and preserve?

Joanne Battiste

Natural Foods

Many cooks today are making an effort to incorporate natural ingredients into their cooking and to cut down on the use of white sugar and flour. This chapter contains recipes of this type—using no white sugar, no more than 50% white flour, and fresh, unprocessed ingredients. A real "purist" will want to do a little adjusting on a few recipes; but for the majority of cooks, this assortment of recipes is very nutritious, wholesome, and DELICIOUS!

Ugly Dip

1 cup celery, finely chopped
1 cup green pepper, finely chopped
2 4-ounce cans chopped black olives
3 7-ounce cans diced green chilies
1 cup chopped fresh tomatoes
1 to 2 tablespoons onion, finely chopped
Garlic salt, to taste
1 tablespoon wine vinegar
1 tablespoon vegetable oil

Mix all of the above and serve from bowl or platter with snack crackers.

Harriet Sullivan

Banana Lo-Cal Shake

Place in blender:

1 frozen banana, cut into chunks (defrost 10 to 20 minutes to remove skin first)
1 cup milk
1 teaspoon real vanilla

Blend until frothy and pour into large glass.

This is especially useful for overripe bananas. Don't throw them away; freeze and use for this refreshing pick-up.

Makes approximately 1½ cups

Tryna Fredregill

Instant Breakfast

1 large glass orange juice (10 to 12 ounces, made from frozen concentrate)
1 raw egg

2 to 3 heaping tablespoons yogurt
1 teaspoon wheat germ
¼ to ½ teaspoon brewers yeast—to taste

Combine all above ingredients in blender and mix thoroughly. Pour in glass and serve.

Pat Wellens

Apple Pancakes

1 cup whole wheat flour
2 to 3 tablespoons wheat germ
1 egg
1 cup buttermilk
½ teaspoon soda
⅛ teaspoon salt
½ teaspoon baking powder

2 tablespoons oil
¼ cup unsweetened applesauce
1 peeled, chopped raw apple
¼ teaspoon cinnamon (optional)

Mix all ingredients in mixing bowl. If needed, add a little milk or water to desired consistency. Cook on hot griddle. Serve with butter and add a little raw honey.

Note: Whenever I use whole wheat flour in baking, I add a little unsweetened applesauce to add moistness. You can't taste it and it really improves the texture.

Serves 5

Bennie Swanson

Cornbread

1 cup cornmeal
½ cup whole wheat flour
1 heaping teaspoon baking
   powder
½ teaspoon salt

1 egg
½ teaspoon baking soda in
1 cup buttermilk
4 tablespoons cooking oil
1 teaspoon honey

Mix all of the above and pour into greased 8x8-inch pan. Bake for 30 minutes at 425°.

Marie Clifton

Crunchy Cassa-Rolls

1 cup milk
1 tablespoon honey
¼ cup butter (half stick)
¾ teaspoon salt

1 package yeast
1 cup whole wheat flour
½ cup unbleached white flour

Grease bottom and sides of 9x9-inch pan or casserole dish.

Heat milk, honey, 1 tablespoon butter, and salt until the butter melts. Pour into another bowl to cool. Meanwhile, melt remaining butter. When milk mixture is cool enough (100° F), add yeast. Stir to dissolve. Add flour and stir until smooth and elastic (dough is sticky). Let rise 30 minutes. Pour half the melted butter in the greased 9x9-inch pan. Stir batter down and drop by heaping tablespoons into pan. Pour remaining butter over rolls and sprinkle with 2 teaspoons wheat germ. Let rise until double. Bake for 30 minutes at 400°.

Hint: Do yourself a favor and time this so you can eat them right from the oven.

Yield: 12 rolls

Phyllis Riesner

Whole Wheat Hamburger Buns

6 tablespoons yeast
3½ cups warm (not hot) water
1 cup vegetable oil
½ cup honey
¼ cup wheat germ

3 eggs, slightly beaten
1 tablespoon salt
8 cups whole wheat flour
2 cups unbleached white flour

Mix first 4 ingredients in large mixing bowl. Let rise 15 minutes. (The amount of yeast used will not cause a "yeasty" taste. A "yeasty" taste is a result of letting dough rise too long.) Then add remaining ingredients. Knead just enough to work all the flour into the lump of dough. Immediately shape into hamburger buns (the shape of a hamburger patty: 12 buns per cookie sheet) and place on lightly greased cookie sheet. Let rise 15 minutes and bake in preheated 425° oven for 10 minutes. Remove from oven and cool for 10 minutes and then remove from pans with spatula and place on racks to completely cool. Slit buns with a sharp bread knife, but not all the way though. Keep one side slightly intact for easier handling. These may then be frozen in plastic bags in quantities desired. Yield: 3 to 3½ dozen buns.

Variation: Make two dozen buns and use remainder of dough to make a loaf of bread. Bread should be cooked longer than buns— 25 or 30 minutes, depending on size of loaf, until golden brown.

Hot dog buns can also be made with this recipe. Just shape buns accordingly. Remember the dough will rise more during the cooking, so be careful not to make the buns too large.

Helen Banner

Honey Wheat Bread

2 to 2½ cups unbleached white
    flour
4 cups whole wheat flour
2 packages dry yeast
1 tablespoon salt
1 cup milk

1 cup water
½ cup honey
¼ cup wheat germ
3 tablespoons shortening
1 egg

In saucepan heat milk, water, honey, and shortening until warm (shortening does not need to melt). In large mixer bowl combine one cup white flour, 2 cups wheat flour, yeast and salt; mix well. Add warm (not hot or it will kill yeast) liquid to dry mix and add egg. Blend at low speed until moistened. Add wheat germ. Then beat 3 minutes at medium speed. Remove from mixer and add remaining flour and mix by hand until you have a firm dough. Use just enough flour so the dough doesn't stick to your hands. Too much flour will make the dough very stiff and bread will be dry. Knead on floured surface for about 10 minutes until smooth and elastic. Put in greased bowl, turning to grease top. Cover with cloth and let rise in warm place until light and doubled in size. I place a pan of hot water in the lower shelf of my oven and the covered bowl on the top shelf. Let rise approximately 1 hour.

Punch down dough and then divide in two parts. On lightly floured surface, roll out with rolling pin each half into a 14x7-inch rectangle. Roll up tightly, pressing dough into roll with fingertips with each roll. This eliminates air pockets. Pinch edges and ends to seal and place seam side down in greased 9x5-inch loaf pans.

Cover, and let rise for 30 minutes or until doubled in size. Bake at 375° for 35 to 40 minutes until golden brown. Remove from pans and cool.

This recipe can be completed in 3 to 3½ hours. It has a sweet, nutty flavor.

Yield: 2 loaves
Helen Banner

Asparagus Quiche

14 whole fresh asparagus
  spears (cooked)
1 unbaked 9-inch whole wheat
  pie shell
4 eggs, slightly beaten
¾ teaspoon salt
Pinch white pepper

1 cup half and half cream
Pinch nutmeg
¼ pound bacon slides, cooked
  and crumbled
1 cup (4 ounces) shredded
  Swiss cheese

Reserve 8 spears asparagus for garnish; chop remaining. Place pie shell in freezer for at least 15 minutes—this helps to keep the shell from shrinking. Preheat oven to 425°. Bake shell 7 to 10 minutes, until pale golden brown. Remove from oven.

Meanwhile, in small bowl, mix next 5 ingredients and chopped asparagus. Sprinkle bacon and cheese over bottom of pie shell. Pour egg mixture into shell. Arrange asparagus spears spoke-fashion on top. Bake at 350° for 35 minutes or until knife inserted in center comes out clean.

Serves 6 to 8   *Becky Denman*

Chicken with Almonds

1 pound chicken breasts
1 egg white
2 teaspoons cornstarch
1 cup whole almonds
2 or 3 green onions, chopped
1 cup chopped celery
2 slices ginger root
1 cup wedged cucumber

¾ cup mushrooms, wedged
6 tablespoons oil
1 tablespoon wine
2 tablespoons soy sauce
1 tablespoon water
1 teaspoon honey
Cooked hot rice

Bone and cube chicken. Mix with egg white and one teaspoon cornstarch. Blanch nuts in 2 tablespoons oil. Remove to small dish. Heat remainder of oil. Sauté green onion, ginger, chicken, and cucumber. Add celery and mushrooms. Add wine, honey and soy sauce. Mix 1 teaspoon cornstarch with water and add to mixture. At this point, you may need a little more water or soy sauce for moisture. Let simmer about 5 minutes. Add nuts and stir. Serve over hot rice with extra soy sauce if desired.

Serves 4   *Janet Holmes*

Fish Cheese Puff

1 pound fish fillet (halibut,
flounder, pike or haddock)
fresh or frozen, thawed (not
breaded)
Melted butter
½ cup dairy sour cream

2 cups grated Cheddar cheese
1 tablespoon chopped parsley
2 egg yolks
2 teaspoons minced onion
¼ teaspoon salt
2 egg whites

Place fish in a single layer on baking dish; brush both sides generously with melted butter. Combine sour cream, Cheddar cheese, egg yolks, parsley, onion and salt. Beat egg whites until stiff; fold sour cream mixture into them. Pour puff mixture over fish, covering well and bake at 350° for 20 to 25 minutes. Serve immediately.

Serves 4

Pat McEvoy

Omelette

8 eggs
¼ cup milk

Salt and pepper

Combine above ingredients in a bowl.

5 fresh mushrooms
¼ cup chopped green peppers
¼ cup chopped pimientos
Bean sprouts, as desired

Grated Cheddar cheese, as
desired
6 ounces bulk sausage,
browned and drained

Sauté mushrooms and green pepper in butter for 5 minutes in a skillet. Remove from pan; pour egg mixture into pan. Cook on medium heat covered until eggs are cooked but still moist on top. Sprinkle sautéed mushrooms and green peppers, pimiento and sausage over half the eggs. Also sprinkle on bean sprouts and Cheddar cheese. Cook covered. When almost done, carefully fold half not covered with mixture over other side. Sprinkle small amount of cheese on top; cook until cheese melts. Flip pan over onto serving platter. Cut into six servings.

Pat Wellens

Split Peasonality

1 pound dried split peas
6 cups water
1 bay leaf
1 cup chopped onion
½ teaspoon ground celery seed
1 teaspoon salt
½ teaspoon ground pepper
1 ham bone (hock) cut into 3
  to 4 pieces with meat

1 cup grated carrot
½ cup broth from cooked peas
3 tablespoons whole wheat
  pastry flour
2 cups whole milk
Chopped black olives
  (optional)

Soak peas overnight in the water OR bring water to a boil and add peas, remove from heat, cover, and soak 2 hours.

Place peas and water in crock pot; turn heat to HIGH. Trim fat off meat and add ham bones, bay leaf, onion and seasonings to pot. Stir, cover, and heat 1 hour.

Turn heat to LOW and simmer about 7 hours. One hour before serving, remove bones and bay leaf. Warm the milk. Mix broth and flour in covered jar and shake briskly and pour into soup. Mix well and add warmed milk. Turn heat to HIGH. Dice about 1 cup of meat from bone and add to soup along with the grated carrot. Stir and continue simmering until soup is thickened and carrot is tender, stirring occasionally. Serve piping hot. Garnish with chopped olives on top, if desired.

This soup is great for a cold snowy evening, served with grilled cheese sandwiches on whole grain bread.

Makes 2½ quarts   *Tryna Fredregill*

Carrots and Grapes

Cut about 2 to 3 cups of carrots into 2-inch sticks and boil in salted water until done. Pour off water and immediately put in a cup of seedless grapes and cover with lid and warm for 2 minutes, until grapes are warm. Add 2 tablespoons butter and 2 teaspoons lemon juice and serve immediately. Delightful combination and very colorful!

Margaret McIntire

370

Oriental Fried Rice

1 stick butter or margarine
4 eggs, beaten well
1 cup sliced onions
(lengthwise)
1 cup sliced green pepper
2 cups fresh bean sprouts or
1-pound canned

1 8-ounce can sliced water
chestnuts
½ cup fresh sliced mushrooms
or 4-ounces canned
1 tablespoon Worcestershire
sauce
1 tablespoon soy sauce
4 cups cooked rice

Optional: 2 cups any kind of meat, cubed (chicken, beef, pork)

Heat large skillet to medium heat and add 1 stick butter or margarine. When butter is completely melted, add the beaten eggs and break up as it cooks. Add onions, green pepper, bean sprouts, water chestnuts, and mushrooms. Mix well and cook covered for 5 minutes. Remove lid and add Worcestershire sauce and soy sauce. Blend well. Then add cooked rice. This makes an excellent rice dish to be served with meat. However, meat may be added to this dish to make a complete meal all in one. Heat all the ingredients together and pour into a large casserole dish (3 quart). Serve immediately or reheat in oven or microwave just before serving.

Main Dish serves 4 to 6
Side Dish serves 12

Helen Banner

Stuffed Zucchini

4 medium zucchini
½ cup diced onion
½ cup diced green chili

½ cup chopped celery
1 cup grated colby cheese
Salt and pepper to taste

Boil squash until almost tender. Cool. Slice in half lengthwise and scoop out loose pulp inside. Drain pulp and mix with onion, chili, celery, and half of the cheese. Salt and pepper to taste. Refill shells and place strips of chili and remaining cheese on top. Bake in 350° oven just until cheese is melted, about 20 minutes.

Serves 8

Joy Everhart

Gourmet Potatoes

6 medium potatoes
2 cups shredded Cheddar
  cheese
¼ cup butter or margarine
1½ cup sour cream
1 teaspoon salt

⅓ cup finely chopped green
  onion
1¼ teaspoon pepper
2 tablespoons butter or
  margarine

Boil potatoes in skin until almost done. (Should not be too soft). Cool. Peel skin off and grate potatoes. In a saucepan over low heat cook cheese and ¼ cup of the butter until almost melted. Remove from heat and blend in sour cream, onion and seasoning. Fold in potatoes (use electric mixer) and turn into a 2-quart casserole. Dot with 2 tablespoons butter and sprinkle with paprika. Bake uncovered for 30 minutes at 350° until heated through.

Serves 6

Joy Everhart

20-Second Mayonnaise

Measure one cup safflower oil (or other light vegetable oil)

Put in blender the following:

¼ cup of the safflower oil
One egg
2 tablespoons cider vinegar

½ teaspoon dry mustard
½ teaspoon salt

Cover blender with lid and blend for 10 seconds on medium or high speed. Remove lid and without stopping blender, pour in the rest of the oil in a slow steady stream. Continue blending another 10 seconds or so, mixing a little with a rubber spatula. The more you blend the thicker it will get, but this is not recommended. Use spatula to help remove mayonnaise into a clean jar. Stores in refrigerator several weeks.

Note: Do not make more than one batch at a time! Successive batches may be made, however, without cleaning the blender, until you have enough.

Yield: About 1 cup

Kim Spitzer

Carob Chip Cookies

1½ cups whole wheat flour
¾ teaspoon salt
1½ teaspoons baking powder
½ cup butter
1 teaspoon vanilla

⅔ cup unsweetened
  applesauce
½ cup honey
1 egg, beaten
1 6-ounce package carob chips
½ cup chopped nuts (optional)

Mix butter and honey. Add vanilla, egg and applesauce. Add dry ingredients and mix in carob chips and nuts. Drop by teaspoons on cookie sheet. Bake at 350° for 15 minutes.

Note: 1 cup raisins or 1 package chocolate chips can be substituted for carob chips.

Kay Anderson

Gorp

Any combination of dried fruit, seeds, nuts, and granola you might have on hand, such as raisins, sunflower seeds, almonds, pumpkin seeds, dried apricots, dried apples, peanuts. Whenever possible, use unsalted nuts. This is a delicious, high energy snack your family will enjoy.

Marsha Immerman Hilvitz

Gorp Cookies

1 cup butter
1½ cups honey
2 eggs
½ teaspoon salt
2 teaspoons vanilla
1 teaspoon baking powder
3¾ cups whole wheat flour

¼ cup milk powder
1 cup sunflower seeds
1½ cups peanuts, roasted,
  chopped
1½ cups raisins
1½ cup carob chips

Cream butter; add honey and beat in eggs, salt and vanilla. Stir together baking powder, milk powder, and whole wheat flour. Add to creamed mixture. Stir in seeds, nuts, raisins, and chips. Bake 10 to 12 minutes at 375°.

Marsha Hilvitz

Honey Cookies

1 cup soft butter
1 cup honey
2 eggs
2 teaspoons vanilla
2⅓ cups whole wheat flour

2 teaspoons baking powder
½ teaspoon salt
1 cup oats
¼ cup wheat germ

Mix well butter, honey, eggs and vanilla. Combine flour, baking powder, salt, oats, and wheat germ and add to honey mixture. Add any of the following optional ingredients:

½ cup raisins
½ cup chocolate chips

½ cup nuts

Bake at 350° for 10 to 12 minutes.

Yield: 4 to 5 dozen   *Candy Quigg*

Vanilla-Oatmeal Cookies

1 cup (2 sticks) butter or
    margarine
1½ cups brown sugar
2 eggs, beaten
2 teaspoons vanilla
2 cups flour (whole wheat or 1
    cup white and 1 cup wheat)

2⅓ cups oatmeal
2 teaspoons baking soda
½ teaspoon baking powder
1 teaspoon cinnamon
2 cups raisins

Cream butter and sugar and then add eggs and vanilla. Combine dry ingredients together and add to creamed mixture. Mix well. Add raisins and drop by teaspoon on cookie sheet. Bake at 350° for 10 to 15 minutes.

Yield: 4 dozen   *Lucky Atkinson*

374

Granola

5 cups old fashioned oatmeal
1 cup each: soya flour, wheat germ, instant milk, sesame seeds,
sunflower seeds, slivered almonds, shredded coconut

Mix together:

1 cup honey
1 cup vegetable oil

Add and mix together. Spread on two cookie sheets and bake
½ hour at 300°, stirring occasionally. Store in jars or plastic bags.

Sue Ann Pumphrey

Natural Candy

¼ pound pitted dates
½ pound dried figs
½ pound dried apricots

1 cup chopped nuts
¼ cup raisins
2 tablespoons shredded
coconut

Grind first 5 ingredients with meat grinder and mix thoroughly.
Moisten hands with water and form into 1-inch balls. Sprinkle
coconut on a sheet of waxed paper and roll each ball in coconut.

Yield: 4 dozen
Donna Pisciotta

Peanut Butter Popcorn

4 to 5 quarts popped corn
1 cup nuts

Mix the above two ingredients. Then in a saucepan heat the
following until blended:

½ to ¾ cup honey
¼ cup peanut butter

1 tablespoon butter
Pinch of baking soda

When well blended, pour over popcorn and peanuts and mix
well.

Marcia Porter

Sesame Street Crunchies

½ cup peanut butter   ¼ cup wheat germ
½ cup honey   ½ cup sesame seeds
1 cup oatmeal

Mix peanut butter, honey, oatmeal, and wheat germ together. Meanwhile, put sesame seeds in a large skillet and cook over moderate heat about 5 minutes, shaking or stirring until light brown. Tip seeds on wax paper and cool. Form peanut butter mix into balls. Roll in seeds until well coated. Store in single layer in refrigerator.

Note: To pack for lunches, wrap each ball individually in plastic wrap.

Makes 40   *Lucky Atkinson*

Solar Fruit Tack

Ingredients:
1 fruit—fresh, frozen, or canned without sugar added; (4 cups approximately will fill one cookie sheet)
                            OR
Combination of *two fruits* like:

Apricot and pineapple   Strawberry and pear
Strawberry and banana   Peaches and plum
Raspberry and apple
Plum and banana   1 to 2 tablespoons honey
Apricot and strawberry   (optional)

Directions: Pit ripe fruits and put in blender and pureé skin and all. Add honey, if desired, for consistency and blend. Cover a cookie sheet with plastic wrap. Pour mixture over wrap so that it is ¼ to ½-inch thick. Cover pan with screening or nylon netting to keep bugs out and place outdoors. The sun will dry mixture in 3 to 5 days, depending on weather. When the fruit tack is no longer "sticky" to touch, it can be removed from the pan by rolling up and wrapping in plastic wrap. This is a great snack and tastes great in the winter.

Donna Pisciotta

man in the kitchen

A refreshingly casual approach
which results in hearty appetite-pleasing
flavor typifies the wonderful flair men add
to the cooking scene whether "in the kitchen"
or in the great out-of-doors with
the aid of a charcoal grill.

Margaritas

5 ounces tequila
2 ounces triple sec
1 can daiquiri mix (frozen)

1 teaspoon egg white
Crushed ice

Blend all ingredients in blender; serve.

Jack Harris

Grandpa's Egg Nog

4 eggs, separated—yolks and
    whites beaten very stiff
½ cup superfine sugar
⅓ cup rum

⅔ cup brandy
2½ cups milk
2½ cups cream
Nutmeg

After yolks are stiff, add sugar slowly. Add liquor slowly. Add milk and cream slowly. Fold egg whites into mixture; add nutmeg.

Serves 12 to 14

Note: For larger groups use:

6 eggs
¾ cup sugar
4 cups milk

4 cups cream
½ cup rum
1½ cups brandy

Tip: Use good rum and brandy—not sweet, fruit-flavored brandy.

Suzie Ware

Onion Straws

Fresh yellow onions (1 per   Flour
  person)   Salt

Peel onions and slice as thin as possible (approximately ¹⁄₁₆-inch). Separate slices into individual rings and place in paper sack with sufficient amount of flour to coat onions. Shake well. Remove onions, shaking off excess flour, put in deep fryer and cook until golden brown. Remove and drain on paper towels; salt lightly. Makes excellent appetizer.

Don Banner

Bob's Supreme Omelette

2 tablespoons butter
5 eggs
¼ cup grated Muenster or
  Monterey Jack cheese
¼ cup grated sharp Cheddar
  cheese
2 tablespoons chopped red bell
  pepper (or pimiento)

¼ cup chopped canned
  mushrooms and juice
½ cup chopped fresh spinach
1 tablespoon chopped onion
½ cup roast beef hash
¼ teaspoon salt
Dash pepper

Grate cheese and chop vegetables. Melt butter over medium heat in large frying pan (or 2 small pans). Do not allow butter to smoke. Meanwhile, beat eggs briskly with a fork in medium bowl until well beaten. Add vegetables, hash, cheese, seasonings, and beat well. When pan is hot enough so a drop of water sizzles in it, pour in egg mixture. Cover pan, turn heat to low, and cook omelette 10 to 15 minutes. As edges begin to firm up, lift cooked portion with spatula and allow uncooked to run under spatula. Repeat around edges every few minutes until center is cooked, but still moist. Cut omelette in half across pan; loosen all of underside of omelette with spatula. Fold each half over and cut it in half. Serve hot with toast and muffins, and sliced apples.

Serves 4

Bob Fredregill

Cheesy Baked Egg Casserole

½ cup butter, melted
3 dozen eggs, slightly beaten

1 pound Velveeta, thinly sliced

Butter 13x9-inch glass casserole dish with the melted butter. Line the bottom of the pan with the sliced cheese. Add to the beaten eggs the following:

1½ cups milk
1 teaspoon salt
¼ teaspoon pepper

1 tablespoon prepared mustard
4½-ounce can sliced
mushrooms

Pour the egg mixture over the cheese and bake one hour at 350°. The pan will be full, but after it is removed from the oven, the casserole will fall. Eggs should be slightly brown and firm. Cut in squares and serve with chili salsa and sliced avocados for garnish.

This recipe will serve 18. Cut the recipe down by ⅓ for 12 servings (2 dozen eggs) or cut recipe for 6 servings by decreasing amounts by ⅔ (1 dozen eggs). Seasonings will vary slightly.

Suggestion: Cook bacon and/or sausage in the oven the same hour it takes to bake the eggs. Everything is ready at the same time without slaving over the stove!

Donald Banner

Bowl Huevos Rancheros

Eggs
Mexican Meat (recipe follows)
Canned or your own enchilada
    sauce
Grated mild Cheddar cheese

Tortillas
Oil for frying tortillas
Chopped onion
Chopped Jalapeño peppers
Ovenproof bowls

In a saucepan, heat about ¼-inch of cooking oil. In another saucepan, heat enchilada sauce. Fry a tortilla for about 3 to 5 seconds on each side. Dip tortilla in enchilada sauce, then place the tortilla in a bowl. Spoon on some of the meat, sprinkle with some cheese, onion and peppers. Prepare another tortilla like the first one and place on top. Cook eggs as desired (1 or 2) and place on tortilla. Sprinkle on more cheese and spoon some enchilada sauce over the top. Place in 350° oven for 10 to 15 minutes to heat through.

Hershell Atkinson

Mexican Meat

3 flank steaks, cut crosswise in
    strips
4 to 6 pork chops, boned and
    cut in small pieces, with fat
    trimmed
2 tablespoons cooking oil
1 large onion, chopped
2 cloves garlic, chopped
2 tablespoons chili powder

1 teaspoon crushed red pepper
1 tablespoon oregano leaves
2 teaspoons cumin powder
1 to 2 Jalapeño peppers,
    chopped (optional)
Salt to taste (about 1
    tablespoon)
1 cup water or beef stock
2 cans green chilies, chopped

Combine all ingredients in a pressure cooker and cook for about 1 hour. Or, cook in a large pot, covered, until meat falls apart. After mixture is cooked, mash the meat apart with a wooden spoon until it's very stringy. If too much liquid remains, simmer uncovered until liquid cooks away. Taste to test seasoning and add desired additional seasonings before simmering away the liquid. This meat can be used for anything—enchiladas, tacos, nachos, tostadas, huevos rancheros, flautas, etc. It freezes well.

Serves 25 when used with Bowl Huevos Rancheros

Hershell Atkinson

Broiled Chicken Perth

1 chicken, 1½ to 2 pounds
3 tablespoons melted butter
2 tomatoes, sliced
2 garlic cloves

Salt
White peppercorns
Parsley

Mix salt, peppercorns, and parsley with some flour. Cut chicken in half by cutting through backbone. Beat the chicken lightly with a rolling pin to loosen major bones. Toss the halves well in seasoned flour. Preheat oven grill (medium hot); melt butter. Brush chicken with melted butter, then place under broiler with skin side up. Broil approximately 10 minutes, turn, butter and broil 10 minutes on reverse side. Brush with butter again. Place tomato slices over cooked upper side; spread squeezed garlic on tomatoes. Sprinkle with more salt and ground peppercorns. Broil to just color tomato (3 minutes), remove. Dust with parsley and serve.

Serves 2   *Len Wilcox*

Individual Pizzas

1 pound pork sausage (hot)
1 pound ground beef
1 15-ounce can tomato sauce
1 4-ounce can sliced
    mushrooms, drained
⅛ teaspoon garlic salt

2 teaspoons oregano leaves,
    crushed
5 English muffins, split and
    toasted
½ cup grated Parmesan cheese
10 slices Mozzarella cheese

In a skillet slowly cook pork sausage for 10 minutes; add ground beef and combine, cooking until browned. Drain. Add tomato sauce, mushrooms, oregano, and garlic salt to meat and stir. Place muffins on baking sheet. Spread each with about ¼ to ⅓ cup meat mixture. Sprinkle each with about 2 tablespoons Parmesan cheese. Top with a slice of Mozzarella. Bake 5 to 8 minutes or until hot and cheese melts, at 400°.

Variations: Add onions, green pepper and black olives. This will make more, so more muffins and cheese will be needed.

Dave Ware

383

Chicken Casserole

2 cups cooked chicken
1 package Noodles Romanoff, cooked, using ¾ cup milk instead of the ¼ cup called for on package
½ cup chopped black olives

1 10-ounce package chopped broccoli, thawed and drained
1 can cream of mushroom soup

Combine all ingredients in covered 1½ to 2-quart baking dish. Bake ½ hour at 350°.

Serves 4   *Sanford Wolfe*

Chow Down Chicken Salad

½ cup mayonnaise
1 teaspoon chili powder
1 tablespoon lemon juice
Salt and pepper
1½ cups diced cooked chicken (or 2 6-ounce cans chicken)

1 16-ounce can whole kernel corn, drained
1 large tomato, cut up
1 green pepper, diced
Hard-boiled eggs, chopped

Combine first 4 ingredients to make dressing. Toss with remaining ingredients, except eggs. Garnish with eggs.

Serves 3 to 4   *Paul Pumphrey*

Creative Chili

1½ pounds ground beef, browned in bacon fat
1 16-ounce can kidney beans, drained
1 16-ounce can pinto beans, drained
2 16-ounce cans chili beans
1 28-ounce can tomatoes, broken up
1 16-ounce can tomato sauce

2 4-ounce cans mushroom stems and pieces, drained
2 cups tomato juice
2 large onions, chopped
1 teaspoon salt
1 teaspoon seasoned salt
1 teaspoon seasoned pepper
3 tablespoons chili pepper
1 tablespoon chopped chives
1 tablespoon parsley flakes

Simmer all ingredients 2 to 3 hours. Add water to thin as desired.

Serves 8   *Mike Stillman*

384

Don K Ranch Tenderloin

Whole tenderloin
Salt
Pepper

Soy sauce
Worcestershire sauce
Salad oil

Sprinkle whole tenderloin with soy sauce and Worcestershire sauce. Salt and pepper to taste. Marinate loin for thirty minutes, turning frequently. Brush with salad oil. Cook on hot barbeque grill for approximately 25 minutes for medium, turning every few minutes.

Don Koenig

Ground Steak and Noodle Bake

2 tablespoons butter,
    margarine, or shortening
1½ pounds ground round
1 clove garlic
1½ teaspoons salt
1 dash pepper
1½ teaspoons sugar

3 8-ounce cans tomato sauce
6 cups small noodles
6 scallions
2 3-ounce packages cream
    cheese, softened
1 cup sour cream
3 cups grated Cheddar cheese

Melt fat in skillet; toss in ground steak, breaking it up in small pieces with fork. Fry till brown, drain. Crush or chop garlic fine and mix into meat with salt, pepper, sugar, and tomato sauce. Cover and cook slowly 15 to 20 minutes. Cook noodles according to directions, drain. Don't overcook. Set oven at 350°. In bottom of casserole put half of the noodles. Mix scallions, cream cheese, and sour cream; spread half of mixture on noodles. Cover with half of meat mixture. Sprinkle with 1 cup of the cheese. Repeat layers; sprinkle with remaining cheese. Bake 20 minutes or till bubbly.

Serves 8

Al Hewitt

Mock Filets

2 pounds hamburger
2 teaspoons salt
1 tablespoon Worcestershire
  sauce
¼ teaspoon pepper

2 eggs
½ pound Cheddar cheese
6 slices bacon
Vinegar

Mix first 5 ingredients well; make into patties (about 3-inches in diameter). Grate cheese. Place 2 tablespoons grated cheese on a pattie; then place another pattie on top. Pinch sides of two patties together and wrap sides with a slice of bacon. Secure with toothpicks. When ready to grill, brush top with vinegar. Brush other side with vinegar when it is turned.

Yield: 5 to 6 filets

Bill Gritton

Mike's Green Chile

3 pounds cubed pork roast or
  steak
1 16-ounce can beef bouillon
¼ teaspoon oregano
½ bay leaf
1½ large onions, chopped
2 12-ounce cans tomatillos or
  3 cups fresh green tomatoes

1 16-ounce can tomatoes,
  chopped
1 clove garlic, minced
Salt to taste
Extra water to cover
3 or 4 8-ounce cans chopped
  green chilies (not hot)

Brown meat in Dutch oven; pour off fat. Add bouillon and rest of the ingredients. Add Jalapeño chilies to taste if desired. Cover and simmer several hours. Add water if needed. It may be thickened, if desired.

Mike Stillman

Tom's El Grand Canoli

1 double crust pizza mix
(includes 2 cans pizza
topping and cheese)
4 cups shredded Mozzarella
cheese
1 pound sausage, crumbled,
cooked and drained

3 4-ounce cans sliced
mushrooms
1 pound hamburger, cooked
and drained
1 8-ounce can pizza topping

Prepare pizza crust per the directions on the pizza mix using both crusts. On a greased cookie sheet spread dough out from the center as you would a pizza, leaving the excess dough on both sides. Sprinkle 2 cups of Mozzarella cheese on the dough. Then layer the cooked, drained sausage on top of the cheese. Then layer half of the mushrooms on top of the sausage. Repeat the layers again by putting the remaining 2 cups of cheese on top of the mushrooms, the cooked hamburger on the next layer, and then the remaining mushrooms. Take the excess dough on the sides and pull up over the entire mixture to cover completely. Cook in oven preheated to 425° for 20 minutes, or until golden brown.

Meanwhile, in saucepan (or glass dish in microwave) heat the topping sauce that came in pizza crust mix with the additional can of pizza topping. When canoli is done and ready to be served, slice in serving pieces and top with warm pizza topping. Pass the Parmesan cheese to sprinkle on top (included in pizza crust mix), if desired.

Variations: Add onions, green peppers, olives, or any other ingredient that you usually enjoy on pizza to the mixture inside the dough. You may want to spice it up by adding Italian sausage in the place of the regular sausage or hamburger.

Serves 6 to 8   *Tom Mullans*

Southern Gulf Sandwich Spread

1 6½-ounce can tuna
3 hard-boiled eggs, diced
1 4-ounce can chopped chilies
(green)

3 tablespoons picante hot
sauce (or to taste)
4 tablespoons mayonnaise

Mix together. Serve on toasted bread garnished with lettuce.

Serves 4 to 6   *Lynn Haney*

Gram's Special Marinade

½ cup olive or salad oil
½ cup Claret or Burgundy wine
¼ cup soy sauce
½ teaspoon black pepper

1 tablespoon curry powder
2 cloves garlic, grated, or garlic salt
2 tablespoons tomato sauce or catsup

Mix all ingredients thoroughly; add no salt (soy sauce provides ample). Marinate meat in refrigerator 12 to 36 hours.

Suggestion: Use 3 pounds sirlion tip, cubed. Turn cubes in marinade several times for flavor. When ready to grill, drain meat, arrange on skewers with raw vegetables. Keep remaining marinade in small saucepan on grill and use to baste.

Yield: 1½ cups marinade   *Richard Gram*

Sunray Soup

1 can cream of asparagus soup
1 can cream of mushroom soup
2 soup cans whole milk

4 ounces canned mushrooms and juice
½ box frozen asparagus tips (cut spears—about 5 ounces)

Put soups in large pot and heat at medium. Slowly stir in milk until well blended; add mushrooms and juice and cover. Continue to stir from time to time while soup is heating—don't let soup stick to bottom. When soup is steamy hot (don't boil) add asparagus. Serve when asparagus is just tender and still bright green. A little seasoned salt and white pepper may be added.

Serves 6 to 8   *Bob Fredregill*

Hot German Potato Salad

Brown 8 slices bacon (diced) in skillet. Remove bacon and drain on paper. Add to bacon grease ½ cup vinegar and ½ cup sugar. Cook until slightly thick and clear. Cook 8 potatoes with jackets on. Cool, peel and dice. Mix potatoes with ½ cup chopped onion, 1 teaspoon salt, and ⅛ teaspoon pepper. Heat through in vinegar sauce; add cooked bacon.

Dave Ware

Barbeque Bacon-Wrapped Onions

Fresh onions, medium to large
   size (one per person)
Bacon

Butter
Heavy-duty aluminum foil

Peel onions and remove center core. Fill center with approximately one tablespoon butter per onion. Wrap onion with two strips of bacon in criss-cross pattern and hold in place with toothpicks. Wrap entire onion in heavy-duty foil and place directly on hot charcoal briquets. Cook approximately one hour, turning every 15 minutes.

Delicious served with charcoaled steak!

Donald Banner

Southwestern Baked Pinto Beans

1 pound dry pinto beans (2
   cups)
¼ pound bacon
1 medium onion, chopped
1 7-ounce can green chili salsa

¼ cup brown sugar
1 teaspoon salt
½ cup catsup
Additional bacon slices
   (optional)

Thoroughly wash beans. Soak beans in water to cover overnight. Cook beans in water in which they were soaked. If they have absorbed a lot of the water, add more so that the beans are covered by two inches. Bring to a boil, reduce heat and simmer, covered, about two hours or until almost done but still firm. Drain beans. Fry bacon until crisp. Drain bacon, crumble and reserve 2 tablespoons of the drippings. Sauté onion in reserved drippings until transparent. Combine onion, bacon, salsa, brown sugar, salt and catsup. Mix well. Add beans. Mix well and place in 2-quart casserole. Arrange additional slices of bacon on top, if desired. Bake covered in oven preheated to 325° for about 1½ hours. Remove cover during last 20 minutes of baking.

Serves 8 to 10

David Ware

Bananas Flambée

5 level tablespoons sugar
8 bananas (or 1 can peach
   halves for peach flambée)
4 tablespoons butter

Juice of 2 fresh oranges
1 jigger Grand Marnier
1 jigger cognac or brandy
6 scoops vanilla ice cream

Melt sugar in a pan (flambée pan made from copper with suitable burner is required, although with improvisation an ordinary pan heated over a stove will suffice). Add butter after sugar has caramelized (turned light brown and melted). Add the juice of 2 oranges (squeezed into the pan) and the Grand Marnier; let it simmer until it becomes slightly creamy. Place the bananas or peaches in syrup, and heat 2 to 3 minutes, spooning warm syrup over top. (Do not overcook and allow to spoil). Pour the cognac or brandy over the bananas and set ablaze (the secret of successful flaming is to remove most of the original syrup before adding cognac. Cognac must be slightly warmed, light immediately after cognac is added). To serve, put bananas on plate top and side with ice cream, and top all with delicious liquer sauce. (A few cocktail cherries put in pan with bananas add a pleasant touch of color and class). "Definitely a dish for the man of the house; it is a display of masculine 'savoir faire'."

Serves 6 to 8

Len Wilcox

Frank's Chocolate Brownies

½ pound butter
4 squares chocolate
4 eggs, beaten
2 cups sugar

1 cup flour
1 cup chopped nuts
1 teaspoon vanilla
¼ teaspoon salt

Melt butter and chocolate in pan. In large mixing bowl, beat other ingredients in order given; then add chocolate mixture and beat. Bake in greased and floured 12x8-inch pan at 350° for 30 minutes.

Fran Hensen

Coffee Fudge Pie

18 cream filled chocolate
  cookies
⅓ cup melted butter
2 squares (2 ounces)
  unsweetened chocolate
½ cup sugar
1 tablespoon butter

1 small can (⅔ cup)
  evaporated milk
1 quart coffee ice cream
1 cup whipping cream,
  whipped with 2 teaspoons
  sugar
½ cup chopped walnuts

Crush cookies and add melted butter. Mix well and press over sides and bottom of 9-inch pie pan. (Deep-dish pie pan works best.) Chill.

Melt chocolate squares over hot water in a double boiler. Stir in sugar and 1 tablespoon butter. Add evaporated milk slowly. Cook over medium heat until thickened, stirring occasionally, about 15 to 20 minutes. Chill in refrigerator.

Take ice cream from freezer and place in refrigerator to soften slightly. Fill pie shell with ice cream, cover with chilled fudge mixture. Whip the whipping cream with 2 teaspoons sugar and spread on top of the fudge. Sprinkle with nuts. Freeze. This is a very rich dessert, so cut small pieces. Delicious with hot coffee.

Serves 8 to 10
Don Banner

Snowy Ice Cream

4 eggs
2½ cups sugar
4 cups milk
4 cups light cream

2 cups heavy cream
3 tablespoons vanilla
½ teaspoon salt

Beat eggs until light. Add sugar and beat until mixture thickens. Add remaining ingredients. Mix thoroughly. Freeze in ice-cream freezer.

Yield: 1 gallon
Merle Brust

Jim's Rum Cake

2 sticks butter
1⅔ cups sugar
5 eggs

2 cups cake flour (sifted 3 times)

Cream until fluffy butter and sugar. Add eggs, one at a time. Sift in cake flour. Pour into ungreased tube pan. Bake at 325° for 1 hour and 10 minutes. Leave in pan and run knife around edge — poke holes in cake one inch apart. Immediately pour Hot Rum Sauce in holes in cake. Let cool in pan.

Hot Rum Sauce:

¼ stick butter
1 cup sugar

½ cup white rum

Heat sauce ingredients until sugar melts; do not boil.

Serves 10 to 12

Fran Hensen

White Raisin Pie

1½ cups white (golden) raisins
6 tablespoons margarine
1 cup sugar
1 tablespoon flour

2 eggs
Dash cinnamon
½ teaspoon vanilla
1 9-inch unbaked pie shell

Put raisins in pan and cover with water. Let them come to a boil and then let drain and cool while preparing the following: Melt margarine. Mix sugar and flour. Stir into margarine and mix well. Add eggs and beat well. Add dash of cinnamon and ½ teaspoon vanilla. Pour cooled raisins into pie shell. Pour other mixture over the raisins. Bake at 325° for one hour or until done.

Serves 6 to 8

T. Chalmers Henderson

weights and measures

Recipes depend upon
clever mixtures of ingredients
which are measured accurately.
The equivalents listed here reflect
the standards used in this cookbook.
High altitude cooking tips will benefit
culinary artists from many
of the western states.

weights
and measures

1 cup = 8 ounces
2 cups = 1 pint
4 cups = 1 quart
4 quarts = 1 gallon
4 tablespoons = ¼ cup
8 tablespoons = ½ cup
½ cup butter = ¼ pound
1 cup = 16 tablespoons
1 tablespoon = 3 teaspoons
1 square chocolate = 1 ounce
1 cup egg yolks = 12-14 eggs
1 cup egg whites = 8-10 eggs
30 crumbled vanilla wafers = 1 cup
9 crumbled graham crackers
   = 1 cup
9 salted crackers, finely
   crumbled = 1 cup
7 salted crackers, coarsely
   crumbled = 1 cup
2 tablespoons flour = 1 tablespoon cornstarch
1 pound rice = 2 1/8
   uncooked cups

Can Sizes

No. 2 = 2½ cups or 20 ounces.
No. 2½ = 3½ cups or 28 ounces.
No. 10 = 13 cups or 6 pounds, 10 ounces.
No. 1 flat = 9 ounces or 1 cup
No. 1 tall = 16 ounces or 2 cups
No. 2 vacuum = 1 3/4 cups or 12 ounces
No 303 = 16 ounces or 2 cups

adjustments for high altitude cooking

Jelly and Candy:

Put your thermometer in boiling water for 10 minutes. Check the temperature and subtract that from 212 degrees. The answer you get is what you will subtract from every candy recipe.

Example:

I have put my thermometer in boiling water for 10 minutes and it reads 202 degrees.

212 degrees
-202 degrees

10 degrees is my answer

I will subtract 10 degrees from every candy recipe.

Jelly gels at 219 degrees; therefore, you will subtract this same answer from 219 degrees to get the temperature jelly will get at your altitude. (Using the above answer—209 degrees).

Home Canning:

Boiling Water Bath:

If processing time is 20 minutes or less, add one minute for each 1,000 feet of altitude. If processing time is more than 20 minutes add 2 minutes for each 1,000 feet.

Steam-Pressure Canner:

Increase the pressure 1 pound for every 1,000 feet above sea level. Increase cooking time 5% for every 1,000 feet above the 2,000 foot mark, 15% at 5,000 for example.

Angel Food and Sponge Cake:

In cakes that use air as the leavening agent, such as angel food and sponge cake, adjustment is somewhat different. Since the leavening agent is air, it is important not to incorporate too much air into the egg whites when beating them. Use eggs directly from the refrigerator instead of letting them warm to room temperature. The eggs should be beaten only until they form peaks which bend over slightly. This increases the moisture in the cake because overbeating eggs tends to reduce the moisture in them and dry them out. The sugar may need to be reduced slightly. In a sponge cake, the eggs and egg yolks should be beaten until they are only slightly thickened. If baking powder is used in the sponge cake, it too should be reduced.

Butter Cakes:

The proportion and balance of ingredients in each cake recipe varies. Therefore it is difficult to give any fast rule for altitude changes. To adjust a standard cake recipe, the high altitude cake adjustment chart given below will be helpful:

Increase oven temperature 25 degrees.

4,500 feet, subtract 2 tablespoons sugar for every cup called for.

5,200 feet, subtract 3 tablespoons sugar for every cup called for.

6,000 feet, subtract 3 tablespoons sugar for every cup called for, and subtract ¼ teaspoon baking powder.

7,000 feet, subtract 3 tablespoons sugar for every cup called for, and subtract 3/8 teaspoon baking powder, add 1 egg.

8,000 feet, sugar same as above; ½ teaspoon baking powder, add 1 egg.

Yeast Breads:

Yeast dough rises in a much shorter time at high altitudes and may become too light if not watched carefully. Over rising gives a yeasty flavor to the bread and may cause it to "fall" or be very porous in texture. It is wise to be guided by "double in bulk" rather than the suggested time. Any standard recipe should be reliable. Do not try to reduce the amount of yeast.

Recipes that generally do not need adjustment:

pancakes	nut breads	cream puffs
roasted meats	muffins	waffles
biscuits	pie crust	baked vegetables
cookies		

Ann Gudger
HOME SERVICE DIRECTOR
Pueblo Gas and Fuel Company

Helpful Hints

Pinch = as much as can be taken between tip of finger and thumb.
Potatoes may turn green if store in a brightly lighted place.
Easy way to sliver almonds: blanch almonds; soak for few moments in boiling water, drain and slip off skins. While still warm and damp slice or sliver almonds.
Dry cut almonds in slack oven; do not brown.
Moderate heat = 350 degrees.
Candy Recipes: = thread stage = 230-234 degrees F.
                soft ball stage = 234-238 degrees F.
                hard ball stage = 248-254 degrees F.
                crack stage = 270-300 degrees F.
                with candy thermometer.
Spaghetti strands frequently stick = during last moments of cooking add 2 tablespoons oil to each 4 quarts water.

Bouquet garni = combination of parsley, thyme, and bay leaf.

Keep fried chicken crisp = when finished frying drain immediately; put into paper bag and keep in a warm oven until ready to serve.

Creaming = finer texture of end product if butter and sugar are completely incorporated.

Scalding milk = rinse pan before starting in ice-cold water; this will prevent scorching.

Vegetables are done when they can be pierced with a sharp knife or fork.

Mushroom sauté = cut mushroom stems flush with caps before sauté to prevent caps from collapsing.

Oven fried bacon = put bacon on broiler pan or shallow pan in slab; do not separate. Bake at 350 degrees, and stir bacon as it cooks. Pour off grease if necessary. End result = bacon curls.

Crust on hard rolls = pan of water in oven while you are baking them.

Scrambled eggs = a dress up would be addition of parsley, mushrooms or mushroom soup, oregano, seasoning salt, chopped green onions, bits of ham and bacon bits.

Hamburgers = to keep the shape and size, poke a hole in the center of each patty with your finger.

Lemon juice = helps keep avocados, bananas, peaches and apples from turning brown.

Boiled potatoes = add a little oil to water to prevent boiling over; works for noodles also.

Too much salt = cook with raw potato to take away excess salt.

1 tablespoon butter and flour with 1 cup heated milk = thin white sauce
2 tablespoons butter and flour with 1 cup heated milk = medium white sauce
3 tablespoons butter and flour with 1 cup heated milk = thick white sauce

CROSS index

401

402

406

411

412

413

414

FROM AN ADOBE OVEN . . . COOKBOOK
Junior League of Pueblo, Inc.
P.O. Box 3326
Pueblo, Colorado 81005

Please send me _____ copies of your cookbook at $8.95 per copy plus $1.50 per copy for mailing. Colorado residents add 6% or 54¢ sales tax

Name _____
please print

Street _____

City _____ State _____ Zip _____
*Proceeds from sale of this book will be applied to the charitable program of Pueblo Junior League.

FROM AN ADOBE OVEN . . . COOKBOOK
Junior League of Pueblo, Inc.
P.O. Box 3326
Pueblo, Colorado 81005

Please send me _____ copies of your cookbook at $8.95 per copy plus $1.50 per copy for mailing. Colorado residents add 6% or 54¢ sales tax

Name _____
please print

Street _____

City _____ State _____ Zip _____
*Proceeds from sale of this book will be applied to the charitable program of Pueblo Junior League.

FROM AN ADOBE OVEN . . . COOKBOOK
Junior League of Pueblo, Inc.
P.O. Box 3326
Pueblo, Colorado 81005

Please send me _____ copies of your cookbook at $8.95 per copy plus $1.50 per copy for mailing. Colorado residents add 6% or 54¢ sales tax

Name _____
please print

Street _____

City _____ State _____ Zip _____
*Proceeds from sale of this book will be applied to the charitable program of Pueblo Junior League.